The Cosby Cohort

Perspectives on a Multiracial America series
Joe R. Feagin, Texas A&M University, series editor

The racial composition of the United States is rapidly changing. Books in the series will explore various aspects of the coming multiracial society, one in which European Americans are no longer the majority and where issues of white-on-black racism have been joined by many other challenges to white dominance.

The Cosby Cohort

*Blessings and Burdens of Growing Up
Black Middle Class*

Cherise A. Harris

ROWMAN & LITTLEFIELD PUBLISHERS, INC.
Lanham • Boulder • New York • Toronto • Plymouth, UK

Published by Rowman & Littlefield Publishers, Inc.
A wholly owned subsidary of The Rowman & Littlefield Publishing Group, Inc.
4501 Forbes Boulevard, Suite 200, Lanham, Maryland 20706
www.rowman.com

10 Thornbury Road, Plymouth PL6 7PP, United Kingdom

British Library Cataloguing in Publication Information Available

Library of Congress Cataloging-in-Publication Data
Harris, Cherise A., 1976-
  The Cosby cohort : Blessings and burdens of growing up black middle class / Cherise A. Harris.
    p. cm. — (Perspectives on a multiracial america series)
  Includes bibliographical references and index.
  ISBN 978-1-4422-1765-2 (cloth : alk. paper) — ISBN 978-1-4422-1767-6 (ebook : alk. paper) 1. African Americans—Social conditions—1975- 2. Middle class—United States. 3. Blacks—Race identity. I. Title.
  E185.86.H357 2013
  305.896'073—dc23
                                                              2012046654

⊗™ The paper used in this publication meets the minimum requirements of American National Standard for Information Sciences—Permanence of Paper for Printed Library Materials, ANSI/NISO Z39.48-1992.

Printed in the United States of America

~

Contents

Contents

~

Preface

Millions of blacks woke up on November 5 [2008] with yet another buppie made better off on their backs while they remain jobless in dangerous
neighborhoods, their immediate futures no brighter for knowing that
cornbread may start appearing at the White House Thanksgiving table.
When we all stop weepily singing "We Are the World" and emailing
each other about what Great-Aunt Bessie would say now if she weren't
dead, we'll find that race is still a festering wound. (Debra J. Dickerson,
"Class is the New Black: How I Had to Look Beyond Race and Learn to
Love Equality." *Mother Jonas*, January 16, 2009)

The election of America's first Black president proved a watershed moment
in American history and reignited old debates about the nature of Blackness.
While public discourse continually noted the level of racial progress that
must have transpired in order to have a viable Black candidate in the race,
Barack Obama faced an abundance of questions that were variations on the
same theme: Is he "Black enough"? All of a sudden, a discussion about racial
identity that had been largely confined to Black beauty salons, high school
cafeterias, and Sunday dinners became part of the national discourse. In large
part, the questions about Obama's Blackness arose in response to his biracial
heritage and unique upbringing, where "certain critics questioned whether a
black man raised by a white mother and grandparents in Hawaii and Indonesia
truly understood the African American experience" (Joseph 2010, 183). Yet,
as journalist Debra Dickerson's statement above suggests, the question was
broader than that. It was a question about social class—about the "buppie"[1]
middle-class attitude toward their working-class and low-income counterparts.

As a graduate of Harvard University, professor of constitutional law at the University of Chicago, and a senator at the young age of forty-three, Obama is emblematic of the success enjoyed by a generation of middle-class (and even upper-middle class) Blacks who have faced fewer prohibitive racial barriers than their progenitors. In an allusion to biblical text, Jesse Jackson Sr. refers to them as the "post-Joshua generation" or the generation that was able to pass through and become successful after Joshua led Moses' (i.e., Martin Luther King's) followers into the Promised Land (Cose 2011). Historian Peniel Joseph (2010) offers important insight into Obama and his generation:

> In large measure, Obama has enjoyed the benefits of both the civil rights and Black Power movements while maintaining a safe distance from both. At forty-eight, he is too young to have marched in civil rights demonstrations or participated in Black Power-era campus protests. Instead, Barack Obama came of political age in the late 1970s and early 1980s in an arid political desert of social change. Though there were ongoing movements to protect Affirmative Action, end apartheid, and stave back Reagan-era economic cuts, this was a time when the left and the black movement in general reacted to, rather than set, America's social and political agenda. (195)

Essentially, the activities of post–civil rights Blacks stand in stark contrast to the generations before them, in part because of the more acute and overt forms of racism during the Jim Crow era, which necessitated a large-scale protest movement. Comparatively speaking, the formative years of post–civil rights Blacks have been marked by a quieter political tone where issues of race have been concerned, and it was within this context that upwardly mobile Blacks like Obama and others of his generation have been able to flourish.

Barack Obama represents a small, highly educated and powerful segment of the post–civil rights Black middle class but one that is often accused of being disconnected from—or, at the very least, ambivalent toward—the rest of Black America. Wingfield and Feagin (2010) suggest as much about Obama when they note that prior to his first presidential race, he was largely absent from the Black political scene:

> Unlike black public figures like D.C. Councilwoman Eleanor Holmes Norton, former NAACP Chair Julian Bond, or Reverend Al Sharpton, Senator Obama had not been present at, or spoken out in support of, the numerous civil rights marches and protest meetings that sought to turn public attention to issues dealing with continuing racial discrimination and inequality. (38)

Thus, embedded in the subtext of the queries over Obama's identity were important questions: *Given the privilege he has acquired, would Obama be able to identify with and relate to the lives of most Blacks? Would his presidency improve the fortunes of Blacks, particularly working-class and low-income Blacks? Furthermore, what are post–civil rights (upper-) middle-class Blacks like him going to do for the rest of Black America, and why haven't they already done more?*

Dating back to slavery, middle-class Blacks have had a long and varied history in the United States. At that time, the middle class was composed mostly of free Blacks and the mulatto elite (for further discussion, see Graham 1999). After slavery and prior to World War II, the Black middle class consisted mostly of Black professionals and entrepreneurs who catered to the segregated Black community (Drake and Cayton 1962; Kusmer 1976; Wilson 1980). Shortly thereafter, however, the population blossomed, where the largest changes in Black upward mobility transpired in the 1950s and 1960s because of increases in Black employment in the government and private sector. These increases were the result of the passage of the Fair Employment Practices Act and postwar economic expansion, both of which sharply increased the size of the Black working and middle class (Watkins 2005, 262). By 1960, the percentage of Blacks in middle-class occupations exceeded 10 percent (Landry 1987). Moreover, throughout the 1960s and 1970s, this segment of the population doubled in size because of "increased economic opportunity through the gains of the Civil Rights Movement and affirmative action programs [which] gave many African Americans increased opportunities to solidify their positions in the American middle class" (Landry 1987, 262).

Michael Omi and Howard Winant's (1994) sociological classic *Racial Formation in the United States From the 1960s to the 1990s* provides an excellent description of the sociopolitical atmosphere and tenor of the post–World War II era when middle-class Blacks were ascending the class ladder. Following World War II, America was excited about its prospects and reveled in their status as the world's saviors. By the 1960s, a "great transformation" began consisting of various social movements, including the women's movement, the civil rights movement, and the Black power movement. As Omi and Winant (1994) discuss,

> Racial minority movements challenged established racial practices simultaneously through direct action, through penetration of the mainstream political arena (electoral/institutional projects from voter registration to community organization), and through "ethical/political" tactics (taking the "moral initiative," developing "resistance cultures," etc.). . . . The unifying element in this

opposition was at first the burgeoning collective subjectivity of blacks—and later that of other minorities—which connected demands for access to the state with more radical demands for freedom, "self-determination," cultural and organizational autonomy, "community control," and a host of other issues. (105–6)

A rash of sit-ins, marches, and other public demonstrations permeated the 1960s and made Blacks increasingly visible on the world stage. Middle-class Blacks, in particular, took center stage during the civil rights movement, as a group of Blacks educated mostly at historically black colleges and universities (HBCUs) organized for freedom. Rosa Parks, Ralph Abernathy, John Lewis, Julian Bond, the members of the Student Non-Violent Coordinating Committee, James Bevel, Diane Nash, Medgar Evers, and, of course, Dr. Martin Luther King Jr. became fixtures on the national scene. Hence, the Black middle class largely set the agenda for the movement where "it was the freedoms that they were most interested in—to attend schools of their choice, to swim in certain swimming pools, to eat in restaurants of their choice, to be able to attend any movie theater, to have the same voting privileges as whites—that came to define their goals" (Jhally and Lewis 1992, 66).

The presentation of self by these men and women included a distinct "politics of respectability" that "demanded that every individual in the black community assume responsibility for behavioral self-regulation and self-improvement along moral, educational, and economic lines" (Higginbotham 1993, 196). The premise of such a strategy was that it would be easier for Blacks to gain White acceptance if they could demonstrate that they shared White standards of child rearing, cleanliness and order, sexual purity, and overall self-improvement (Higginbotham 1993, 139; see also Gaines 1996; Giddings 1984). As a result, a group of middle-class Blacks—cloaked in the politics of respectability; clad in their Sunday-best suits, dresses, and hats; and speaking an impeccable Standard English—would win many White allies and introduce middle-class Blacks on the world stage. However, it would also reinforce the idea that if Blacks wanted to advance, they would have to do it on Whites' terms and according to their particular norms.

Social change in the 1960s and 1970s would seemingly come at a snail's pace. While the civil rights movement flourished in the South, Black communities elsewhere continued to suffer from poverty and the confines of institutional racism and felt under siege by police forces in their neighborhoods. Police brutality became the catalyst for urban rebellions in dozens of cities. These conditions consigned working-class and low-income Blacks to rather dire circumstances. Nevertheless, some Black Americans began to gain ground. For example, during these decades, a new generation of Black politicians arose in a host of these urban cities, including Cleveland, Gary, Newark, Atlanta, Detroit, and Philadelphia (Joseph 2010). In this way, the spotlight continued to shine on upwardly mobile Blacks. Yet their fortunes—and indeed the fortunes of all Blacks—would be compromised by a country floundering for its footing on the global stage.

By the 1970s, America felt itself losing ground as a global superpower. The country began plunging into increasing debt and was facing significant economic decline. By 1973, inflation and unemployment were on the rise. That same year, a Harris poll found that the number of Americans feeling "alienated" and "disaffected" by the general state of the country had risen from 29 percent in 1966 to over 50 percent (Zinn 2003; see also Etzioni 1973). The number of those designated as "legally" poor rose 10 percent just from 1974 to 1975, eventually reaching 25.9 million people. Americans became increasingly concerned that hard work and saving money wouldn't be enough to accomplish the American dream. Moreover, the cultural shifts precipitated by social movements, the Vietnam War, Watergate, and other national and global events further alarmed Whites who were part of the American corporate elite and led to a feeling of unrest among Whites in general (Zinn 2003; see also Etzioni 1973; Hine et al. 2006). As a result, a racial reaction began to brew in opposition to the egalitarian ideals of the 1960s and in opposition to a state that many Whites felt no longer reflected their concerns.

Despite this national tone of disenchantment, middle-class Blacks continued to increase in visibility and power. During his term as president, Jimmy Carter appointed Blacks to important positions in the administration. Patricia Harris was appointed secretary of the Department of Housing and Urban Development, Andrew Young was appointed ambassador to the United Nations, and Sam Brown was appointed as the head of the Domestic Youth Service Corps. Marian Wright Edelman continued to serve in her capacity as the director of the Children's Defense Fund and played a visible role in Carter's lobbying for benefits for the poor (Zinn 2003). According to Hine et al. (2006), "Carter's black appointments were practically and symbolically important. Never had so many black men and women occupied positions that had direct and immediate impact on the day-to-day operations of the federal government" (609). Further, in 1972, Shirley Chisolm ran for president, receiving the support of not only the Black Panther Party but also White feminists (Joseph 2010), and succeeded in raising the visibility of Black voters overall (Hine et al. 2006). In these ways, upwardly mobile Blacks shined brightly at a time when the economy was in significant decline. In part, this would provoke a backlash that would come to define the 1980s and 1990s.

Nevertheless, Blacks who became upwardly mobile at this time represented the first sizable generation of middle class Blacks, and therefore, for the purposes of this study, they are referred to as "the first generation." By the 1980s, the increase in their population led to a growing body of literature on "the Black middle-class experience." To be sure, defining the meaning and boundaries around the term "Black middle class" has proven complicated in the sociological literature. However, occupation is frequently used as a primary indicator, where Blacks with white-collar jobs (broadly defined as professional, managerial, or clerical jobs) have been included in the category "Black middle class" (see Landry 1987; see also Coner-Edwards and Edwards 1988; Feagin and Sikes 1994; Higginbotham and Weber 1992; Oliver and Shapiro 1995; Pattillo-McCoy 1999). Most of the first generation were located in lower-middle-class occupations as teachers, foremen, government bureaucrats, office assistants, entrepreneurs, firefighters, and receptionists (Pattillo-McCoy 1999). On the whole, their occupations were less lucrative and stable than those of their White counterparts, who tended to have upper-class occupations, such as professional, entrepreneurial, managerial, and executive jobs (Pattillo-McCoy 1999).

The first generation experienced significant difficulty in their climb toward upward mobility. They were tasked with integrating White neighborhoods and workplaces (Collins 1997; Cose 1993; Feagin and Sikes 1994) and combating the discrimination within. Their other challenge was maintaining and nurturing relationships with poorer Black counterparts. Research and popular discourse on Black interclass relationships have always been fraught with tension and controversy. In part, this is because the fairly small yet powerful population of middle-class Blacks, estimated at anywhere from a quarter (Attewell et al. 2004) to a third (Pinkney 2000; Sue and Sue 2003) of the Black population, are sometimes perceived as having left their poorer brothers and sisters behind (Anderson 1990; Evans 1993; Frazier 1957; Feagin and Sikes 1994; Wilson 1987). As a result, research frequently discusses the complex relationships that exist particularly between first-generation middle-class Blacks and their working-class and low-income counterparts (Boyd 2008; Drake and Cayton 1962; Dyson 2005; Frazier 1957; Hyra 2008; Jackson 2001; Lacy 2007; Nunnally 2010; Pattillo 2007; Robinson 2010; Wiese 2004).

Arthur S. Evans (1993) details some of these complexities in his article "The New American Black Middle Classes: Their Social Structure and Status Ambivalence." In living and traveling in the predominantly White spaces mandatory for successful assimilation, middle-class Blacks find themselves in the role of "the stranger" who must constantly employ strategies for acceptance and tolerance (Evans 1993). Yet, when attempting to reestablish social ties with the larger Black community, they find themselves in the role of "homecomer," who returns after leaving the group for a significant amount of time. To their chagrin, homecomers sometimes find that, while away, they and the community to which they are returning have undergone psychocultural changes, causing them to be uncomfortable among their own and also unwelcomed by them (Evans 1993). At times, homecomers are dismayed by the changes that they have seen in the community, perhaps causing them to become standoffish, while the community perceives homecomers as "putting on airs." Thus, the class and cultural lines are drawn, and it is within this context that middle-class Blacks must constantly negotiate the tensions between upward mobility and maintaining ties to the larger Black community and culture (Collins 1997; Cose 1993; Feagin and Sikes 1994; Lacy 2007; Nunnally 2010; Pattillo-McCoy 1999). Despite these difficulties, researchers maintain that middle-class Blacks, particularly those of the first generation, feel connected to other Blacks and successfully nurture and maintain relationships across class lines (Dawson 1994; Higginbotham and Weber 1992; Hochschild 1995; Jackson 2001; Pattillo 2007; Pattillo-McCoy 1999). The question remains, will subsequent generations feel this same sense of connection?

The question must be raised because the second generation's[2] experience, in particular, has been qualitatively different than their parents'. Capitalizing on an ever-changing same sociopolitical structure, first-generation Black middle-class parents took great pains to ensure that their children would have even greater access to opportunity than they did. In the face of the sharp decline in manufacturing jobs and increasing violence in urban communities that were characteristic of the 1980s (Dougherty 2008; Dyson 2004; Hill 1999; Wilson 1987), the first generation departed the inner cities and other areas in which they had grown up or were familiar in exchange for life in majority White and majority Black suburbs. From 1960 to 1980, more than 3.5 million Blacks moved into suburbia (Wiese 1993, 30). The population of Black suburbanites soon grew from 6.1 million (approximately 23 percent of all Black Americans) in 1980 to a record high of just under 12 million (roughly a third of all Black Americans) in 2000 (Wiese 1993, 51; Wiese 2004, 255). By 2000, 38 percent of Blacks lived in suburbs (Nicolaides and Wiese 2006, 409).

As Wiese (1993) says, "In the popular consciousness, the very word *suburban* has connotations of affluence: of quiet rows of homes surrounded by equal-sized lawns, two-car garages, and station wagons" (33). This was the case for a segment of middle-class Blacks in the 1970s and 1980s who experienced "unprecedented residential freedom" (Nicolaides and Wiese 2006,

409) that allowed them to move into spacious new houses in White neighborhoods with quality schools and access to public services. Thus, where the first generation grew up in Black communities and were "grounded by their upbringings and socialization in more humble black surroundings" (Pattillo 2007, 297), their children were more likely to grow up in White spaces, absent this context. For another segment of middle-class and working-class Blacks, their journeys led them to poorer, older, and less financially secure neighborhoods (Nicolaides and Wiese 2006) that were spatially closer to other Blacks, which ultimately facilitated interclass relationships (see Pattillo-McCoy 1999).

By 1990, Black suburbanites earned 55 percent more than their counterparts in central cities and averaged $32,000 per year—only slightly below the national median of $35,000 (Wiese 2004, 255). While clearly concerned about issues of employment and safety for their families, the first generation's other concern was social reproduction (see Bourdieu and Passeron 1990) or passing down their class position to the second generation and beyond (Robinson 2010; Wiese 2004). Suburbia would offer these parents the opportunity to raise their children in safe neighborhoods with better school systems than the ones they had experienced in the cities, thus giving their children the opportunity to maintain or even elevate their class position in adulthood. With these intentions in mind, Black middle-class parents embarked on a mass exodus to the suburbs and went about the business of raising and training the second generation in predominantly White environments that were conducive to success. Included in this movement were my own parents.

When I was born in the mid-1970s, my parents were living in a small, majority Black, working-class city in New Jersey with a notoriously poor educational system. My mother grew up working class—her father was a postal worker, while her mother worked several jobs at a time, including secretarial, seamstress, and laundering jobs. Neither of my maternal grandparents had a college degree, nor did my paternal grandparents. My father grew up in a low-income household. As children, he would tell us stories about having only two outfits to wear to high school and nothing but potatoes to eat for dinner. Like many young men of his time, as a teenager, he was drafted into the army as a result of the Vietnam War. He would later end up with a hardship discharge when his mother passed away of cancer while only in her late thirties and he was just nineteen years old. Nevertheless, my father's military benefits and sales experience along with my mother's college education and success in corporate America gained them entrance into the Black middle class. As their young family kept growing, they realized that they needed not only a larger house but also one located in an area with a better school system. At their first opportunity and while they were still in their early thirties, they moved their three daughters to a predominantly White, middle-class suburb of New Jersey with an excellent school system where we could get superior educational preparation.

My parents provided us with a very comfortable standard of living where we had everything we needed and a good deal of what we simply wanted. Nothing was emphasized more in my family than academic excellence in the hope of securing our futures. As early as I can remember, my parents and my grandmother (who played a significant role in raising us) stressed the value of obtaining a college degree and doing whatever was necessary to achieve that goal. Because so much emphasis was placed on our education, earning any grade below a B was not an option in my house, and the consequences could be great. In addition to emphasizing education, my parents taught typical assimilationist values: the importance of hard work, fluency in Standard English (as opposed to slang or the Black English Vernacular), establishing social networks with others who were "going places," and wearing conservative styles of dress and hair.

Essentially, my parents and other parents of this generation always knew that because more intense levels of prejudice and discrimination are reserved for Blacks (Feagin 2010; Sears 2008; Sears et al. 1999, 2003; see also Gans 2008), in order for their children to get ahead, they would have to be able not only to compete but outperform Whites and all other groups of color as well. Where other groups of color were concerned, when I recently asked my father about the groups he perceived as our competition, he immediately said, "The Asians." (Included in that category was the large Asian Indian population in our part of the state.) My mother agreed and said that whenever she took us on trips to the public library on weekends, she would see Asian children studying for school and knew that they would be tough academic competitors (and, later on, tough competitors in the workplace). The touting of Asians as the "model minority"[3] would only reinforce their fears. When I asked them if they perceived Latinos to be a threat as well, my mother said, "Well, we knew from our own experiences that Whites would rather give the best opportunities to anyone other than Blacks. They'd even rather give it to Hispanics." Indeed, research conducted around the time of our formative childhood years indicates that, at the most basic level, Whites preferred to interact with Latinos rather than Blacks (Bobo and Zubrinsky 1996; Collins 1997; Herring and Amissah 1997). These groups aside, by far the greatest threat they perceived was from Whites, and they needed to look no further than their own lived experience to know that was the case.

My mother learned early on when a White classmate wouldn't hold her hand during Catholic school prayer that "the color line separating Blacks and Whites is more rigid and impermeable than the category lines separating Whites from any other minority groups" (Sears 2008, 141). My father, who spent some time growing up in Jim Crow Virginia, always knew that "no other group in the American context [has] faced such systematic lower caste treatment" (Sears 2008, 136). And, as indicated by most narratives of the challenges middle-class Blacks face in White spaces (Collins 1997; Cose 1993; Feagin and Sikes 1994; Feagin and McKinney 2003; Lacy 2007; Wiese 2004), my parents knew that arriving into the middle class didn't exempt one from dealing with racism. My mother, in particular, figured this out when she was part of the small cohort of Blacks integrating corporate America in the 1970s and discovered that even with her bachelor's degree from Rutgers and her 3.7 grade-point average, she was being paid significantly less than a White woman who had only one semester of college.

These experiences etched a new habitus within my parents, which intentionally and unintentionally influenced their child-rearing motivations. Bourdieu (1984) refers to "habitus" as a fluid and constantly reformulated set of dispositions that are created through personal and social history and compose a particular lifestyle. These dispositions structure individuals' actions in the social world and operate at every moment as a matrix of perceptions, tastes, and behaviors. Moreover, habitus "operates at a conscious and subconscious level, as individuals reproduce practices and ideas about themselves and the world around them without complete cognizance of actually doing so" (Young 1999, 203). This was certainly the case for my parents, whose adult experiences as first-generation middle-class Blacks prompted them to push their three girls toward success. As my mother recently said to me, "I knew that having all the tools in your arsenal didn't mean you would land 'the perfect job' or ideal job of your choosing. But I also knew that [with the best education and credentials] it would be more difficult for you to be denied that position."

And so, there we were, my two sisters and I, being raised with assimilationist and achievement-oriented values in a mostly White middle-class suburb of New Jersey. We were academically proficient and would go on to accumulate three bachelor's degrees, four master's degrees, and two doctorates between us. In many ways, we were the embodiment of the Huxtable family from the iconic sitcom *The Cosby Show*. As we anxiously gathered around the television every Thursday night at 8:00 during the show's run from 1984 to 1992, we watched the adventures of Cliff, Clair, Sondra, Denise, Theo, Vanessa, and Rudy and saw a closer approximation of who we were as Blacks as opposed to sitcoms that focused on working-class and low-income Blacks, like *Good Times* and *What's*

Happening. We were hooked from the pilot episode ("Theo's Economic Lesson," aired September 20, 1984) when the middle child and only son, Theo, brings home a bad report card, thus drawing his mother's ire. When Clair sends Cliff up to talk to him about it, Theo says the report card doesn't matter because he doesn't want to go to college and just wants to be "regular people." Cliff proceeds to use Monopoly money to illustrate to Theo how difficult it is to live on the salary of someone who didn't go to college. Still, Theo remains obstinate, and the following exchange occurs:

> *Theo:* You're a doctor and Mom's a lawyer. And you're both successful and everything and that's great. But maybe I was born to be a regular person and have a regular life. If you weren't a doctor, I wouldn't love *you* less, because you're my dad. And so, instead of acting disappointed because I'm not like you, maybe you can just accept who I am and love me anyway, because I'm your son. (*Audience applause*) (Leeson and Weinberger 1984)

At this point, we were expecting Cliff to cross to Theo, hug him, and tell him he is right. That was the kind of scene that would come to characterize White middle-class shows of the 1980s like *Family Ties* or *Full House.* Instead, Cliff's response was unexpected and priceless:

> Theo . . . (*pause*) That's the dumbest thing I've ever heard in my life! No wonder you get D's in everything! Now you are afraid to try because you're afraid that your brain is going to explode and it's going to ooze out of your ear. Now, I'm telling you, you are going to try as hard as you can! And you're going to do it because I said so! I am your father. I brought you in this world, and I'll take you out! (Leeson and Weinberger 1984)

The Harris girls were officially hooked after that episode because we knew Cliff's response would have also been our parents' response if we had used Theo's logic. In this very first episode of the iconic show, the writers—and indeed Cosby himself—outline one of the show's key emphases: the importance of achievement and upward mobility. Here, Cliff Huxtable makes it clear that academic achievement is a priority for the Huxtable children, and he and Clair spend the remainder of the nine seasons reinforcing that point with all of their children. There is considerable angst when Vanessa brings home a D, when Denise begins failing college, and when Sondra decides to scrap her Princeton education and open up a wilderness store with her new husband, Elvin. It is clear that the Huxtable children were meant to be upwardly mobile and, in many ways, embody basic American values, including its notions of meritocracy.

It was also clear that we were meant to be upwardly mobile, and being "regular people" wasn't exactly my parents' intention either. Because the show resonated for us in these ways, it became a permanent fixture in our lives and was even used as a punishment for failing to complete household chores, not finishing homework, or getting a bad grade (i.e., "Maybe you don't need to see The Cosby Show this week and put in some extra study time until you can bring up your geometry grade."). In a pre-DVR era, this was fairly devastating and prompted a good deal of begging for a very simple reason: this was an entertaining look into the lives of Blacks who were a lot like us. The Huxtable parents and children spoke perfect Standard English and had White friends (and friends of other racial groups as well), and their parents were serious about their academic achievement and upward mobility.

Yet growing up in the context of 1980s and 1990s Black America, where "authentic" Blackness became tied to a hip-hop culture emphasizing anti-intellectualism and a general distance from mainstream values, these characteristics were often perceived as "acting White." They were never positioned that way on The Cosby Show, but data from Blacks who watched the show back then indicated that some felt that the Huxtables were acting White (Jhally and Lewis 1992), as this designation gained momentum in the 1980s and the 1990s. In our real lives, the accusation led to us being ostracized by the few Black students in school. However, we also didn't fit in among our White friends either. While traveling in predominantly White circles, I became the token Black girl, but it was always clear to me that I didn't belong in this circle either, as my family did not have the same money or lifestyle as my White friends. I also wasn't invited into their sacred social spaces, like the prestigious swim club in town. In these ways, I found I had little in common with them, yet I wasn't accepted among Black peers either.

As a result of this experience, I became a person without a community and experienced a sense of rootlessness. I did not fit well into the White world, nor did I fit well into the Black world. I was subjected to constant teasing and ridicule by other Black children who threw about terms like "wannabe," "sellout," and "oreo" (i.e., Black on the outside, White on the inside) that, as a kid, often felt like daggers through the heart. I was ostracized from Black lunch tables, not invited to parties that Black children had, and then, around age twelve, was no longer invited to parties that White children had.[4] The sting I felt most, however, was the rejection by other Blacks. Somewhere around middle school to early high school, I began to reject them back. Despite my parents' and grandmother's efforts to provide examples of good Black role models and their recounting of important events in Black history, these weren't enough to make me feel grounded in the Black community, particularly when most of the Blacks I encountered seemed to reject me based on our class differences. I began to feel a great deal of confusion over my racial identity and began to approach other Blacks with caution, always fearful of "imminent discreditation" or being exposed as "inauthentically Black." These feelings lasted for me up until my last few years of high school where I found other Blacks who also were not asked to sit at the lunch table with the "cool" Black kids. We were all in the honors and music arts courses together and began to form our own clique based on those commonalities. This, in turn, strengthened my racial identity, which only became stronger during my college years, when I found even more Black friends who shared my childhood experiences.

Despite having found a handful of friends with an experience similar to mine, I still believed for a long time that our lives were rather unique. However, on a sunny Georgia afternoon in 2001, I was sitting in the inimitable Patricia Bell-Scott's graduate course on the Black family when I heard a story that sounded much like mine. By this point in my graduate school career, I had taken several courses with Pat, to the point where it may have appeared that I was majoring in her, not in sociology. Yet I kept returning because her courses emphasized that personal experience is an integral part of one's knowledge and that theory can be applied to that experience (see also Feagin 2001). On this particular day, a woman named Debra[5] began talking about her life as a second-generation Black middle-class child. She began talking about the stressors associated with being upwardly mobile as well as the difficulties of not fitting into either the Black or the White world as a child. Her childhood world was filled with displacement, frustration, and the ever-present pressure to achieve. After listening to her speak for a few minutes, I realized that she was telling my story.

Indeed, as time went on in graduate school, I would hear my story many times over from other people who grew up all over the United States. In another graduate class on racial identity, we were discussing Tatum's (1997) *Why Are All the Black Kids Sitting Together in the Cafeteria?* when I met Jim, a Black man in his early thirties, who also grew up middle class and was not asked to "sit at the table." When he began to sit at a lunch table with White boys who did accept him, his Black peers began calling him "oreo" and "wannabe." As a result of these childhood experiences, he felt ambivalent about socializing with other Blacks in his adult life. I would hear more stories like ours from undergraduate students in my early years of teaching. As these stories mounted and multiplied, I began to ask questions. What are some of the experiences of second-generation middle-class Blacks, and how might they differ from the first generation? What does their experience tell us about how some Black middle-class children internalize and make meaning of the race and class socialization imparted by their families? What effect does social class background have on racial identity development throughout the life course? Essentially, what can the life experiences of second-generation middle-class Blacks tell us about the price of assimilation in childhood and the challenges of Black racial identity formation that continue into adulthood? And, finally, what can they tell us about some of the current tensions that exist between middle-class Blacks and the rest of Black America? In other words, are there aspects of this experience that in some ways account for some post-civil rights middle-class Blacks' current spatial and emotional disconnect from their working-class and low-income counterparts? The stories presented in this book give us some indication of the answers to these questions.

In part, there remains scant research on the Black middle class because, since the 1960s, scholars have devoted disproportionate attention to low-income Blacks. This was particularly the case after William Julius Wilson's (1980, 1987) seminal works *The Declining Significance of Race* and *The Truly Disadvantaged*, both of which provoked heated debates on the structural roots of Black poverty and the plight of the underclass. For this reason, the lives of middle-class Blacks have been underresearched in the sociological literature in lieu of research and theory on working-class and low-income Blacks (Pattillo 2005). However, while the problems of middle-class Blacks may appear less emergent, these problems recur in multiple contexts, such as in interactions with Whites in public settings (Cose 1993; Collins 1997, 2000; Feagin 1991) and in forging a personal racial identity and attachment to other Blacks (Cose 1993; Early 1993; Feagin 1991; Garrod et al. 1999; Jackson 2001; Nunnally 2010; Tatum 1999; Thompson 1991). Therefore, while middle-class Blacks may enjoy a degree of privilege through their class standing, it is often tempered by the realities of being a racial minority group and the attendant interracial and intraracial expectations.

Since the 1990s, scholarly focus has shifted to the Black middle class. Still, it is most often the adult experience that is examined. These scholars offer stirring accounts of the challenges adults face in the workplace (see Collins 1997; Cose 1993; Feagin and McKinney 2003; Feagin and Sikes 1994), neighborhoods (see Feagin and Sikes 1994; Lacy 2002, 2007; Tatum 1999; Wiese 2004), and public spaces (see Feagin 1991; Feagin and Sikes 1994; Lacy 2007). Some research also details the difficulties adults have in negotiating a racial identity in light of having a foot in both the White and the Black world (see Jackson 2001). Largely missing from the landscape of studies on the Black middle-class experience are the stories of the second generation who grew up in predominantly White areas in the 1980s and 1990s and were forced to negotiate the gauntlets of racial integration and assimilation at very young ages. Using the childhood recollections of these Blacks, this book explores their journey through issues of race, class, and identity over the life course and how their experiences as children have shaped their racial identities and the trajectory of their lives. Primarily, I draw on the social constructionist framework and the symbolic interactionist tradition, which hold that "people use their own reflective processes to make sense of the world around them" (Hill 1999, xvi–xvii).

Because I spend a great deal of time focusing on childhood experiences and centering on this point of view, it may seem at times that first-generation middle-class parents are being portrayed rather harshly. It may appear that they are being attacked for choosing to raise their children in White spaces with a mainstream orientation. *To be sure, there is nothing inherently wrong with the strategies for upward mobility that these parents used to raise their children.* One would be hard pressed to argue that providing children with safe neighborhoods, quality schools, or a multitude of extracurricular activities are unnecessary in a world of declining middle-class fortunes where every advantage and strategy must be employed. These parents have done their very best to ensure that their children would become upwardly mobile and maintain (if not elevate) their class status in adulthood. Moreover, unlike White middle-class parents, they were forced to do so within a context of racial discrimination. Therefore, any pressures they put on their children were a response to these kinds of forces beyond their control. Yet we are still left with the question: What are the unintended consequences of raising children this way? How did these consequences manifest themselves in the lives of second-generation, post–civil rights middle-class Blacks? What can their experiences tell us about future generations of Black middle-class children in White spaces and the burdens of assimilation? Finally, what are the implications for racial identity and attachments to Black people and culture throughout the life course? These are questions that merit attention regardless of parental intentions and are the centerpiece of this book.

~

Acknowledgments

It is no exaggeration to say that completing this book took a village, and I am eternally grateful to the many people who have been part of my village.

Without my family, none of this would have been possible. My parents' story is briefly mentioned in the preface of this book, but the sacrifices they made for my sisters and I to have a better life cannot be captured in words. It is with profound gratitude that I dedicate this book to Denise and Clarence Harris. I would like to thank my mother specifically for the grueling, hands-on work that she did with this project out of sheer love for her daughter. Likewise, my father let me cry, whine, and complain throughout the process but never judged, always listened, and always had a joke at the ready. I love both of you more than I can say in words.

My sisters are two of the most brilliant and amazing women I have ever known. Thanks to my sister Dawne for her proofreading, for her comments on those very early and rough first drafts, and for listening to my emotional outbursts. Thanks to my sister Deena for being unintentionally hilarious and for providing many light moments when they were desperately needed. I must also thank my nephews, "The Furbies," also known as Masai, Naim, and Caiden, who are givers of life in their smiles, giggles, and the little quirks that make them uniquely them. I must also extend my gratitude to my extended family for always being my cheerleaders, specifically Dorothea and Arthur Pierson; Edna Jones; Dottie Charity and Sherri Porter; Ruth Whitaker; the "Golden Girls"—Daisy Briggs, Janice Freeman, Sylvia Seabon, and Adele Carter and family; the entire Ridley family; the Franklins, Harrises, and

Mitchells for being "surrogate" aunts and uncles; the Boykins; the Crawfords; and all of the other Hart, Harris, and Miles relatives who have sustained me on my journey through college, through graduate school, and now in writing this book. I love all of you very much.

My sister-friends compose a great and important segment of my village. I am beyond grateful for their incredible friendship. I have to send a special shout-out to my "bestie" of more than twenty years and my third sister, Ayesha Abdullah, who has always offered unconditional love and exceptional care; no one has more patience or a bigger heart. I am also indebted to the phenomenal Rosemarie Roberts for talking me off of many ledges as this project was coming to fruition and for holding my hand every step of the way. Very special thanks to my many other sister-friends who have also held my hand along the way: Kelly Manley, Michallene McDaniel, Stephanie McClure, Marybeth Stalp, Kerri Smith, Lauren DeFlorio, Keisha Edwards Tassie, and Jocelyn Briddell. They are among some of the smartest, strongest, and most passionate women I've ever had the honor of knowing. Thank you also to Dante' Clay for things that can't be quantified.

I am grateful to a host of other colleagues at Conn who provided emotional or professional support and/or who lent their expertise, including Ron Flores, Jennifer Domino Rudolph, Jim Downs, Monique Bedasse, Dana Wright, Robert Gay, Abby Van Slyck, and Roger Brooks. In addition, I would like to thank the members of my accountability group who gave me much-needed reality checks: Griselda Thomas, Viviana Quintero, and Edna Viruell-Fuentes.

Because this project started in graduate school, I must thank my committee members at the University of Georgia for all of their hard work. Thank you to Reuben May, E. M. "Woody" Beck, William Finlay, and Jerome Morris. Thanks also to Joya Misra, Cynthia Hewitt, Michael Hodge, Linda Grant, and Jim Coverdill for all of their encouragement during my grad school years. And my endless gratitude goes to the inspirational Patricia Bell-Scott, who gave me the strength, courage, and insight to pursue this line of research in the first place.

My village in Chicago graciously lent their assistance as I was beginning this project in earnest. I am grateful for the support of Heather Dalmage, who gave me direction for the manuscript. I am also grateful to Michael Maly and Lynn Weiner, who were very supportive during my time at Roosevelt, especially Mike, who encouraged me to see this project through. I would also like to thank the Chicago Write-on-Site group—Marisha Humphries, Glenda Morris Burnett, and Tanya Golash-Boza—who were instrumental in cheering me on when I was writing the first full draft. I am grateful as well for Leanne Silverman, who offered her feedback while I was still in Chicago.

There aren't enough adjectives and superlatives to describe the mentorship and aid that I have received from the extraordinary Kerry Ann Rockquemore. It was simply transformative to be a part of her Write-on-Site group in Chicago and later have her as my coach for the Faculty Success Program that she created. Without these, I would never have finished this book. Kerry Ann has been an endless source of advice, support, and good ideas. I thank her also for reading and giving feedback on some early drafts and for giving me the courage to aim higher and never settle for crumbs.

David Brunsma was easily the turning point in this project for me. His openness of spirit and generosity of heart will always remain with me as a model for what it means to be a mentor. Moreover, I benefited a great deal from his scholarly brilliance and his encouragement to do and say things I didn't think I could.

I had an abundance of help from students at Roosevelt University and Connecticut College. My thanks to my incredible research assistants: Tim Bauer, Tim Wateridge, Marija Jurcevic, Rachel Becker, and Jane Sternbach. Thanks also to my awesome teaching assistants who freed me up to get much of this research done: Samantha Sgourakes, Leah Feutz, and Natalie Abacherli. Additionally, I must thank the students who read and commented on various incarnations of this book, including my Spring 2009 Black and White Racial Identity students at Roosevelt and the Spring 2011 and Fall 2011 Middle Class Minorities students at Conn. I am also appreciative of the support of three other special students as well—Breanne Timura, Loretta Char Vereen, and Rasheed Mitchell.

Along this journey, there were several medical professionals who played an integral role in my survival. I would be remiss if I didn't thank the surgical team at the University of Illinois–Chicago, as well as Bernadette Golden, Anne Procyk, Kristina McGillis, and Robyn McDonald.

It has been my distinct honor to have completed this book with the guidance of the brilliant and passionate Joe Feagin, who offered invaluable feedback. I am also extremely grateful to Sarah Stanton, Jin Yu, Kathryn Knigge, Elaine McGarraugh, and the team at Rowman & Littlefield who have given me such an incredible opportunity. Special thanks as well to Badia Ahad, whose editorial talents on the book proposal and the manuscript helped me to get both out the door. I am also indebted to the anonymous reviewers of the manuscript whose comments made this a better book.

Finally, I would like to thank the interviewees whose stories are told here for their willingness and bravery. I am forever beholden to all of you.

Additional Dedication
To the angels who watch over:
June Hart (1925–1996)
Iris Grimes (1932–1970)
William Hart (1915–1984)
Joyce Harris Crawley (1948–1994)
And to the little souls on their way . . .

CHAPTER ONE

~

The Genesis of the Cosby Cohort: 1980s–1990s

In the 1980s and 1990s, Black middle-class families faced daunting challenges as they attempted to integrate White workplaces and White suburban neighborhoods and schools. Many first-generation middle-class Blacks spent their days hitting their heads against the glass ceilings of corporate America in hostile work spaces (Collins 1997; Cose 1993, 2011; Feagin and Sikes 1994; St. Jean and Feagin 1998). They spent their nights and weekends dealing with hostile neighbors and suspicious Whites in retail stores and other public spaces (Feagin and Sikes 1994; Jacobs 2001). Meanwhile, their children found themselves negotiating similar yet different journeys that would shape their childhoods (and, later, adulthoods) in salient ways. Impeding these families' journey through the gauntlet of assimilation was an increasingly anti-Black political, social, and public discourse that permeated the Reagan, Bush Sr., and Clinton administrations from the 1980s to the 1990s. Examining the sociopolitical climate at this time illuminates the context in which these families struggled to survive and carve an identity and existence for themselves. Indeed, these decades were marked by the increasing visibility of upwardly mobile Blacks on the national stage but in the context of intractable White resistance, which ultimately served to reinforce Blackness as a master status from which the Black middle class couldn't escape.

The Sociopolitical Landscape and the Visibility of Upwardly Mobile Blacks: 1980s–1990s

The lives of the first-generation Black middle class were shaped considerably by the social, political, and economic changes of the 1980s and 1990s. As a result of the economic downturn of the 1970s, by the 1980s the United States no longer enjoyed world dominance (Omi and Winant 1994). While the economic changes were troubling, the changes to the cultural landscape proved equally troubling, particularly to Whites who felt disconnected and disenchanted with what they perceived as a "liberal interventionist state" that "obstruct[ed] the economy's 'natural' tendencies toward recovery" through its use of social programs (Omi and Winant 1994, 115). Their discontent manifested in an increasingly bitter public discourse. For example, after President Reagan dismantled the Federal Communications Commission's "fairness doctrine" requiring airtime for dissenting views, talk radio attracted millions of listeners who were "treated to daily tirades from right-wing talk-show 'hosts,' with left-wing guests uninvited" (Zinn 2003, 564). In addition, groups who had become dissatisfied with the changes of the 1970s developed powerful political organizations (e.g., anti–equal rights and anti–abortion rights organizations, among others) that ultimately rooted themselves in the Republican Party (Hine et al. 2006). In these ways, America's increasing economic decline exacerbated White fears that the country was changing in ways that were disadvantageous to them.

Their fears frequently became couched within racial subtext. Conservatives argued that the state only made its poorer citizens' problems worse by encouraging dependency, specifically asserting that taxes were being used to expand the welfare state and finance recipients of color at the expense of hardworking (White) taxpayers (Omi and Winant 1994, 116). The country's welfare program, which included Aid to Families with Dependent Children, food stamps, and Medicaid, was slashed considerably, and most families received $500 to $700 per month in aid, which was well below the poverty level of roughly $900 per month. During Reagan's tenure, new requirements also eliminated free lunches for nearly 1 million poor children, many of whom were of color and part of the population that was officially declared "poor." For Whites looking to reverse the gains of the civil rights movement, scapegoating people of color, specifically Blacks, became an easy way to "reestablish" a White dominance that they felt was slipping away in the 1980s and 1990s (Omi and Winant 1994).

The other major target of White conservatives' wrath, according to Omi and Winant (1994), was affirmative action policies—an oppositional stance that bode poorly for upwardly mobile Blacks. According to the right, a new form of racial inequality originated from the great transformation of the 1960s and 1970s—one that granted privilege and "preferential treatment" to minority groups: "Through its reckless intervention, conservatives alleged, the state committed 'reverse discrimination'—*whites* were now the victims of racial discrimination in education and the job market. The dislocations which began in the 1970s, then, were often understood *racially*" (Omi and Winant 1994, 116; for data on White views of affirmative action in the 1980s–1990s, see also Jhally and Lewis 1992). In the eyes of many Whites, the state had gone too far and now served to enfranchise Blacks at the expense of Whites, particularly White men.

White discomfort was only exacerbated by an economy that continued to decline in the 1980s. The unemployment rate increased under Reagan; in 1982, 30 million people were unemployed all or part of the year. By the end of Regan's second term, the gap between the rich and poor had grown exponentially: "Where in 1980, the chief executive officers (CEOs) of corporations made forty times as much in salary as the average factory worker, by 1989 they were making ninety-three times as much. In the dozen years from 1977 to 1989, the before-tax income of the richest 1 percent rose 77 percent; meanwhile, for the poorest two-fifths of the population, there was no gain at all, [and] indeed a small decline" (Zinn 2003, 581). Hine et al. (2006) report that "the real income of the highest paid 1 percent of the nation . . . increased from $312,206 to $548,970 during the 1980s" (617). Of course, the losses were particularly heavy for Blacks, Latinos, women, and young people. During the Reagan–Bush years, Black families were hit the hardest; at least a third of Black families fell below the poverty level (Zinn 2003, 582), and Black unemployment was at least twice that of Whites (Hine et al. 2006, 617). This, combined with the reduction in development funding to inner cities, led to a destabilization of inner-city neighborhoods—neighborhoods where 56 percent of the residents were Black (Hine et al. 2006, 617). With increased poverty came an increase in crime and violence, which further demonized Blacks in the White imagination. It also led to a mass migration of Black middle-class families into White suburbs.

Despite the right-wing assaults on people of color, Blacks advanced in the 1980s. It was perhaps most evident in the rise of Black political power, where "the growing black middle class sought to use electoral politics to share fully in America's educational, social, and political institutions" (Hine et al. 2006, 616). In 1983, Harold Washington became mayor of Chicago, thereby joining a small cadre of Black mayors in major cities like Atlanta, Los Angeles, and Philadelphia. The following year, Jesse Jackson ran for president of the United States and galvanized Black voters for the purposes of gaining leverage for Blacks within the Democratic Party. His "Rainbow Coalition" emerged at a crucial time in American history and was designed largely to even the political playing field (Joseph 2010). Having Blacks in such visible leadership positions alerted Whites to the increasing power of Black Americans, ultimately posing a threat to White hegemony.

George H. W. Bush's presidency (1989–1993) would retread the same brand of racial resentment that permeated the Reagan years and ignite new clashes and tensions over race. Ethnic Studies scholar Ronald Takaki (2010) adeptly outlined the racial tensions during that era:

> What is fueling the debate over our national identity . . . is America's intensifying racial crisis. The alarming signs and symptoms seem to be everywhere—the killing of Vincent Chin in Detroit, the black boycott of a Korean grocery store in Flatbush, the hysteria in Boston over the Carol Stuart murder, the battle between white sportsmen and Indians over tribal fishing rights in Wisconsin, the Jewish-black clashes in Brooklyn's Crown Heights, the black-Hispanic competition for jobs and educational resources in Dallas, which *Newsweek* described as 'a conflict of the have-nots,' and the Willie Horton campaign commercials, which widened the divide between the suburbs and the inner cities. (50)

These ever-present racial tensions were perhaps most evident in the discourse following the Los Angeles uprising in response to the Rodney King case. According to Takaki (2010), the "reality of racial tension rudely woke America like a fire bell in the night on April 29, 1992" (50; see also Omi and Winant 1994) when the officers caught on tape brutally beating King were acquitted of all charges. The ensuing fires and devastation awakened America to racial tensions that had been lying just beneath the surface. The *Los Angeles Times* and the *Chicago Tribune* demonized the Black participants in the uprisings as "criminals and opportunists," and ABC News characterized their actions as "mindless, infectious, and random" (Jacobs 2001, 223). The *Chicago Tribune* perhaps best expressed the nation's bewilderment over these events: "Even after all these years of apparent progress, of affirmative action and equal opportunity, of an expanding black middle class and of a decline in the kind of boiling race hatred that filled the screens of the first video generation in the 1960s, racism remains the nation's incurable malignancy" (May 10, 1992, A1, cited in Jacobs 2001, 227).

As a result of these patterns, the racial reaction that began in the late 1960s and early 1970s had developed into yet another widespread effort to reinterpret and reframe the meaning of race in America. However, because it was difficult to outright dismantle the political gains of racial minorities, racial rhetoric had to be rearticulated to fit a society no longer dependent on overt manifestations of racism. Anti-Black sentiment soon became encapsulated in code words like "justice," "law and order," and "equal opportunity" (Omi and Winant 1994, 123–24; see also Doane 2003). This coded rhetoric worked and positioned the right as "an apparent alternative to ghetto riots and white guilt, to the integration of northern schools and the onset of stagflation," thereby increasing their appeal to the majority of the electorate (Omi and Winant 1994, 124). Furthermore, the New Right resented any mobility on the part of what they perceived as lower-status groups and expressed a great deal of anger toward groups that represented both an economic and a cultural threat.

The threat to a perceived common culture was particularly onerous for Whites. The late 1980s and early 1990s ushered in an era of multiculturalism and "political correctness" that set off a panic about racial divisions (Omi and Winant 1994). As a result of this hostility and the increasing fears of Whites, Blacks, and other people of color were forced to tackle racial issues in more covert ways. It soon became more advantageous for racial movements to work within this newly articulated racial state than confront it (Omi and Winant 1994; see also Feagin 2010). Indeed, confronting it could lead to disaster, especially for upwardly mobile Blacks, as demonstrated by the Lani Guinier controversy.

Guinier was the first tenured Black female professor at Harvard Law School and was a nominee for assistant attorney general for civil rights in the Clinton administration. She had openly written and discussed racist voting practices like racial redistricting and was an advocate of affirmative action, albeit without set-asides or quotas. Nevertheless, because she had been so vocal on racial issues, her record and writings were distorted, and she was soon dubbed the "quota queen" in a *Wall Street Journal* op-ed piece—a term that was an obvious play on Reagan's previous mythic "welfare queens." As Omi and Winant (1994) claim, "Guinier's sin, it is clear in retrospect, was not her supposed radicalism, but her willingness, indeed her eagerness, to discuss the changing dimensions of race in contemporary U.S. politics. She sought an open and democratic dialogue, to be held in legislative, academic, journalistic, and judicial fora, on the meaning of race in the post-civil rights era" (156). For this, she paid a heavy price, and her nomination was withdrawn by President Clinton. During his presidency, Clinton would continue to appoint more people of color to government posts than his Republican counterparts, but, as in the Guinier case, he abandoned them quickly when they became too outspoken or became a political liability. In another example, Surgeon General Joycelyn Elders, a Black woman, was forced by Clinton to resign following her suggestion that masturbation should be taught in sex education.[1] Again, upwardly mobile Blacks gained high profiles on the national stage but were dismissed quickly when they posed a perceived or imagined threat to White hegemony. Such high-profile incidents often become messages to middle-class Blacks that advancement requires silence on racial issues or anything else that challenges the White patriarchal power structure (see Feagin 2010[2]; Wingfield and Feagin 2010).

While Clinton was accused by some of "doing just enough for blacks, women, and working people to keep their support" (Zinn 2003, 644), others lauded the Clinton presidency where he was considered in some circles "the first Black president" and also "the first woman president" for his support of equal rights (Hine et al. 2006). He appointed several Blacks to high-profile positions that had little to do with race, such as Hazel O'Leary who served as secretary of the Department of Energy, Alexis Herman as secretary of labor, and Ron Brown as secretary of commerce (Hine et al. 2006). Despite gains among middle-class Blacks, poorer Blacks continued to receive the nation's scrutiny.

The attacks on crime and welfare were particularly damning for low-income Blacks as they again became the proverbial "boogeymen" under the Clinton administration and continued to fall further behind. The "Crime Bill" of 1996, geared mostly toward punishment, extended the death penalty to even more criminal offenses, called for $8 billion for new prisons (Zinn 2003), and created the "three-strikes" law of stiffer penalties for those with two prior convictions (Hine et al. 2006). Moreover, the 1990s ushered in an era where both Democrats and Republicans played on economic fears in order to "reform" welfare. Clinton ultimately passed the Personal Responsibility and Work Opportunity Reconciliation Act of 1996, restricting poor families to a lifetime limit of five years on assistance and issuing work requirements for many of them. In these ways, Clinton contributed to the disenfranchisement of poor Blacks, however covertly, and even balanced the national budget largely by withdrawing government assistance from families in need (Zinn 2003; see also DeFazio 2006; Hays 2003; Katz 1996).

Despite these setbacks for many Blacks, the Black middle class began to grow in leaps and bounds. For example, reporter Alec Klein (2004) found that "the portion of black households making $75,000 to $99,999 . . . increased nearly fourfold between 1967 and 2003, rising to 7 percent of the black population" (A1). By 1995, there were approximately 7 million Blacks employed in middle-class occupations, which often included social workers, receptionists, insurance salespeople, and government bureaucrats (Dyson 2005, 62; see also Pattillo-McCoy 1999). The Clinton years brought about a great deal of prosperity for the country at large, and middle-class Blacks were able to benefit in the process.

Still, the pattern of Black prosperity and visibility existing in tandem with White hostility remained in the 1990s. For example, the Clinton years brought about another racially polarizing case: the O.J. Simpson trial and verdict. Watched by over 107 million Americans (Jacobs 2001), Simpson was declared not guilty of murdering his White ex-wife and her White male companion. The verdict further underlined the Black–White tensions in America during the 1990s. Ronald Jacobs (2001)[3] writes, "Television cameras focused on the celebration of African Americans and the anger of whites, largely ignoring those whose opinions did not fit the narrative of racial division, and largely ignoring the voices of Asians and Latinos" (234). Moreover, while the Rodney King verdict uncovered racial division and distrust, the O.J. Simpson verdict showed that the racial chasm was even deeper than previously imagined (Jacobs 2001). The *Los Angeles Times* perhaps captured it best: "The stunning pictures of blacks cheering while whites muttered or choked back tears when the verdict was announced chillingly captured the widening separation of interests that increasingly define[d] American life in the 1990s" (October 9, 1995, A5, cited in Jacobs 2001).

The 1980s and 1990s were a period marked by racial antipathy, particularly toward Blacks, at the same time that the Black middle class began to grow and become more visible. To be sure, a racial dichotomy existed where race was specifically understood in Black–White terms (Hacker 1995; Jacobs 2001; Omi and Winant 1994). As such, Blacks were increasingly singled out for particular scrutiny and discriminatory treatment. This is a phenomenon that sociologists have referred to as "Black exceptionalism" (Sears et al. 2003, 2008; see also Gans 2008). The term is used to describe the more intense levels of racism reserved for Blacks that significantly impede their journeys to assimilation and upward mobility.[4] In part, Blacks remain the exception to racial progress because of systemic racism or the "complex array of exploitative and discriminatory white practices targeting Americans of color" (Feagin 2010, viii). These practices are borne out of an intractable White racial frame that justifies White privilege and dominance (see also Feagin 2006). Feagin (2010) describes this frame as "an overarching worldview . . . that encompasses important racial ideas, terms, images, emotions, and interpretations" (3) and typically leads to discriminatory actions. Indeed, sociological and psychological research indicates that in the past and present, Blacks have been targeted for the most central oppression in American society in large part because Whites often accord Blacks primacy in their feelings and everyday thoughts about race (Feagin 2010; Frankenberg 1993) and also unconsciously link them to negative traits (Dasgupta et al. 2000; Vendantam 2005). This makes structural assimilation,[5] integration, and upward mobility more difficult for Blacks than any other racial group. [6] Moreover, as the next chapter discusses more fully, their ability to do so successfully has been largely dependent on their understanding of and adherence to the White norms and ideas embraced under the White racial frame. As upwardly mobile Black families were negotiating these obstacles in the 1980s and 1990s, a fictional Black middle-class family would capture the American imagination and make the lives of middle-class Blacks visible for the first time.

Enter the Cosby Cohort

In the 1980s, middle-class Blacks were not only visible on the national level, but through the medium of television, they became hypervisible when the first episode of *The Cosby Show* debuted on September 20, 1984, and instantly became a cultural juggernaut that single-handedly revitalized NBC's flagging lineup. The show was the top-rated television series of the 1980s and remains one of the most-watched sitcoms in television history (Innis and Feagin 1995). In its eight-year run, it represented a turning point in portrayals of Blacks in the media, as it was the first all-Black program that avoided racial stereotyping (Innis and Feagin 1995) and offered a bird's-eye view into the lives of (upper-) middle-class Blacks. The parents, a doctor (Cliff) and a lawyer (Clair), embodied the civil rights generation of Blacks whose promise had been fulfilled while their children represented the post–civil rights seeds that they had planted, each imbued with the promise of upward mobility. Because "television characters, especially those whom we recognize as realistic, become part of the framework within which we make sense of the world" (Jhally and Lewis 1992, 23), the success of the parents signaled to many White viewers in the 1980s and 1990s that America had indeed become "postracial" where institutional discrimination and racial inequality were a thing of the past. As such, the show suggested that affirmative action was no longer required because Blacks had achieved the upward mobility for which the policy was intended, and thus Blacks who hadn't succeeded failed because of some character defect of their own (Gates 1992; Innis and Feagin 1995; Jhally and Lewis 1992).

The Cosby Show frequently drew criticism for its rather assimilationist portrayal of Blacks, as the Huxtables spoke impeccable Standard English, maintained friendships across the racial and ethnic spectrum, emphasized educational achievement and excellence, and frequently depicted a politics of respectability. Examples of some of these themes can be found in a notable season 2 episode. In "Close to Home" (episode 20, written by Carmen Finestra [original air date March 13, 1986]), Theo and his friend Cockroach announce that they are going to do a rap for speech class and disappear into Theo's room to begin working on it. After they depart, Cliff's friend Dr. Morgan arrives, and the audience is reminded several times that he attended Morehouse College when he and Cliff engage in a friendly rivalry over their HBCU alma maters (Cliff's is the fictional Hillman College that would spawn the spin-off, A Different World). Dr. Morgan's Morehouse education and medical degree cement him firmly in the (upper) middle class for the audience. During the episode, he expresses his lament and shock over the fact that his daughter Cindy has become a drug addict despite he and his wife's loving efforts and the good home they provided. It is an episode in which the audience is reminded that even kids from "good homes" can fall off the track to upward mobility if they make the wrong choices. There are no structural reasons attributed to Cindy's downfall; she simply made bad choices. This suggests that all who engage in drug use or activity are similarly making bad "choices."

Later in the episode, Theo and Cockroach reemerge with their first attempt at the rap for speech class. Their initial effort yields a rap that glorifies the party life and getting girls. They are only a few lines in while performing it for Cliff and Clair when Cliff interrupts, saying, "Can't you have some fun talking about something productive?" He prompts the boys to try again, and they return back to Theo's room. The meritocratic subtext (and, to some extent, the politics of respectability) are eventually reified in this episode when Theo and Cockroach appear in the final scenes with their second attempt at the rap. The song glorifies the value of hard work and the spirit of meritocracy in its lyrics and particularly in its imploring hook:

> HOOK: This is your life to do something with, don't be too scared to compete. Don't stand around and keep losing ground or you'll end up on the street.
>
> FIRST VERSE: Hey, you gotta do somethin' with your life, don't be too scared to try. And then develop a frown and just stand around until life just passes you by. And when you do wake up and begin to see that life ain't a piece of cake, whether you win real big or lose real bad, you gotta sleep in the bed you make.
>
> FIRST REPEAT OF HOOK
>
> SECOND VERSE: You gotta keep burnin' that midnight oil cuz that's a fact that still remains. Hey boy, you gotta study hard, you gotta study long, you gotta exercise your brains. Because . . .
>
> SECOND REPEAT OF HOOK (Finestra 1986)

The significance of the lyrics and the juxtaposition of the drug storyline are not lost on the audience. The party life as embodied in Theo's first rap and in the off-screen character of Cindy is the road to nowhere. All that is re-quired for upward mobility and success is "studying hard" and being unafraid to compete. Failure to use these opportunities "wisely" means "you gotta sleep in the bed you make." Ultimately, the episode manipulates cultural Blackness (rap) to promote a meritocratic agenda devoid of any of the so-ciopolitical implications and consequences of Blackness as a minority status. Indeed, in 1980s America, there were many Black children "studying hard" to no avail in crumbling, impoverished school systems, and given the rise in Black poverty at that time, they sought solace as well as economic relief in the ingesting and/or selling of drugs. They didn't simply make bad choices like Cindy; their "choices" were a function of deteriorating cities and a lack-ing opportunity structure. Nevertheless, *The Cosby Show* oversimplified these issues (in large part for the sake of entertainment) and reinforced the idea that Black mobility was dependent on individual effort, perseverance, and adherence to American meritocratic ideals.

As alluded to above, a distinct politics of respectability also permeated *The Cosby Show*'s weekly story lines. Lessons on proper decorum were com-mon, such as Cliff's tutorial on restaurant etiquette once given to Rudy and her merry band of multicultural friends. In the context of more serious issues, peripheral characters were used to illustrate the politics of respectability. For example, in the episode called "The Shower" (season 3, episode 19, written by Matt Williams [original air date February 26, 1987]), Denise's college-aged friend Veronica intentionally gets pregnant out of wedlock in an effort to manipulate her parents into giving their approval to marry her boyfriend—a storyline suggesting that pregnancy necessitates marriage for respectability's sake. To her chagrin, none of Veronica's plans are working out the way she and her fiancé had hoped. She complains to Denise, "I can't get a decent job without a college degree" (Williams 1987). Dejected and concerned for her friend, Denise seeks out her mother for comfort and counsel, at which point Clair stubbornly denies that Veronica's situation would ever occur in her household. When Denise expresses a desire to help Veronica, Clair tells her,

> Denise, I know you feel this way and I'm glad you feel this way. But honey, you have got to learn how to care about people without taking on all their problems. Now Veronica has created this situation for herself. This is for her to deal with, not you . . . As her friend, the most that you can do is to love her and to let her know that you're here for her. (Williams 1987)

In other words, Veronica has made a foolish choice by getting pregnant out of wedlock and getting married young, and thus has "made her bed" and must lie in it. The storyline, including Clair's responses, underscore the show's politics of respectability and its emphasis on "proper," morally circumspect behavior as an avenue to upward mobility. It also suggests that Blacks who don't do this and make "bad choices" deserve no assistance and must pay for their mistakes on their own.

As indicated above, *The Cosby Show* offered a world absent of structure and the sociopolitical implications of Blackness. For example, most of the Huxtables' Black friends and acquaintances were middle class or upper middle class (Jhally and Lewis 1992) and therefore similar in background to the Huxtables. As Dyson (2005) pointed out, the show "hardly ever uttered a sentence about racial or class struggle. In fact, no sign of poor black folk was spotted until near the end of the series' run when a visiting relative of modest means was embraced by her wealthier kinfolk" (28; see also Jhally and Lewis 1992). Thus, notably absent were depictions of working-class or low-income Blacks—a fact that is particularly salient considering that the percentage of the Black poor increased dramatically during this period (Jhally and Lewis 1992; Dyson 2005). Hence, by and large, the Huxtables' affinity toward Blacks and Blackness, was toward middle-class Blacks and a very specific middle-class Blackness—a Blackness built firmly on upward mobility, the politics of respectability, and a seamless assimilation into White society.

The Cosby Show also absented structure from the lives of middle-class Blacks. For the most part, the world of the Huxtable family was largely a raceless one (Innis and Feagin 1995; Jhally and Lewis 1992) characterized by unfettered Black middle-class ascendance. Some middle-class Blacks were critical of the fact that the show presented "an upper middle class Black family that never experience[d] problems, especially racial problems" (Innis and Feagin 1995, 698). For instance, the show presents Cliff and Clair's professional ascension as one uncomplicated by being passed over for a promotion or saddled with the low expectations of supervisors and coworkers. At a time when middle-class Blacks were having these kinds of difficulties in the workplace and social spaces (see Cose 1993; Collins 1997; Feagin and Sikes 1994; Innis and Feagin 1995; Jacobs 2001), the fact that the Huxtable family never encountered White hostility rang false to some. In the end, this very popular depiction of carefree middle-class Blacks that was fairly ubiquitous in the 1980s and 1990s left the audience with a salient impression:

> The overall impression [from the show] is that the American dream is real for anyone who is willing to play by the rules. We are shown substantial upward mobility in only one generation and led to believe that mobility will be even more pronounced for the Huxtable children because they too are playing by

the rules. We are left with the impression that they will not face any barriers
or obstacles in the quest for a good life. (Innis and Feagin 1995, 709; see also
Jhally and Lewis 1992)

As this study shows, for real-life Vanessas, Denises, and Theos who grew up
second-generation Black middle class in the 1980s and 1990s, the journey
wasn't so easy.

As indicated earlier, Blackness isn't simply about minority status; it is
also about cultural identity. On *The Cosby Show*, cultural Blackness was
presented with a distinctly middle-class sensibility as represented through
the inclusions of Black art and jazz, which some White viewers even read
as a type of "high" or sophisticated culture (see Jhally and Lewis 1992). Lisa
Price, who performed production and writing duties on the show, reported,
"I saw [Cosby] fight many battles to make sure black people were represented
respectfully. He paid attention to every detail. All artwork had to be ap-
proved by Mr. Cosby. Black publications, such as *Ebony* and *Black Enterprise*,
were always placed prominently on the living room table" (Price and Beard
2004, 118; see also Jhally and Lewis 1992; Pouissant 1988, cited in Innis
and Feagin 1995). Some Black viewers interpreted the strategic placement
of Black cultural artifacts on the show as a reason for why it was "authentically Black" (Jhally and Lewis 1992). In these ways, the show offered some
depictions of cultural Blackness, even as it ignored the impact of Blackness
as a minority status. Ultimately, *The Cosby Show* was able to make White
viewers comfortable because of this rather glaring omission; instead of being
presented with the ugly realities of racism, the White audience could seek
comfort in the Huxtables' aesthetic tastes in art, jazz, and auctions—tastes
that made Whites see them as "cultured" and people with whom they could
identify (Jhally and Lewis 1992, 78). Perhaps because of this, the show was
able to survive and even thrive in the context of particularly virulent anti-
Black cultural, social, and economic discourses.

Noticeably deemphasized on *The Cosby Show* was an engagement with
Black culture and events as they existed in the 1980s and 1990s and outside
of a middle-class sensibility. Aside from a few instances, hip-hop culture was
minimally featured, and, when it was, it was used in a way that reflected or
supported the politics of respectability. For example, in season 4, episode
5 (titled "Shakespeare," written by Matt Robinson), Cockroach and Theo
converted parts of *Julius Caesar* to rap. This revision represented a decenter-
ing and co-opting of 1980s/1990s rap away from its moorings in race-class
inequalities and toward a literary classic emblematic of high culture. In the
1980s and 1990s, hip-hop was in its "Golden Age" (Ogbar 2007; see also

Kitwana 2002) and heavily political in nature, specifically centering on Blacks' experience of inequalities. Groups like Public Enemy were prominent on the music scene and rapped about poverty, police brutality, and the drug epidemic sweeping inner-city neighborhoods. Yet, when employed on *The Cosby Show*, rap was featured in such a way as to promote meritocratic or assimilationist ideals.[7] Other than this, current[8] manifestations of Blackness were largely absent.

In many ways, *The Cosby Show* serves as a mirror, albeit a funhouse mirror, to the real lives of middle-class Blacks, specifically second-generation middle-class Blacks who spent their formative years in the 1980s and 1990s. In this book, I refer to this group as the "Cosby Cohort"[9] as a means for (1) locating their lives in the time period and social context of the 1980s and 1990s when the show was at its pinnacle, (2) situating them in the race-class nexus that they shared with the Huxtables as middle-class Blacks, and (3) referencing the privilege they enjoyed as a result of this class background, much like the Huxtable children. In listening to their stories captured in this book, we see that their lives resembled the Huxtable children's in key ways. Most grew up in two-parent families at a time when the political discourse convinced most of America that this was an anomaly for Black children. In addition, as children, these Blacks traveled abroad like Theo, were peppered with taunts of "rich girl" like Vanessa, tested their parents' boundaries like Denise, and eventually ended up at law school like Sondra. They were children of privilege. However, unlike the Huxtable children, the Cosby Cohort composed of real-life second-generation, solidly middle-class Blacks who grew up in the 1980s and 1990s led lives that were deeply affected by the salience of race.

During this era, race was a paramount issue for Black middle-class families as they witnessed the hostility of the anti-Black discourse and felt the gains of affirmative action and Black progress potentially slipping away. This necessitated a host of preventive measures employed by parents in order to ensure their children's upward mobility, including moving them to White suburban neighborhoods and schools. As a result, the Cosby Cohort's privilege forced them to confront the realities of race at a very young age. This represents a significant departure from *The Cosby Show*, which never directly addressed the impact of White racism. In real-life Black middle-class families, it was clear that achievement was necessary in order to compensate for the realities of racial discrimination. Reminders of that minority status were part and parcel of the Cosby Cohort's childhoods, where their achievement and inclusion in White spaces were meant to cement their upward mobility in spite of it.

As the remaining chapters demonstrate, while Blackness as a minority status was stressed in the home, there was an appreciable lack of emphasis on *cultural* Blackness in these families where children were taught a minimum of Black or African history and sporadically attended Black cultural events (or didn't at all). Much like with *The Cosby Show*, cultural Blackness was rarely emphasized or took on a distinctly middle-class sensibility (e.g., trips to museum exhibits featuring Black inventors or the inclusion of books featuring Black characters). Excluded or minimized in the daily lives of these families were more obvious and current manifestations of cultural Blackness, such as hip-hop culture (e.g., dress, language, and sometimes music). Furthermore, respondents reported receiving very few messages about Black solidarity and Blackness as a group identity as children, where the messages they did receive often cast Black culture and people in a negative light. As a result of all of these factors, for some members of the Cosby Cohort, race was more "accidental" to their identity, thus manifesting in tenuous connections to non-middle-class Blacks and more ambivalent racial identities. Their stories tell us much about how "privileged" Black Americans must conform to and also resist oppressive contexts and the repercussions of such a fight over the life course. To date, there is very little research on the experiences of second-generation middle-class Blacks.

Previous Research on Second-Generation Middle-Class Blacks

Negligible research exists on the lives of this generation and fairly small cohort who faced considerable challenges around issues of assimilation and upward mobility. However, there is anecdotal and statistical evidence that suggests that all was not well for Black middle-class children growing up in suburbia during the 1980s and 1990s. For example, fifteen-year-old Edwin Jones Jr. lived in suburban Chicago, where his father was both a police officer and a minister. He was a cymbal player in the high school band and president of his youth group at church. His stepmother, Shauna, described him as a neat child who was well groomed and cared a lot about his appearance. Tragically, in November 1997, Edwin was found in his family's basement, dead of a self-inflicted gunshot wound. In his room upstairs was a suicide note that he left on his bed beside a picture of himself. In the note, Edwin discussed having recently failed a subject in school for the first time in his life and his despair over this: "By the time you receive this note, you're gonna know I received an F, and I'd rather be dead than to get a whooping" (Public Broadcasting Service 1998). His suicide came as a shock to his father and stepmother. Shauna noted that she worried about "the pressures Edwin put himself under" to get good grades and achieve (Public Broadcasting Service 1998). Yet, from Edwin's suicide note, it seems that the pressure he was under wasn't completely self-imposed but was in some part the result of the pressures he felt from his parents to achieve.

In reference to the Jones case and the trend of rising Black adolescent suicides in the 1980s and 1990s, Dr. Carl Bell surmised that the unique experiences of Black middle-class children may be a key factor in suicide and suicidal ideation: "For the middle class black child, they're sort of marginal in between the poor working class black world and in between the white professional world, and they don't fit in either world to some extent. So they're also at risk for getting a depression and then being alienated and isolated" (Public Broadcasting Service 1998). Indeed, the Centers for Disease Control (CDC) declared that between 1980 and 1995, the suicide rate for Blacks ages ten to nineteen increased by 114 percent (CDC 1998). In the report, the CDC speculated that a possible factor for the increased rate was the growth of the Black middle class: "Black youths in upwardly mobile families may experience stress associated with their new social environments" (CDC 1998). A handful of case studies on Black middle-class children indicate that there are social and psychological challenges that can exist among this group and thus that a closer examination of their experiences is in order (e.g., Boyd-Franklin 2003; Day-Vines et al. 2003). Still, since the CDC's report, there has been little more than conjecture about the pressures of growing up Black middle class in White environments, leaving us to wonder what life might be like for other second-generation middle-class Blacks like Edwin Jones and members of subsequent generations as well.

An abundance of literature in the past thirty years has detailed the ways in which Black parenting has been shaped by the realities of integration and assimilation (Boykin and Toms 1985; Hill 1999, 2005), particularly for middle-class Blacks in White-dominated spaces (Feagin and Sikes 1994; Hill 2005; Lacy 2007; Reynolds 2010; Tatum 1999). Much of this research discusses the ways in which parents teach their children how to navigate and succeed in a White world. In many cases, a common message is that as Blacks they will have to achieve more than their White counterparts in order to compete and get ahead. While Black parents most often stress the Black–White color line, there is every reason to believe that they recognize Asian and Latino competition as well. For example, in a qualitative study done by Coard et al. (2004), one mother admitted to teaching her child, "We have to be better than any other race . . . in order to succeed . . . we have to be so much better. So much smarter" (287). The National Black

Parents Association (NBPA) also recognizes the competition from other minority groups when they state on their Facebook page, "NBPA works tirelessly to mobilize black parents to reform public education and eliminate the academic achievement gap between black students and their white, Asian and Hispanic counterparts" (NBPA n.d.). In these ways, and as other accounts of middle-class Blacks have already noted (Lacy 2007; Lareau 2003), the challenge for these parents is to employ strategies that will help their children to compete successfully above all others and ultimately achieve successful structural assimilation.

However, there remains scant research on how those who grow up in such a structure and atmosphere are affected by this socialization. Essentially, their stories would indicate the difficulties and challenges inherent in the Black assimilation process if even the most privileged Blacks (who had access to many of the same opportunities and amenities as some White children) were still forced to negotiate a multitude of racialized obstacles that impacted their quality of life and sense of identity. For the Cosby Cohort in particular, this was a battle fought at a time where White hostility and resentment was notably strong because of the increasing integration of neighborhoods, schools, and public places. Unlike the adults profiled in so many accounts of Black middle-class life in the 1980s and 1990s, they were children who had to navigate these waters without the benefit of adult experiences and racial wisdom with which to contextualize and understand their experiences. In other words, at young ages, they were pushed toward achievement while also being constantly exposed to the realities of racism. They did not have a great deal of practice in making sense of these realities or navigating successfully through them. This experience proved frightening, frustrating, intimidating, and overwhelming for some detailed in this book, which indicates the vulnerability of Black middle-class children whose life histories and experiences clearly merit more scholarly consideration.

Despite the privilege that many Black middle-class families have enjoyed, historically there has been a certain fragility to their class status that is manifested in a variety of statistics and measures on income, education, occupation, wealth, and downward mobility (see Jackson 2001; Pattillo-McCoy 1999). For example, a little over fifteen years ago, when much of the Cosby Cohort was graduating from high school, Andrew Hacker (1995), author of *Two Nations: Black and White, Separate, Hostile, Unequal*, explained, "While there is now a much larger Black middle-class, more typically, the husband is likely to be a bus driver earning $32,000, while his wife brings home $28,000 as a teacher or a nurse. A white middle-class family is three to four times more likely to contain a husband earning $75,000 in a managerial position" (104–5). In other words, Black middle-class families tend to be dependent on two incomes where parents' combined salaries still fall far below a single-earner White middle-class family. Moreover, because of their lower-than-average incomes and the legacy of slavery and institutional discrimination (e.g., residential segregation, discriminatory lending practices, etc.) that have prevented wealth accumulation in Black families, middle-class Blacks typically possess less wealth than their White counterparts. During the Cosby Cohort's formative years, Oliver and Shapiro (1995) found that middle-class Blacks earned seventy cents for every dollar earned by middle-class Whites but possessed only fifteen cents for every dollar of wealth held by middle-class Whites. Thus, for Black middle-class families in the 1980s and 1990s, economic security was far from certain.

For parents who were (1) experiencing their own class insecurities as first-generation middle class and (2) concerned with social reproduction for their children, the pursuit of class goals may have been all-consuming. These goals might have prompted them to push their children to achieve high grades in accelerated courses or to excel in a plethora of extracurricular activities in order to increase their odds of being admitted into a good college. Perhaps of lesser importance was ensuring that their children maintained a strong and viable racial identity. The 1980s and 1990s era of White resistance may have convinced parents that it would be better to play down cultural Blackness for their children, which complicated their racial identity development. When I speak of racial identity, I am drawing primarily from Broman et al.'s (1988) concept, namely, "the feelings of closeness to similar others in ideas, feelings, and thoughts" (148). I am also referring to Stryker's (1980) concept of *identity salience*, which refers to the importance of an identity in the definition of self. Essentially, I refer to identity in terms of not only whether a Black middle-class individual perceives him- or herself as having something in common with other Blacks but also the extent to which he or she feels that being Black is central to his or her personal identity and the extent to which he or she feels a cultural affinity to Blackness.

A great deal of research claims that racial and cultural socialization is common in Black families and is employed in order to provide a racial identity for Black children (Bowman and Howard 1985; Boykin and Toms 1985; Demo and Hughes 1990; DuBois 1903b; Hill 1999; Hughes and Chen 1997; Marshall 1995; Neckerman et al. 1999; Peters 1985; Phinney and Chavira 1995; Stevenson 1994; Stevenson et al. 2002; Tatum 1999; Thompson 1994; Thornton et al. 1990; Willie 2001). Black middle-class parents even claim they provide this type of socialization (Lacy 2007), but the stories told by their children yield a different picture.

To be sure, having a strong racial and cultural identity is of the utmost importance in a country that organizes and coalesces around the concept of race. In a debate in *Harper's Magazine*, Cornel West noted the personal and sociopolitical importance of racial identity:

> People identify themselves in certain ways in order to protect their bodies, their labor, their communities, their way of life; in order to be associated with people who ascribe value to them, who take them seriously, who respect them; and for purposes of recognition, to be acknowledged, to feel as if one actually belongs to a group, a clan, a tribe, a community. (Klor de Alva et al. 1997, 483–84)

Dalmage (2000) further suggests, "Some sense of unity, of an 'us,' is necessary when groups are struggling for greater justice. This sense of community is necessary for both countering the feelings of alienation created by oppression and building political struggles" (12). As both statements indicate, in addition to the personal salience of racial identity, there are obvious sociopolitical implications when people have organized around issues they feel are important to the community in which they *feel* they belong. Thus, racial identity salience may be a requirement for social and political action related to group concerns (Thompson 1999).

Yet the personal salience of racial identity cannot be ignored or underestimated. For individuals marginalized by race, feeling attached to a culture and community is vital to a sense of belonging (Lacy 2004), as "Blacks feel a sense of affirmation when other blacks accept them as black" (Dalmage 2000, 112). In addition, the more affiliated and connected Blacks feel to their community, the less vulnerable they are to psychological distress (see Kaslow et al. 2004) and the more they are able to lean on the community as a buffer against discrimination (Sellers and Shelton 2003). Finally, having a strong racial identity is tied to other processes that improve life chances, including academic achievement (Bowman and Howard 1985), college performance (Sellers, Chavous, and Cooke 1998), perceived academic and career efficacy (Smith et al. 1999), and self-esteem and self-efficacy (Smith et al. 1999). For all of these reasons, racial identity is quite important for the individual.

However, for this racial class (and for children especially), forging a viable racial identity becomes increasingly difficult when caught in the status inconsistency of being both Black and middle class. A status inconsistency occurs when an individual has two (or more) statuses of varying levels of prestige (Lenski 1954, 1967) and "is a source of stress for individuals, especially when the inconsistencies are substantial since individuals prefer to think of themselves in terms of their higher status or statuses, while others have a tendency to treat them in terms of their lower status" (Lenski 1967, 298). In other words, while middle-class Blacks are privileged by class, they must still deal with the realities of belonging to a racial minority group subject to racial discrimination. This stress was all the more acute among adults who were pioneers in desegregating neighborhoods, schools, and other White spaces in the 1980s and 1990s. We know even less about how the children at that time made meaning of their dual statuses or the difficulties with racial identity development that conflicting statuses present throughout the life course.

In the last twenty years, the childhood experiences of second-generation middle-class Blacks have begun to receive some attention in the scholarly literature. For example, Beverly Daniel Tatum's (1999) ethnography *Assimilation Blues* details the lives of Black middle class parents raising children in a White suburb in California in the 1980s. Mainly, Tatum presents an account of parental intentionality where parents discussed how they were raising upwardly mobile children and the advantages that *they believed* they were providing for them by raising them in a White suburb. The story is told almost entirely from the parents' point of view, with the voices of the second generation receiving very little attention. Only in the last few pages of the book does Tatum interview two young women who spent their childhoods in predominantly White communities; their briefly mentioned stories indicate the difficulties Black middle-class children sometimes have in reconciling their race and class. Nevertheless, because her analysis focuses almost entirely on the parents, there remain unanswered questions about how the second generation experienced and made meaning of this process.

Arguably, Pattillo-McCoy's (1999) *Black Picket Fences* remains the seminal work on the post–civil rights Black middle class. Pattillo offers an ethnography of a rather fragile middle class living on the South Side of Chicago and in the shadow of the ghetto. The book offers a great deal of insight into second-generation Black middle-class children but focuses singularly on urban residents who live in close proximity to impoverished areas, meaning that they must constantly negotiate issues of crime and the lure of ghetto culture that stresses easy money over hard work. That lure proved too great for some of the children in this area, making upward mobility a significant challenge for her respondents. Pattillo's research speaks to a Black middle class that is financially insecure and that, in many ways, experiences a life similar to their low-income neighbors, complete with drugs, crime, and an emphasis on materialism. Their well-being is compromised by living in this space. But, because Pattillo's text is centrally focused on the Black middle class within urban communities, there remains a gap in the literature where the experiences of that same generation who were raised in White suburban communities is missing. Also missing are the ways in which that experience has affected their racial identity over the life course.

Lareau's (2003) classic study *Unequal Childhoods: Class, Race, and Family Life* touches briefly on a more secure Black middle class living in mostly White suburban areas. However, only two of the twelve case studies offered in her book focus specifically on middle-class Black children. Those case studies are told mostly through the lens of the research team observing the parents and children and also include accounts from the parents themselves. Again, this offers limited information from the second generation's point of view. Nevertheless, Lareau offers a wonderful in-depth account of the transmission of cultural capital in these families and introduces the concept of "concerted cultivation," or the ways in which middle-class parents purposefully nurture their children's talents and abilities and teach them communication and interaction skills that facilitate upward mobility. The research presented here expands on Lareau's concept of concerted cultivation in Black middle-class families. Still, one of the main criticisms of her work is that she suggests that there is very little difference between how White and Black middle-class children are raised, asserting that "race did not appear to shape the dominant cultural logic of childrearing" (133) in Black middle-class families. The accounts of the respondents in this book challenge this claim as race remained firmly at the center of their lives in a variety of different and unexpected ways.

Finally, Karyn Lacy's (2007) *Blue Chip Black: Race, Class, and Status in the New Black Middle-Class* accounted for several of the gaps in the previous literature. In thirty in-depth interviews with couples, Lacy details the lives of two very secure populations of "blue-chip" middle-class Blacks, known as the "elite" (e.g., those with occupations requiring more than a bachelor's degree and whose household income is likely over $100,000) and the "core" (e.g., those with occupations requiring a bachelor's degree and who have a household income between $50,000 and $100,000). Both populations lived in either White suburbs or Black suburbs, far from the ghettos and disenfranchisement detailed in Pattillo's book. Lacy offers a thorough analysis of how Black middle-class adults negotiate racial, class, status, public, and suburban identities and how they transmit related messages to their children.

Still absent is any indication of how the second generation internalized these messages and how these experiences shaped their views around racial identity and identification. Additionally, like Lareau and Tatum, because her account focuses primarily on parents and how they transmit cultural capital and manage their own identities, we still have little indication of the second generation's perspective on growing up Black middle class and the short- and long-term effects that such an experience has on a racial identity development.

The Present Study

In this book, I close some of the gaps in the previous literature by using interviews from members of the Cosby Cohort to answer four central questions. First, how have the lives of suburban second-generation middle-class Blacks been shaped in response to racism and the attendant challenges of assimilation, class mobility, and racial identity development? Second, what are the unintended and unanticipated costs of being raised in White-dominated spaces and constructing lives around successful assimilation and integration? Third, how do the childhood events and experiences of the Cosby Cohort indicate the presence of inequality in the lives of even the most privileged Blacks?

A fourth major question posed by this study is, what are the residual effects of growing up Black middle class in White environments? In particular, now that they are adults, how connected does the second generation feel toward Black people and culture given their childhood experiences? Much has been written on the Black middle class's alleged disconnect from the rest of the community (Drake and Cayton 1962; Dyson 2005; Frazier 1957; Nunnally 2010; Robinson 2010; Wiese 2004; Wilson 1980), and other research contests these claims (see Dawson 1994; Higginbotham and Weber 1992; Hochschild 1995; Jackson 2001; Pattillo 2007; Pattillo-McCoy 1999). However, questions remain about how connected middle-class Blacks—specifically those of the second generation—feel toward the rest of the community. Their level of attachment may depend largely on the racial identity that they have pieced together in the context of White places and spaces. Yet the literature on racial identity offers little information about identity development within this group. Existing studies are limited in key ways: (1) most utilize quantitative measures, thus obscuring the socialization process in Black families, (2) they are heavily reliant on a survey of Black adults during the 1979–1980 wave of the National Survey of Black Americans (NSBA) and are therefore dated and exclude the experiences of children growing up around that time, and (3) they frequently examine identity among poorer Blacks rather than middle-class Blacks (e.g., Demo and Hughes 1990; Thornton et al. 1990; Thompson 1999). In light of these limitations, several important questions remain unanswered: (1) given their childhoods spent in White spaces in the 1980s and 1990s, to what extent does the Cosby Cohort identify with and feel attached to a Black community that mainly consists of working-class and low-income Blacks; (2) what meanings have they attached to being both Black and middle class; and, perhaps most important, (3) how much of their racial worldview is the result of their childhood socialization?

The Cosby Cohort: Blessings and Burdens of Growing Up Black Middle Class[10] focuses on the childhood socialization and racial identity development of thirty-three second-generation middle-class Blacks between the ages of twenty-three and forty who grew up in White spaces in the 1980s and 1990s. This particular age range was chosen in order to produce a sample that (1) was slightly more mature and would have at least a small measure of life experience by which to gauge their childhood experiences and (2) had likely completed a bachelor's degree and moved into the workplace or postgraduate work, thus making them more solidly middle class. Participants were drawn from a medium-size city in southeastern Georgia[11] and solicited through Black graduate student and faculty listservs and through the use of snowball sampling, which offered access to professionals outside of academe. The primary criterion for the study was that respondents had to grow up in a household where at least one of their parents or guardians held a white-collar (i.e., professional, managerial, or clerical) job or was an owner of a successful business. Second, each respondent had to meet the same criteria themselves or be graduate students studying to obtain a white-collar job. Similar criteria have been used in other studies on middle-class Blacks (see Blackwell 1985; Coner-Edwards and Spurlock 1988; Feagin and Sikes 1994; Higginbotham and Weber 1992; Kronus 1971; Landry 1987; Oliver and Shapiro 1995; Pattillo-McCoy 1999; Wilson 1995).

In adulthood, these respondents became the corporate managers, grade school teachers, researchers, doctors, lawyers, and professors that their parents struggled so diligently to raise. In many ways, they have "made it" and are now in a position to use their financial, social, political, and cultural capital on behalf of the rest of the community. Thus, using this sample and method accomplishes a number of tasks and illuminates several sociological phenomena. First, because the respondents in this sample ultimately became upwardly mobile professionals, their narratives become indicators of all that is required to negotiate the unique problems of assimilation for Blacks. Second, because a great deal of research indicates a divide between today's Black middle class and their lower-income counterparts, these narratives (and to some extent life histories) give us a better indication of how that may have come to be the case. Finally, by using the childhood recollections of these adults rather than the accounts of actual children in the sample, we obtain a more expansive, reflective, and nuanced picture of growing up Black middle class in White spaces.[12]

A particular challenge of this research is its reliance on memory. The questions posed to the interviewees required them to recall specific events and emotions from their childhood; these are events from over fifteen years ago (and longer in the case of older respondents). Memories of past events are not as accurate as recent ones (Peterson 1980), and recall bias can occur, particularly if there is a large gap in time between the events in question and the data collection (Lesane-Brown 2006). Moreover, memories play an integral role in the construction of the self (Crawford et al. 1992), which means that they are subject to being constructed and reconstructed in ways that feel congruent with whom an individual imagines him- or herself to be.[13] In these ways and others, memories can sometimes be unreliable (Onyx and Small 2001). Nevertheless, it seemed that the interviewees had very little trouble remembering the not-too-distant past, and many were even moved to tears as they recalled some of the events, particularly childhood identity events. This is consistent with research indicating that when people reflect on the past, they are more likely to remember what they felt at the time rather than situational details about the event (Peterson 1980). This was beneficial to the study, as respondents were more likely to give an accurate account of the emotions surrounding their childhood experiences where the particular sequence of events was less important. Furthermore, the remarkable similarity in the life events and memories of different respondents suggests that their recollections were fairly accurate representations of the realities of growing up Black middle class.[14]

Participants were first asked some preliminary questions designed to glean demographic and background information. Data were collected on their parents' occupations; their hometown(s); the number and type of activities they participated in as children; the racial compositions of their neighborhoods, schools, and friendship circles; and any other information that would establish a context for the interviews. Following the preliminary questionnaire, I asked one series of questions about their family lives, socialization, schooling, social difficulties, and racial identities in childhood. I then asked a second series of questions about their racial identities as adults. All interviews were transcribed, which resulted in thousands of pages of hand-coded transcripts.

In terms of sample characteristics, 64 percent of the respondents ($n = 21$) grew up in the South, another 15 percent in the Northeast, 6 percent in the West, 9 percent in the Midwest, and a remaining 6 percent grew up all over the country (mostly because of a parent's military service). The fact that this is mostly a Southern sample is notable because most of the previous research on middle-class Blacks (except for Karyn Lacy's) discusses non-Southern samples. Thus, this study offers a bird's-eye view into desegregating communities in the South, particularly during the 1980s and 1990s. For these respondents, the southern context might have yielded more intense feelings surrounding race and identity given the South's troubled racial history. In these ways, the study may be slightly less "generalizable" to those who grew up outside of the South. Nevertheless, there is a remarkable consistency in the stories of respondents who grew up in the South as compared to those who grew up in places like Nevada, New Jersey, California, Maryland, Illinois, and various other places outside the South. This suggests a similarity to the experience of growing up Black middle class during this period in America.

In terms of the racial composition of the neighborhoods in which respondents grew up, 49 percent ($n = 16$) grew up in neighborhoods that they considered predominantly White. Another 27 percent ($n = 9$) grew up in neighborhoods that they believed to be more racially mixed, either with an equal half Black–half White mix or with a true mixture of all races. Twenty-four percent ($n = 8$) grew up in neighborhoods that they classified as majority Black. Thus, the majority grew up in White neighborhoods and attended primarily White schools. Even those who grew up in more racially mixed neighborhoods reported attending White schools or being immersed in White social circles because of their class status.

Respondents' parents held jobs as corporate managers, civil servants, professors, judges, principals, nurses, pilots, military personnel, and various other white-collar jobs. In terms of Black middle-class status, 85 percent ($n = 28$) grew up in what Lacy (2007) regards as the "core" Black middle class, where parents' occupation required a bachelor's degree and the household income was likely between $50,000 and $100,000. The remaining five respondents would likely fit the category of the "elite" Black middle class (see Lacy 2007), where parents had occupations that required more than a bachelor's degree and whose household income was likely over $100,000. Regarding gender, 76 percent of the interviewees were women, and 24 percent were men. That this sample is mostly female may offer a somewhat one-sided account of this experience. Overall, however, there appeared to be few salient differences between the experiences of men and women. Finally, in terms of age, the mean age was twenty-eight years, where 76 percent percent of respondents (*n* = 25) were between the ages of twenty-three and thirty at the time of the study.

The data presented in this study suggest that despite the privilege afforded by their social class, as children, second-generation middle-class Blacks were forced to negotiate and compensate for the direct and indirect effects of race. In terms of direct effects, in living and interacting in majority White spaces, respondents were forced to manage the overt and covert racism offered by neighbors, school administrators, and various significant others in their lives. The indirect effects essentially manifested themselves in the pressures and stressors of achievement inherent in the process of social reproduction in Black middle-class families. In other words, much of the Cosby Cohort's lives were spent in pursuit of achievement and upward mobility as a way to overcome the racism directed toward them as children and the discrimination their parents anticipated them facing as adults. Ultimately, these strategies bore fruit and they became the upwardly mobile adults that their parents strived to raise. Yet they paid a price. First, as children, respondents were burdened with intense pressure from parents to achieve that in many ways served to abbreviate their childhoods. Second, they were expected to achieve and thrive in environments that were racially isolated and hostile, which appeared to add an additional stressor and presented significant challenges to racial identity development. Third, because parents placed achievement and pursuit of class goals at the center of their children's lives, class became a more salient part of their identity than race. This left most respondents with ambivalent or limited attachments to Black people and Black culture in adulthood.

The findings in this book extend our knowledge of the heterogeneity of the Black experience while raising additional questions as well. For example, a recent survey indicates that 70 percent of Blacks believe that there is a monolithic "Black experience" (Harris 2008, 4), and previous research has suggested the same (see Gwaltney 1980; Marable 2002). The data presented here indicate that this is not the case. Middle-class Blacks, particularly those raised in White areas, inhabit a vastly different world than the majority of Blacks. For the Cosby Cohort, their childhood socialization into a culture of mobility and their years spent in predominantly White environments distanced them both spatially and experientially from other Blacks. For this reason, forging a viable racial identity became a tricky proposition, as they had little familiarity with other Blacks or with aspects of Black culture in general. Their stories indicate the ways in which middle-class Blacks struggle to fit comfortably in both the White and the Black world, forever trying to reconcile their double consciousness (DuBois 1903b).

In this book, we journey through the childhood recollections of the Cosby Cohort and the distinct advantages and disadvantages associated with their childhood experiences. As much as possible, I try to let the voices of the respondents be heard because "personal narratives [can] provide a strong sense of experiential impact" (Thompson-Miller and Feagin 2007, 111). In chapter 2, "Training for the Race: The Cosby Cohort and the Black Middle-Class Culture of Mobility," I use the Cosby Cohort's experiences to explore the Black middle-class culture of mobility, which consists of a series of strategies, opportunities, and amenities designed to ensure children's upward mobility and the ability to compete successfully with White counterparts. These strategies include access to safe neighborhoods, stable family environments, superior school systems, enriching extracurricular activities, and proficiency in Standard English. However, in return for these opportunities, respondents as children were expected to sacrifice large amounts of time and energy toward taking full advantage of these prospects. In many ways, this led to abbreviated childhoods and saddled them with adultlike concerns at an early age. Their socialization into the culture of mobility often included purposely separating children from non-middle-class Black counterparts and transmitting negative messages about this group. Negative messages about Whites (also part of the culture of mobility) appeared to complicate the issue where, as children, they found themselves distant from this group as well, leaving them with no "home" among either Whites or Blacks. These experiences not only left respondents extremely stressed but also left them floundering to find a place where they belong—both then as children and now as adults.

In chapter 3, "Race Lessons: What the Cosby Cohort *Really* Learned about Blacks and Blackness," I explore the content, quality, and extent of racial, cultural, and intraracial messages in Black middle-class families in order to understand how the Cosby Cohort has acquired a racialized worldview and racial and cultural identity. Findings indicate that respondents were far more likely to receive messages that emphasized the negatives of being Black (e.g., inequality and discrimination) rather than messages emphasizing the positive cultural aspects of Blackness and Black people. In addition (and contrary to an abundance of previous research), while some respondents received a good deal of racial and cultural socialization, a fairly sizable portion received little or none of this type of socialization, leaving them with no Black counterframe (see Feagin 2010) to help them negotiate racial discrimination or to teach them how to be proud of being Black in the context of a racist society. Furthermore, parents frequently transmitted negative messages about non-middle-class Blacks that suggested that they were not as smart, capable, or worthy as middle-class Blacks. These findings suggest that class socialization (detailed in chapter 2) rather than racial and cultural socialization took center stage in the Cosby Cohort's lives, which left respondents with racial identity issues in childhood that ultimately shaped their understandings of Blackness as well as their interactions with other Blacks.

In chapter 4, "Cast Out of the Race: The Reality of Childhood Intraracial Rejection," I examine how the combination of the culture of mobility (discussed in chapter 2) and parental racial, cultural, and intraracial socialization (discussed in chapter 3) affected the racial identity development of the Cosby Cohort and their interactions with and feelings toward other Blacks. In large part, their adoption of the culture of mobility influenced their Black peers' perceptions of them in childhood, which led to a series of events in which their racial identity was questioned or challenged (hereafter referred to as "identity events"). Frequently, they were accused of "acting White"— a designation that often precipitated being cast out of Black social circles. While previous research suggests that this accusation causes children to underperform academically (Fordham and Ogbu 1986), other research convincingly refutes these findings (Carter 2005; Cook and Ludwig 1998; Tyson et al. 2005). Certainly, for middle-class children raised under the culture of mobility, underperforming was not an option. Still, as is consistent with previous research (Neal-Barnett et al. 2010; Peterson-Lewis and Bratton 2004), the "acting White" accusation played a pivotal role in respondents' lives. This chapter moves us beyond the literature that merely focuses on the accusation's impact on academic performance to instead focusing on how it affects attachments to Black people and culture over the life course. Much of this chapter discusses (1) the consequences of the Cosby Cohort's inability to approximate an acceptable Black performance as children, (2) their strong emotional responses to the acting White accusation, and (3) their parents' effective and ineffective responses to these events.

Chapter 5, "Losing the Race? Attachment, Ambivalence, and Retreat," explores the cumulative impact of these childhood experiences on adult racial identity. First, I offer a general profile of the second-generation Black middle-class adults whose childhood experiences are detailed in this study. These children turned into the successful adults that their parents strived to raise, which represents a positive outcome of the Black middle-class culture of mobility. However, it appears to have come at great cost to their racialized sense of self. Twenty-six of the thirty-three respondents in the study indicated either ambivalent or limited attachments to Black people and culture in adulthood, while only seven indicated much stronger attachments. For those with ambivalent or limited attachments, their attitudes are largely the result of (1) a childhood focused on matters of social class and upward mobility; (2) negative or inconsistent racial, cultural, and intraracial socialization; and (3) negative interactions with other Blacks in childhood. Thus, as a result of their unique life experiences, some members of the Cosby Cohort are more distant toward poorer counterparts than the generation before them. In this way, the current study continues to raise questions about feelings of solidarity among Blacks and indicates the ways in which the middle class's response to systemic racism can result in alienation from self and community.

In the final chapter, chapter 6, "Passing the Baton," I conclude that we must look much more closely at the ways in which responses to racism carry significant sociopolitical consequences. Essentially, I explore how the potential divestiture of this privileged segment of Black America negatively affects the group as a whole, resulting in a potential crisis in leadership as well as decreased political support for social problems affecting poorer Blacks. Previous research suggests that regardless of class, Blacks will consistently vote for a pro-Black agenda (Dawson 1994; Hajnal 2007; Hochschild 1995; see also Sears 2008; Sears et al. 2003). However, the data presented here raise questions about such an allegiance. Furthermore, the question may not be about whether middle-class Blacks will vote for a pro-Black agenda, but how strongly they will support it. Simply voting for Black issues may be less effective than active, grassroots-level organizing and support. Given their childhood socialization and a lifetime of feeling distant from other Blacks, will this generation be willing to use their resources for the good of the entire community? Research presented here suggests that, for them, this might be a challenge. Yet without their support and commitment to social justice for all segments of the community, Black advancement may prove difficult.

It is my hope that the research in this book will give us another way to think about middle-class Blacks and the ways in which racial issues remain at the center of their lives and are further complicated by issues of class.

CHAPTER TWO

~

Training for the Race: The Cosby Cohort and the Black Middle-Class Culture of Mobility

You have to be one on top of them if you want to stay ahead.—Alexis

In the magical world of *The Cosby Show*, the Huxtable children thrived within a multiracial community in Brooklyn, where there was little stress and strife save for the normal challenges of being a kid. Nested comfortably in their brownstone, the Huxtables hosted gatherings and parties full of White, Latino, Asian, and biracial guests who also seemed to be middle class. They existed in a world of racial harmony even though that time in Brooklyn (and New York City in general) was anything but. However, exposing the racial tension in New York in the 1980s and 1990s does not exactly make for good sitcom material. It is exceedingly difficult to set a laugh track to Black–Hasidic tensions in Crown Heights or the anti-Black sentiment in Bensonhurst that were characteristic of New York City at that time (and perhaps even today). Thus, it is understandable that *The Cosby Show* offered viewers a Black middle-class oasis of racial harmony devoid of racial and even class strife. Yet for real-life second-generation middle-class Blacks of the Cosby Cohort, life was far less smooth than it was for the Huxtable children.

Black middle-class parents in the 1980s and 1990s who were raising children during a discourse of Black ressentiment were forced to make very difficult decisions regarding their children's lives. Gaining access to and succeeding within the public institutions and organizations of White society (i.e., structural assimilation) requires providing children with as much cultural capital as possible, regardless of sacrifices required on behalf of both parents and children. Bourdieu and Passeron (1979) use the term "cultural capital" to refer to the knowledge, skills, behaviors, or dispositions that can be converted into prestige and/or financial capital and transmitted through generations. In American society, the "knowledge, skills, behaviors, or dispositions" required are ones valued by Whites as the dominant group. Having this kind of cultural capital reaps rewards and can raise one's social or economic status. In the postdesegregation era, having the "right" cultural capital (e.g., education, values, dispositions, orientations, and knowledge that can often be found in the "right" neighborhoods and schools and with the "right" friends) became critical to the success of middle-class Blacks who were finally integrating resistant White places and spaces (Tatum 1999; Wilson 1980) as a result of affirmative action and equal opportunity legislation.

It perhaps cannot be stated strongly enough that the first generation's desire to acquire the right cultural capital for their children is a response to the White racial frame (Feagin 2010) or the country's dominant "frame of mind" where matters of race are concerned. Among other things, that frame includes racial stereotypes, narratives, and images as well as racialized emotions toward people of color. Fairly often, these conceptualizations manifest in discriminatory actions (Feagin 2010). According to Feagin (2010), this frame developed early in the country's history and has become a hegemonic worldview that stresses White superiority and virtue. It is also a frame that early on centered on Black Americans, reserving the most discriminatory treatment for this particular racial group (Feagin 2010). It is through this frame that Blacks are frequently depicted as unintelligent, lazy, unruly, violent, unattractive, and hypersexual, among other negative characteristics. It is because of this frame that a politics of respectability was established early on by middle-class Blacks as a way to dispel Black stereotypes and gain access to White institutions. Similarly, it also plays a key role in the development of a minority middle-class culture of mobility that parents of color have had to establish in order to ensure their children's upward mobility within a racist structure.

Neckerman et al. (1999) use the term "minority middle-class culture of mobility" to refer to "a set of cultural elements that [are] associated with a minority group and that [provide] strategies for managing economic mobility in the context of discrimination and group disadvantage. . . . [It] draws on available symbols, idioms and practices to respond to distinctive problems of being middle class and minority" (949). The Black middle-class culture of mobility, in particular, provides two interactional guides: one for interactions in majority White settings and another for interactions with non-middle-class Blacks. Mastering the two interactional guides has proven to be the key that opens many doors to success in White America—even the door to the most prestigious office in the land. According to scholar Orlando Patterson (2009), President Obama's success can in large part be attributed to his proficiency in both interactional guides:

> [Obama's] success is not, as is often superficially claimed by others, due to his transcendence of race. His life and achievement, rather, is the perfect exemplification of the value of cultural integration. White Americans, including many with persisting racial biases, could look beyond race in judging him precisely because they also saw in him someone who had achieved mastery in both the formal and informal areas of American culture. And [he] was able to do so in part because of his socialization into the private domains of both white and black[1] private life. (15)

In other words, while mastering the culture of mobility may not change racial biases, it makes it more difficult for them to prevail after one has become bicultural and adept in managing White and Black interactions.

The next chapter focuses more extensively on the guide to interactions in Black settings provided under the culture of mobility. This chapter focuses on the guide to interactions in White settings and the ways in which parents prepare their children to interact in the White world and compete more successfully with White counterparts. As Neckerman et al. (1999) note, this culture and the strategies contained within are a response to a racist social structure and, most particularly, one that practices Black exceptionalism (see Gans 2008) by reserving most of its hostility for Blacks. In this chapter, I extend Neckerman et al.'s concept of the Black middle-class culture of mobility to explore how the constellation of strategies and knowledge employed by parents is experienced by their children. By the time Black middle-class children reach adulthood, the invisibility of the socialization process can make it appear as if their successes were effortless rather than the result of a deliberately crafted, strenuous training program created during childhood and designed to compensate for racial discrimination. However, through their own lived experience, parents realized that Black middle-class status didn't exempt one from racist treatment or the looming threat of downward mobility. In anticipation of these realities, the parents of the Cosby Cohort attempted to provide their children with enough cultural capital to transcend racial prejudices and discrimination, thus ensuring their children's ultimate success. Yet this process deeply affected the private worlds of the Cosby Cohort as children.

Research on middle-class Blacks discusses the myriad ways in which cultural capital is transmitted in these families. For instance, as briefly discussed in the previous chapter, Lareau's (2003) concept of "concerted cultivation" describes the ways in which Black middle-class parents develop their children's talents in an organized and purposeful fashion through participation in extracurricular activities (see also Lacy 2007). Others have discussed additional assimilation-ist strategies, such as wearing conservative styles of dress and hair and striving for academic and professional excellence (see Coard et al. 2004; Cose 1993; Fordham and Ogbu 1986; Jackson 2001; McKnight 1993; Neckerman et al. 1999; Pattillo-McCoy 1999; Tatum 1999). Meticulous neighborhood (Lacy 2007; Tatum 1999) and school selection (Diamond and Gomez 2004; Lareau 2003; Toliver 1998) also rank among key strategies employed for the purposes of ensuring children's ultimate success. Scholarship on cultural capital in Black middle-class families tends to use parents as the primary subjects who discuss with the researcher (1) the strategies they invoke in order to help their chil-dren navigate and negotiate the White world, (2) the need for such strategies as well as the challenges of executing them, and (3) what *they perceive* as the outcome of their efforts (for examples, see Lacy 2007; Lareau 2003; Tatum 1999). Collectively, these studies reveal a carefully crafted Black middle-class culture of mobility where parents arrange all external conditions in a way that will yield the best possible outcomes for their children.

What these arrangements also reveal is an exacting script that children must follow and from which they must not deviate. This was decidedly the case for the Cosby Cohort, whose lives were structured around upward mobil-ity. In order to better understand the implications of their parents' strategies, the experience must be articulated from their point of view as the assumed beneficiaries of this culture of mobility. Only then can we gauge the impact of these practices on their lives and sense of self. Epistemologically speaking, closer examination of these stories indicates the ways in which the realities of racism loom large in the Black consciousness when (1) a set of strategies emerge in response to it[2] and (2) those strategies and life experiences reveal the extent to which even privileged Blacks are affected by race. Finally, examining these experiences offers an indication of the drastically different world the Cosby Cohort inhabited as compared to their working-class and low-income peers, which ultimately shaped their racial politics and their connections with other Blacks.

This chapter reveals the uncompromising, rigorous, and daunting training ground that the Cosby Cohort faced on their way to upward mobility as seen through *their* eyes. Here, I extend Lacy's (2007) work on Black middle-class children in White spaces and other researchers' work on the transmission of cultural capital by pushing us past the realization that this process exists to asking how Black middle-class children conceptualize and make meaning of it. In other words, what are the social and psychological implications of being pushed toward upward mobility as the Cosby Cohort remembers it? Additionally, what are the advantages and disadvantages to such a process?

I specifically look at how the Cosby Cohort experienced family, neighborhood, schooling, language, values, and messages about Whites as a culture of mobility designed to guarantee their long-term academic and professional success. The findings show that while these strategies and dispositions provided invaluable cultural capital, they also (1) required great sacrifices of time and energy that led to abbreviated childhoods for many respondents and (2) placed spatial, philosophical, and experiential distance between them and poorer Black counterparts. For many, the latter led to a sense of alienation and isolation, as they were outsiders in the White spaces they inhabited but also in the Black spaces where they visited. Furthermore, the culture of mobility is often laced with implicitly and explicitly negative messages from parents about other Blacks and Blackness in general, which complicated racial identity development for the Cosby Cohort throughout their lives. Thus, while the strategies for mobility helped them get ahead, they also disconnected them from Black peer groups (and, in large part, Black culture) while also saddling them with adultlike pressures and concerns as children. In this way, parents' concern with social reproduction sometimes resulted in unintended and negative social and emotional consequences for their children. Yet because parents knew that the stakes were high for their children, they aimed to provide them with the "right" kind of life—one that they believed would help them conquer a White-dominated world replete with racism and discrimination. Often, their quest began with neighborhood selection.

The "Right" Neighborhood

Neighborhood selection is a key component of the culture of mobility. Since the 1950s, Blacks have flocked to suburbia (to the extent that such opportunities weren't limited by residential segregation) in order to raise their families in areas that would provide "adequate play space for children, good schools, safety and quiet, good property maintenance, and congenial neighbors of roughly equivalent income and educational background"—a place where children could "skate, bike ride, and keep pets" (Grier and Grier 1958, 17–18, cited in Wiese 2004). The "right" neighborhood provides little distraction for children who are being trained to study, work hard, achieve, and create important social networks. It also limits access to negative influences, for, as Pattillo-McCoy (1999) states, "youthful rebellion can [only] go as far as the local options allow" (106). For a more secure middle class like the one detailed in this study, parents had the means to select a neighborhood with few distractions and limited access to "bad influences"—spaces that they felt were fundamental to their children's long-term success.

The majority of the Cosby Cohort respondents (49 percent) recalled living in neighborhoods they estimated to be either majority White (i.e., well over 50 percent White) or neighborhoods they perceived as predominantly White with a greater racial mix (i.e., 50 percent White and 50 percent Black or minority; 27 percent of respondents). This well-illustrates the racial turnover in neighborhoods of the 1980s and 1990s that was common at this time (see Wiese 2004). When I asked these respondents to describe their neighborhoods, their responses evoked notions of wholesome White middle-class living. For example, Shayla's response was, "I don't know if you've seen *Father of the Bride*, [but] that's pretty much what my neighborhood was like." This description of large two-story houses, with manicured lawns, flower gardens, and white picket fences featured in the film, was a neighborhood environment common to many in the study. Shayla grew up in Kentucky, but similar descriptions were given by interviewees who grew up as far away as New Jersey, California, Florida, and Nevada. These descriptions indicate the level of affluence in these families and stands in stark contrast to the urban neighborhoods in which many Black children live, both then and now.

In most cases, parents moved to White middle-class neighborhoods because of the safety, cleanliness, amenities, or high-quality public schools that these communities offered. As Pattillo-McCoy (1999) states, "A neighborhood's racial makeup is frequently a proxy for the things that really count" (30). Debra's story confirms this reality:

[My parents] moved to neighborhoods that matched their personality, their desire, their expectations, which in this country are White neighborhoods. So, it wasn't [that] my parents [were] *trying* to live in a White neighborhood; it's [that] my parents [were] moving into a certain neighborhood because it has good schools. Because it's clean. Because the houses are nice. And unfortunately, in this country, that's a White neighborhood.

Her statement is a compelling commentary on the realities of neighborhood segregation, particularly in the 1980s and 1990s when she was coming of age (see Lipsitz 2006; Massey and Denton 1993; Wiese 2004). At this time, racially restrictive covenants and inconsistent fair housing enforcement constrained housing options for Blacks (Cashin 2001; Massey and Denton

1993; Wiese 2004) and relegated many to poor Black neighborhoods with substandard amenities. Both then and now, children of color attending schools in minority neighborhoods receive a lesser-quality education than those attending schools in White neighborhoods. As a result and as Debra's story indicates, Black middle-class parents must sometimes move to racially isolated neighborhoods so that their children can attend better-quality schools and flourish in a space that will support their efforts toward upward mobility. This was particularly the case for the Cosby Cohort.

Yet living in majority White communities also exposes children to an increased level of racial prejudice and discrimination and is frequently isolating. As children, White neighbors tended to paint respondents and their families as outsiders and thus cast doubt on their sense of belonging in the neighborhood. For example, Olivia talked about her transition from a Black suburban neighborhood in Georgia to a White one and the difficulty of the adjustment:

> Our house was one of the biggest houses in the neighborhood—so we had a lot of [White] kids question us about whether we were drug dealers . . . . So, they would ask my brother if he was a drug dealer and if my parents sold drugs, and how did we get that big ole house. . . . Like, we could go to a McDonald's and they would be like, "Aren't y'all the people that live in that house?"

Being identified as the people who live in "that house" and therefore as potential drug dealers likely signaled two important facts to Olivia: (1) that other Blacks don't have houses like hers, which made her feel different from them, and (2) that her White neighbors' skepticism over their presence in the neighborhood meant that they wouldn't find full acceptance there. For Olivia and others profiled in this study, these experiences foreshadowed a life often spent outside both White and Black social worlds.

In her interview, Olivia indicated that the scrutiny and rejection from White neighbors was painful and eventually prompted her to complain to her parents, "Why don't we move back? Why [did] y'all sell that house? Why did we move out here? I hate this house, I hate [it] out here!" Given the residential segregation during this time period, there were few other viable options for Black middle-class families like hers. As a result, families were forced to manage life in the context of racial hostilities, which included physical threat. Olivia recalled a particular incident that occurred when she was thirteen and living in her new White neighborhood:

> And on one occasion, [my brother and I] were walking back home like we always did, talking. And we got to this stop sign, this four-way stop sign and

this red truck pulled up beside us and they were like, "What are you f——ing niggers doing in this neighborhood?" . . . And they like come up behind us like real slow with a gun out the window and twirling the gun and cussing us like, "You f——ing niggers!" and all.

Being threatened at gunpoint and targeted with racial slurs communicated to Olivia that she and her family were not welcome in their new White suburban neighborhood. It bears note that Olivia was one of the many southern respondents in the study who were integrating White neighborhoods at a point in time where the South was barely getting used to the idea.[3] Incidents like these are frequent occurrences for Black middle-class adults in White spaces and have proven to be quite emotional for the victims (Dent 2006; Feagin and Sikes 1994;[4] Wiese 2004).

However, for children, episodes like these are likely to be even more frightening because a child does not have the cognitive skills and life experience that understanding and contextualizing these incidents requires. For example, where an adult might be able to rationalize incidents like these by reminding themselves that Whites have a long history of intimidating Blacks whom they perceive as invaders and that such incidents reflect larger structural dynamics more than anything else, a child may have neither the cognitive ability nor previous similar incidents to draw on in order to make sense of events like these. Moreover, because this incident involved the threat of deadly violence, it was probably even more frightening for Olivia, who was barely a teenager at the time. It also brings up the issue of identity for the child who may feel like a stranger in this neighborhood where people who do not look like her are using physical threats to inform her that she does not belong there. The ensuing sense of isolation is further exacerbated by the absence of people who *do* look like her (i.e., other Blacks), whose presence could potentially offer a sense of belonging and reassurance.

Because even adults have difficulty reacting to such situations (Feagin and Sikes 1994), parents may not know how to respond in a way that lessens the child's fears and concerns. Upon hearing what had happened to their children that day, Olivia said that her parents were outraged and alarmed but felt there was little that could be done other than letting she and her brother ride the bus home for the rest of the school year. Even though situations like these may happen to their children, middle-class parents are sometimes forced to take the risk if it means the chance of better education or opportunities for their children. Besides, such a negative outcome isn't guaranteed, as at least one respondent, Chuck, said that his family was the only Black family in the neighborhood, but "everybody knew everybody, so it was just one big happy type thing." However, shortly after this statement, Chuck admitted that perhaps his parents protected him from these tensions, which subsequently left him unaffected. Thus, it is possible that parents may be able to shield their children from neighborhood racism.

Nevertheless, living in racially isolated areas can be a lonely experience, particularly when there aren't other children who can relate to this predicament. For example, at one point in her interview, another respondent, Debra, recalled,

> There were few other Blacks—not many—from the middle class who kinda understood what I was going through and may have been going through it themselves. . . . I didn't really see other people going through what I was going through, but I knew that I could not be the only one.

Her story suggests that even when there are other Black middle-class children in these spaces experiencing similar incidents, they may not reach out to each other and as such have little sense of the commonalities between their experiences. In her case and others, this led to increased alienation and isolation.

Ariel's story offered additional insight into the lack of connection between Black middle-class children living in the same neighborhood. She grew up in neighborhoods that she estimated were at least 90 percent White and detailed how this complicated her social life, particularly as she entered adolescence:

> When you're in a White neighborhood, a lot of times you don't hang around those White kids, especially when you get older. You know what I'm saying? It's just like, *Oh gosh, we really don't have anything in common or anything like that.* And so, you just feel like you're by yourself. . . . Like, you want to talk to other Blacks but they just seem like they don't really want to talk with you. And then if you do have friends that are in your neighborhood who are Black, sometimes, I know from my own experience, some of them were still trying to hold onto their White friends when it was obvious that their White friends were just totally dissing them or whatever.

Ariel's statement is freighted with several implications. First, it reflects patterns found in previous research that suggest that feelings toward Whites may change by adolescence (see also Tatum 1997) when Black children perceive that their White friends have a different lifestyle or value system. This may preclude them from pursuing friendships with Whites. For Ariel, her options narrowed even more when the few middle-class Blacks who lived in the neighborhood eschewed relationships with other Blacks in an attempt to curry favor with White peers. Her story indicates the sense of displacement and isolation that accompanies life in White surroundings. This is one of several ways in which assimilationist strategies designed to compensate for racism ultimately complicate Black middle-class children's intraracial relationships by leaving them with few options for meaningful same-race friendships. For many of the Cosby Cohort, this was the case. Because of the external hostilities and social difficulties presented by life outside of the home, life *inside* the home took on greater importance.

The "Right" Family Life

In addition to finding a safe neighborhood in which to live, providing a stable family life also makes for fewer distractions and helps Black middle-class children focus solely on education and other avenues to upward mobility while simultaneously offering them sanctuary from the racism of the larger society. Family both acts as a transmitter of cultural capital and can be a form of cultural capital in and of itself, where being from a "good" family becomes a measure of prestige. Where the Cosby Cohort was concerned, family served three important functions: (1) to construct their lives in ways that increased their life chances and odds for upward mobility, (2) to set boundaries that kept them on the path to mobility that parents had so painstakingly constructed, and (3) to reassure them of their personal worth. While integrating hostile White spaces in the 1980s and 1990s, these functions provided by family life proved critical in this cohort's lives and offered them a safe place to fall. Their stories are also a far cry from the negative images of Black families that dominate scholarly literature, network news, and entertainment media.

Most respondents described their family atmospheres as fairly tranquil, thus allowing them to thrive without the distractions of tense relationships between parents or siblings. Some specifically mentioned the relationship between their parents, like Vivian, who said that while growing up, she never witnessed her parents fighting. When she once asked her mother why this was the case, her mother responded, "Well, I believe that children's things ought to be with children and adults with adults. I remember when you were born, we just made a conscious effort not to fight each other while you were around." Shayla also mentioned how well her parents got along when she fondly said of her mother and father, "Together, they are oil and vinegar, but they are each other's best friends and are in love with each other just as much as they were the first time they met." In these ways, parents consciously modeled a peaceful and loving family environment and a sense of stability that gave their child a sort of emotional anchor.[5]

The handful of respondents who grew up in single-parent households or families where a parent was frequently away also reported that both of their parents remained involved in every aspect of their lives. While growing up, Monica's parents were divorced, but "it was still pretty much like I had both parents whereas I saw my dad all the time . . . like all my sporting events and those types of things." Similarly, Zara's father was often away because of his military service[6] but remained committed to supporting all of her activities:

> My dad would sometimes be stationed at a military base that was three hours away, and it didn't matter. I would know that he would be there. He would drive three hours to go to a band concert, and other kids would have parents that lived *in* the city and would never show up. . . . But that gave me a certain amount of confidence. I knew that when they said stuff was a priority that it was a priority.

From stories like Monica's and Zara's, it is clear that being involved in their children's lives was a top priority for middle-class parents and a way of providing constancy for them regardless of the changes or special circumstances that the family was experiencing at that time. Staying close to children and maintaining an active presence in their lives reinforces the culture of mobility and parental expectations while also creating a supportive environment in which children can succeed.

In part, the ability to provide a stable and congenial atmosphere is a function of social class. Comparatively, these families had fewer worries about financial difficulties and daily survival than their working-class and low-income counterparts, which might have made it easier to provide a pleasant family atmosphere. Indeed, descriptions of daily life from the respondents suggested that these families were in suburbia enjoying each other and living out the American dream with few significant problems. For example, Deidre talked about how her family did everything together and how all of the siblings attended each other's activities. Olivia recalled how she and her five siblings would make dance tapes and fake commercials with their parents' video camera. Others compared themselves to television families, like Belinda, who said that as a kid, her friends called her family "the Black Brady Bunch," and Langston, who indeed said that his family was "Cosby-like" because it was very comical and everyone got along.

The Sunday church ritual further reinforced family relationships for this cohort and also served the culture of mobility by providing children with a moral center that kept them on a productive path. Elijah Anderson (1999) discusses how Black low-income "decent" parents use the Black church to provide their children with a strong moral base; Black middle-class parents are no different in that regard (see also Pattillo-McCoy 1999). Parents feel that rooting their children in the church and biblical scripture as well as encouraging heavy church involvement serves as a deterrent to deviant activities (e.g., drugs, teenage pregnancy, and so on) that will derail their child's journey to upward mobility. Since many respondents grew up in the "Bible Belt" of the South and a few were children of ministers, most of Sunday was spent in church. In 1999, it was estimated that 82 percent of Blacks were church members, where the middle class composed a significant portion of that population (DiIulio 1999; see also Gilkes 1998; Pinkney 2000). More recently, the U.S. Religious Landscape Study conducted by the Pew Research Center Forum in 2007 found that more than half of Blacks (53 percent) report attending religious services at least once a week, 76 percent say they pray on a daily basis, and 88 percent are absolutely certain God exists. In these ways, Black Americans are "the most religiously committed racial or ethnic group in the nation" (Pew Forum on Religion and Public Life 2009). This pattern was well reflected in the church-related activities of the respondents where even those who didn't grow up in the South spoke about how "all day Sunday [was] church." For others, several weeknights were spent in church as well.

The Sunday dinner ritual often followed church services. Sunday dinners are used by Black families to strengthen and maintain attachment among family members and create and reinforce the family's culture or sense of identity (Baxter and Clark 1996). For most, Sunday dinner involved only the immediate family and was mandatory, which meant that all other activities took a backseat. As Marissa said, "But Sundays, yes, if I was at the mall, [my parents would say], 'You need to be on the way home now because dinner is almost ready.'" The few respondents in single-parent families also reported eating family Sunday dinners, like Iyana, who said, "We definitely ate together on Sundays after church." Of particular note is that only one person, Belinda, reported that Sunday dinners were a way to connect with the *extended* family:

> Sundays would be dinners at my grandmother's house where all of her children that lived in the area would come together and have dinner at her house right after church. And my mom would be in the habit of fixing food either that Saturday night or Sunday morning. . . . We would go to our grandmother's house, drop the food off so we were fresh for church, then go to church and come home and have a big family dinner. So that was really nice.

Only a handful of others recalled having these types of regular interactions with extended family members. Some, for instance, reported the presence of grandmothers who picked them up from activities, while others grew up with cousins, aunts, and uncles nearby.

These stories aside, a significant portion of respondents said that their extended families lived rather far away. In the context of the 1980s and 1990s, moving to remote areas away from extended family members was often necessary for parents' pursuit of upward mobility (see Tatum 1999). That was indeed the experience for several in the study, like Alexis, whose father accepted a job on the West Coast, which meant they had to leave behind their extended family in the Northeast. Most of the military children had the same experience where, in pursuit of their fathers' military careers, they moved all over the United States and abroad, which regularly distanced them from their extended family. Still, it appears that military parents made some effort to stay in touch with the extended family by visiting them on vacation. For example, Chuck said, "It was Easter vacation, and a lot of it was going back and forth seeing other family members." Likewise, Camille, who grew up in Georgia, stated,

> My dad's family is from Alabama, and my mom's family is in Tennessee. We would go every summer and stay with my mom's family for about a month in the summer. And with my dad's family, we didn't see them that often. And my parents don't fly anywhere, so we always had to drive. So, we drove everywhere and we stayed at home quite a bit. But we didn't see them that often, but there was always contact weekly with the families [by phone].

In the stories above, the physical distance from extended family can be a burden because it places these children far away from those who may offer them unconditional love and acceptance. At a time when Black middle-class children spent much of their time in hostile White spaces (and even hostile Black spaces, as discussed in chapter 4), the constant love and care of extended family members might have been beneficial. Moreover, extended family members may have provided meaningful levels of racial and cultural socialization for the Cosby Cohort (Lesane-Brown et al. 2005; Thompson 1994), which might have been helpful during their childhoods immersed in hostile White spaces. This is yet another way in which the tension between race and class manifests itself in the lives of middle-class Blacks attempting to accomplish successful assimilation; while their social class allows them to live privileged lives and offers many opportunities for success, they must sometimes do it in relative isolation from other Blacks, including their extended family. In these ways and others, they pay the price for upward mobility. The sacrifice is a latent consequence of the culture of mobility, which also includes an array of values that children are expected to adopt and embrace as their own at an early age.

The "Right" Values

If there was a defining feature of *The Cosby Show*, it was the parents' desire and continual efforts to socialize their children with the "right" values. Cliff and Clair demanded that their children do their best on any task requested of them, adhere to "the golden rule," and keep their eyes firmly fixed on their future. These were values that Black middle-class viewers were excited to see: "I am glad to see them portraying Blacks in middle class roles, and realizing that Black people, Black middle class people, have some of the same values as White middle class, Hispanic middle class, or Oriental [sic] middle class. It's not necessarily a race that determines it, it's just middle class people sometimes have similar values" (Innis and Feagin 1995, 703). Imbuing children with these kinds of values that are conducive to success is a critical component of the Black middle-class culture of mobility. All respondents in this study reported that their parents emphasized mainstream ideals like self-reliance, hard work, and moral responsibility.[7] According to them, the most common values taught by their parents were those concerning the work ethic, sacrifice, delayed gratification, and gratitude. However, this section shows that there were also more covert messages transmitted in this process, namely, (1) messages about the burdens of being a racial minority and (2) subtle (and not-so-subtle) judgments about non-middle-class Blacks and their value system. Messages surrounding the latter, in particular, have been largely omitted or deemphasized in previous research detailing the parents' point of view. As such, telling the story from the second generation's point of view offers a more comprehensive picture of the race and class socialization offered in Black middle-class families.

When asked, "What values did your parents teach you while growing up?," more often than not, messages surrounding the work ethic immediately came up, where every respondent reported receiving these messages. This is unsurprising considering that the culture of mobility is built around the work ethic and meritocratic ideals. Hence, respondents reported that their parents tried to instill in them the idea that through hard work, all things were possible. For many, this message was tempered with the idea that racial discrimination might limit their success. For instance, Gabrielle said,

My parents would make it known that you need to get an education because while you'll have your education, you'll have to work twice as hard in order to be considered equal to White people as far as your career path goes. . . . And so, that was pretty much their goal—to continue to push to educate yourself to be considered equal with White people.

More of these messages are detailed in the next chapter, as they are an integral part of racial socialization in Black families (Boykin and Toms 1985). Still, since the minority middle-class culture of mobility is its own type of racial socialization, they are mentioned here as well because they bring several important issues to light. First, while these children may be living a life of privilege that is similar to their White peers, they must still deal with the salience of race in their lives by striving to achieve above and beyond Whites just to be considered equal. While White middle-class children are also being pushed toward achievement, they are unlikely to receive the message that their race will be an obstacle to their success. Second, this is a message that emphasizes the negatives of being Black, namely, the perils of discrimination. Although this is undoubtedly a reality for all Blacks and is an important message for parents to send their children, it should be counterbalanced with positive messages about being Black, like the richness of Black/African culture, among other things. For the Cosby Cohort profiled in this study, this wasn't always the case (more on this in the next chapter).

Notably, messages about the importance of hard work exist within a narrative of sacrifice and delayed gratification commonly promoted in Black middle-class families. This narrative is an essential part of the culture of mobility designed to show children that prolonged hard work reaps long-range rewards. For respondents like Gabrielle, formal messages about sacrifice were unnecessary, as she merely had to observe the role of sacrifice in her parents' lives. For instance, when I asked her about the disadvantages of growing up Black middle class, she replied,

Probably a disadvantage is, in order to make [opportunities] possible, you're having to really sacrifice in some areas. So, for instance, my father worked a lot in order to make sure those things were possible for us. I remember that the majority of my childhood, he was probably tired a lot. . . . And that's probably a huge disadvantage in the sense that you are able to enjoy some things, but you really work hard in order to be able to enjoy them.

During the interview, she disclosed that in addition to being a minister, her father worked the night shift as a police officer, which meant that she and her brother would have to tiptoe by his room during the day so as not to wake him. Gabrielle's experience points to the fragility of Black middle-class status where parents sacrifice a great deal to make sure that their children have the best opportunities and that children ultimately recognize this as part of what it means to be part of this racial class. However, as Gabrielle's statement also indicates, the children must sacrifice as well in that they may end up with a de facto absentee parent because that parent is working to provide them with a privileged lifestyle and a lifetime of opportunity. In many ways, this harkens back to income inequality where middle-class Blacks have fewer monetary resources than the White middle class (Bureau of the Census 2010; Oliver and Shapiro 1995) and therefore must work more, thus having less time to spend with their children. Had Gabrielle's father had the choice, he might have opted to work less and spend more time with her and her siblings, but for Blacks trying to succeed within a context of inequality, choices are often very limited.

A few reacted to the sense of responsibility and guilt they felt over their parents' sacrifice by altering some of their behaviors and goals. For instance, Scott confessed, "I was in honors classes only because I knew it would make [my mother] happy. I really didn't care about school that much . . . school was never a big priority for me." He admitted in his interview that he felt this sense of responsibility toward his mother because she was raising him and his brother alone, yet struggled to provide them with a middle-class lifestyle. In a similar way, Marissa talked about the fact that she very reluctantly became a pre-med major because her father said he wanted one of his children to be a doctor; she ultimately dropped that major because it proved a poor fit. These stories indicate the sense of responsibility Black middle-class children feel for the sacrifices their parents make and the desire to avoid parental disappointment at all costs.

In a rather extreme example of this, one respondent confessed that she and her friends (who were also Black middle class) were sexually active, but were so fearful of disappointing their parents that they took secret trips to the neighborhood clinic for birth control and even abortions. As she so plainly put it, "You couldn't put the baby up on the wall like a degree." In these ways, children are clear that they are expected to reap a return on their parents' investment in them and that nothing must stand in the way of their achievement.[8] The stories in this section are similar to those of children of first-generation immigrants who also feel a sense of responsibility to their families for the struggle and sacrifices made for their betterment (Barajas and Pierce 2001; Portes and Rumbaut 2001; Suarez-Orozco and Suarez-Orozco 1995; Vallejo and Lee 2009; Zhou et al. 2008). Of course, the irony lies in the fact that Blacks have been in America for nearly four centuries, but because of continuing racial inequality, even Blacks with an elevated class status experience emotional lives analogous to recent immigrants. Moreover, in the end, the theory of Black exceptionalism suggests that the hard work that Black middle-class children put in may not reap the same dividends for them as it might for middle-class Latinos or Asians.

Nevertheless, Black middle-class parents persevere in socializing their children toward success, where the values of sacrifice and delayed gratification are paramount in this process. As indicated above, these values were often informally socialized into the Cosby Cohort but at times were formally socialized and conveyed in much more obvious ways. For instance, a few reported feeling deprived of fancier clothes and toys by their parents, even though they felt that their parents could afford them. Jamika was one of these respondents. By the time she was a teenager and started driving, she wasn't allowed to drive her car that often because, according to her, "I was being taught a lesson to appreciate certain things." While her White friends were driving BMWs, she was granted very limited access to the family car where her parents reasoned, "You need to understand that [having a car] is a privilege and you haven't earned it." Similarly, when Jamika complained about not having the fancy clothes her friends had, her grandmother washed up all of her clothes and made her spend the entire weekend ironing them so that she could see that she in fact had all she needed and would stop complaining.[9] These became lessons for her not only in gratitude but also in delayed gratification and the futility of materialism.

In another example of the socialization of these values, Zara complained to her mother that she wished she could have all of the clothes and jewelry that one of her Black friends had. Her mother asked her where her friend lived and drove her there. When Zara saw that the neighborhood was run down and her friend's house was not as nice as her own, her mother said,

> Now, you have a choice. I could spend our money now and buy you some earrings and some necklaces and we could live here. Or I could take our money and we could save part of it and we could pay for you to go to college. And you could live in a house where you could leave your bike outside and not worry about somebody stealing it.

Zara's story indicates that Black middle-class parents strive to teach that delayed gratification and sacrifice of material items make some of the more important opportunities in life possible. However, what is also implicit in her mother's statement is the idea that poor Blacks spend their money on things that have little value, while being middle class means that one is more careful with their money and invests it toward opportunities that bring long-range rewards. While these lessons are very useful for children striving for upward mobility, they are infused with negative messages about non-middle-class Blacks, which complicated racial identity development for the Cosby Cohort. Ultimately, it began to create a racial worldview in which other Blacks were constructed as different and unequal—a sentiment that also came through in parents' concerns about their children's friends.

The "Right" Friends

Black middle-class parents are very anxious about the company their children keep. For instance, Rema Reynolds's (2010) article on parental socialization of Black middle-class boys finds that parents warn their sons[10] about "guilt by association" at school and instruct them "to separate from their Black friends if [they] seemed to be getting a little too loud or rambunctious" (156). While the parents in Reynolds's study felt uneasy about giving them this advice, they believed it necessary to their academic success, particularly given the fact that their children stood out as such a small population on the school's campus. Although the parents in her study don't specify that it was low-income children that needed to be avoided per se, she indicated that the parents were concerned about their children engaging in behaviors that reflected Black stereotypes (Reynolds 2010). Often, said "stereotypes" are ones associated with low-income Blacks. Parents in Lacy's (2007) *Blue Chip Black* made this connection explicit when they expressed worry about their children associating with "children from 'cheaper' sections" of town who might cause their kids to "pick up traits" (e.g., bad attitudes, head shaking, etc.) or in other ways negatively influence them (177).

Respondents in this study discussed how their parents were very careful about which children they spent time with and whose houses they visited. Parental supervision was often stringent because parents were fearful of their hanging out with other children who might veer them off the path of mobility and jeopardize their success. For instance, Camille's parents were so concerned about whom she spent time with that they preferred her friends to come to their house and play. Camille explained,

> Unfortunately, you are judged by the company you keep. And also, people who don't care or who aren't about anything and they see you succeeding, a lot of times they will try to bring you down to where they are. And so, that was also my parents' philosophy. So, they always met all of our friends like before we would be able to leave with them and stuff.

Black friends who weren't middle class drew particular suspicion from respondents' parents, where parental messages implied that they were somehow different and unequal. Usually, respondents attempted to avoid saying that their parents wanted them to steer clear of poor Black children by referring to them as "children with values different from our own." By way of example, Felicia said,

> I do recall them, to a degree, being somewhat classist because there were certain of my [Black] friends whom they approved of more because they seemingly came from a home that was similar to ours. You know, they looked down on some of my friends. I do recall that there were some friends who came to my house who were not allowed to come up to my bedroom. . . . I think they were concerned about the influence those children would have on me because I think they felt that the homes those particular kids came from did not hold the same values that my parents held.

Keeping poorer friends out of the private and distant reach of an upstairs bedroom seems to be an attempt to "protect" their children from low-income Blacks who might be a bad influence. Moreover, Felicia clearly states that her parents were class conscious, which (perhaps unwittingly) sets up a contrast in the child's mind between low-income Blacks and middle-class Blacks.

While peer group relationships are discussed in greater detail in subsequent chapters, it bears mention here because friendship selection is a key part of the Black middle-class culture of mobility. Parents attempt to surround their children with other children whose families subscribe to similar philosophies of hard work, achievement, and morally circumspect values.[11] However, negative messages about Black friends construct an in-group (i.e., middle-class Blacks) versus out-group (i.e., working-class and low-income Blacks) comparison, which suggests that the out-group is not as smart, capable, or worthy. This confuses some middle-class children's racial identity development as they are Black like the out-group, yet their parents characterize that group in a negative fashion. As indicated in this chapter and the next, this significantly complicated racial identity development for the Cosby Cohort.

The "Right" Education

Perhaps the most important part of the Black middle-class culture of mobility is the emphasis put on education. Black parents often laud education as the ultimate key to their children's success (Blau 1981; Cole and Omari 2003; Higginbotham 1981; Higginbotham and Weber 1992; Hill 1999; Manns 1997; Pattillo-McCoy 1999) and their ability to overcome racial discrimination.

McAdoo (1978) suggests that since these parents sometimes lack wealth, the greatest gift they feel that they can give their children is the motivation and skills necessary to succeed in school. Arguably, those who eventually become upwardly mobile cannot do so without a superior education and academic proficiency. In that spirit, nearly all respondents reported receiving an excellent education at predominantly White schools outfitted with computers, vast library resources, after-school activities, field trips, and active parent-teacher associations. This is an indicator of the importance of education particularly to first-generation parents attempting to capitalize on the gains of the civil rights movement and the opportunities that were opening up for middle-class Blacks in the 1980s and 1990s. For them, education was the only way to propel their children toward greatness, and all strategies were employed in this pursuit. As Debra's statement earlier in the chapter indicated, when quality public schools weren't available in their neighborhood, parents moved to other neighborhoods where these schools were available. However, if moving wasn't an option, many opted to send their children to private or magnet schools in surrounding areas that typically ranked among the best in the state.

Sending children to schools outside of the neighborhood required a great deal of expense and sacrifice on the behalf of not only the parent but also the child. For example, Alexis remembered having to wake up earlier than her friends in order to battle the busy Los Angeles freeways to get to a predominantly White public school located eleven miles from her home. She was frequently late because traveling during rush hour made it "a lot harder to get to school." When I asked her why she didn't attend the schools in the neighborhood, she replied, "Most of the schools around me were predominantly Black and Latino, and the education was just terrible." This is again an indication of the residential segregation of the 1980s and 1990s that made it challenging for middle-class Blacks to procure the best outcomes for their children. To compensate, Alexis's parents sent her to a school far outside of the neighborhood, which necessitated a commute that she found exhausting. Moreover, because the school was predominantly White, she had limited access to same-race peers. In these ways, the culture of mobility leads to other unexpected forms of inequality (e.g., physical exhaustion, long commutes, and loss of time and energy) and limits access to other Black children. It also begins to condition the child to see these dynamics as normal. In other words, they begin to construct a worldview that normalizes (1) sacrifice in the pursuit of upward mobility and (2) distance from other Blacks. This is an outlook that would have a powerful impact on the Cosby Cohort's adult racial identities.

Even when respondents attended schools with larger percentages of students of color, they often ended up in all-White courses. In their efforts to ensure that their children received a top-notch education and were able to compete successfully with Whites, respondents' parents encouraged them to take honors courses where they were frequently the only Black child in the class. In cases like Marissa's, parents had to fight administrators in order to get their child into these courses:

> I think that as far as my schooling went, I was discouraged a lot from taking upper-level classes, honors classes, AP classes. I think that it was because of my race and the school administration not being used to Black people trying to excel in that kind of way. But, I mean it wasn't too much of a battle because, you know, any time I wanted to take AP or whatever, I would pick up the phone and call my parents, and they would see a mother and father walk in for a Black child, and they'd drop it.

Marissa's statement indicates the lengths parents will go to in order to make sure their children are in the most challenging courses, even facing the racism of school administrators in the process.[12] It also illustrates the extent of class privilege and the value of cultural capital when a call or visit from a parent is enough to quickly change an administrator's mind.

Nevertheless, there is a burden of loneliness that children in these accelerated courses bear, which was articulated by Alexis in her interview:

> My dad was like, "You're going to be in honors and AP." And he went up to the school and said, "These are the classes she's going to take." And so those classes were predominantly White. . . . So, I was the only Black person in my class all day. And these were my cohort, and then I come out of class, and I don't know any of the Black people because I'm in class all day.

Alexis's and Marissa's experiences, much like other respondents in the study who went to majority White schools or were enrolled in predominantly White courses, indicate the sense of exile that came with spending all of their time with White peers. While being immersed in Whiteness offers them important exposure to White cultural norms that they must master in order to become upwardly mobile, it nevertheless serves to distance them from Black counterparts.

When children expressed resistance to being in White schools or classes, parents tended to dismiss their concerns and instead stressed the value of education. For example, Will expressed to his mother that it was difficult to be around the wealthy White children at his all-White boarding school because those students had little previous exposure to Black people. He told her that he constantly felt like the representative for his race, which at times became uncomfortable for him. His mother's response was, "Just worry about what you are there for. You're there to get an education more than anything." Langston had a similar experience when he complained to his mother that he had tested out of the classes that his Black friends were in:

> Mom and Dad would always say, "Just keep your head up. You say you desire to go to college and you want to do these things. Sometimes there are going to be people you aren't going to be able to hang with because they're not going to be in those classes, because they're not going to have the same goals and drives."

To be sure, for Black boys and their parents, navigating the educational terrain is more difficult than it is for Black girls (Reynolds 2010), where an abundance of research indicates that boys battle lower teacher expectations, are labeled with negative stereotypes, are absent from higher-track courses, and are more likely to be suspended or expelled for minor offenses (Delpit 1995; Haddix 2009/2010; Kunjufu 1995; Mendez and Knoff 2003; Morrell 2007; National Association for the Advancement of Colored People 2005; Noguera 2003b). In these ways, parents are correct to be vigilant about their children's education, particularly their sons'. Nevertheless, in both Will's and Langston's cases, parents indicated that becoming upwardly mobile meant sacrificing contact with other Blacks. Essentially, given few other options for upward mobility in a White-dominated society where Whites only see Blacks through the White racial frame, class aspirations outranked personal discomfort and isolation from other Blacks. The message from Langston's parents specifically suggested that other Blacks simply don't work hard enough to be in the accelerated courses, which again sets up the negative in-group/out-group comparison. While it may be the case that parents were unaware of the challenges these kinds of messages posed to their children's racial identity development,[13] the outcome was still the same: as children, the Cosby Cohort began to experience a world where class goals were placed above intraracial connections.

As the emphasis on quality schools and advanced courses indicate, education was extremely important to the parents of the Cosby Cohort, who demanded that their children excel academically. In terms of grades, respondents said that their parents generally would accept As and Bs; Cs were usually acceptable only if they were in a difficult subject like chemistry or calculus, where it was obvious that the child had tried their best, but a C was the best grade they were able to earn. Parents even hired tutors for the more challenging courses, but some still had difficulty. These were the only cases in which "bad" grades were accepted.

Generally, respondents reported a great deal of angst around grades. For example, a few remarked that if they received all As one marking period, they were expected to do that *every* marking period. This put a great deal of pressure on them as children, particularly when they were trying to earn these grades in advanced courses. Parental scrutiny could be overwhelming, where Jaime recalled,

> I wrote a paper and my mom tore it apart and my dad tore it apart. And then they told me why they tore it apart, and then I had to correct it. So this was every single paper, homework, etcetera. Report cards came home, and they knew when they were coming out. We knew our grades, they knew our grades. They would have conferences with our teachers just to see how we were doing. . . . So they were very involved in our academics.

Taking the time after a full day's work to critique every homework assignment while staying constantly abreast of the child's academic development further suggests that the most important component of the Black middle-class culture of mobility is education. Additionally, it indicates the degree of sacrifice that parents are willing to make in pursuit of their child's education because of the role it can play in compensating for minority status. However, what is also clear is the pressure this puts on children to succeed. This was further indicated in the fact that over half of all respondents reported that some sort of punishment would be involved for receiving bad grades; punishments ranged from yelling sessions to withdrawal from activities, spankings (like in the Edwin Jones case), or groundings.

One of the most stunning stories of parental expectations came from Danyelle, a second-generation woman of Caribbean descent. Danyelle told me that in her house, As were the *only* grades allowed. Papers with As went up on one wall in the family room; papers with anything less than an A (including A-minuses) were put up on a different wall, which became known in the house as "the failure wall." To drive the point home even further, her homework desk was placed in front of the failure wall so that she could be reminded of her shortcomings as she did her work. If there was a spelling word that she had missed or a math problem that she had miscalculated that caused her to get less than an A, she had to write that word or problem over and over again to her parents' satisfaction. While Danyelle admitted that in some ways these practices were good because they "made me take school very seriously," she also admitted to being stressed out: "I was really anxious in a way other kids weren't." According to her, it wasn't until college that she realized that she didn't have to get an A on everything and that an A-minus was indeed "good enough." Anxiety represents yet another outcome of compensating for racial discrimination and is an indication of the inequalities inherent in this process of upward mobility. To be sure, White middle-class children also experience achievement anxiety (Levine 2006), but for Black children and particularly those of the Cosby Cohort who grew up in the 1980s and 1990s, this reaction was in part a response to racial realities.

Attending college was a forgone conclusion for nearly all of the respondents in the study. Their parents assumed that they would go to college, and there was little choice in the matter. Getting a college education was also emphasized by extended family members like Camille's grandparents (former sharecroppers) who urged her to get an education because "that's the one thing that no one could take from you." Some parents were more explicit in explaining to their children that college was a way for them to not only maintain their middle class status but also transcend it. For example, Gabrielle recalled,

> My parents have always said, "You're supposed to be a step better than we are. The purpose of us training you and sending you out into the world is so that you will do better than what we're doing. Maybe you won't have to work as hard as we have or maybe you won't have to feel that these are the only types of positions that were available to you because you are Black. You'll have a wider variety to choose from, hopefully." . . . The idea is that you're supposed to be able to retire and be able to live off of your retirement . . . that's how they measured success.

When I asked Gabrielle how early she received this message that her retirement was dependent on getting a good education, she said that she first heard it while still in elementary school. As her story illustrates, the "training" that is part and parcel of the culture of mobility takes place at a very young age and presents pressures that are additional to the ordinary pressures any child feels while growing up. The training evolves out of their parents' understanding of how racial inequalities have shaped their own lives. Because of the unyielding nature of racism, they realize that this is a cross their children must also bear, which justifies the training they set up for their children.

The "Right" Extracurricular Activities

The pressure of achieving academically is only complicated by (over)involvement in extracurricular activities. Throughout their childhoods, Cosby Cohort respondents reported being involved in six different extracurricular activities on average, where some reported as many as fifteen. Almost all were involved in at least three or more activities throughout middle school and high school. The stories presented here indicate that Lareau's concept of concerted culti‑vation is racially motivated and a response to both perceived and potential anti‑Black prejudice and discrimination. In other words, Black middle‑class parents employ this as yet another strategy for making sure their children have an advantage in a society that discriminates on the basis of race.[14]

Frequently, respondents performed an intricate balancing act because of their involvement in these extracurricular activities. For example, in the sixth grade, Will was enrolled in a program for gifted students that took place at another school. During the academic year, he was required to attend the program every Wednesday night and all day on Saturdays. The program also ran several days a week throughout the summer. Will recalled,

> So, I think that year, that sixth‑grade year, when I was balancing going to basi‑cally two schools at the same time, it was real intense. . . . I think the pressure was more like, I don't get to hang with my friends as much as I want because I need to sit home and do homework, 'cause I have an assignment due on Mon‑day. Or, I have something to do Friday night because I have class on Saturday all day. So, I can't really hang out as much as I really want to at that age.

When I asked him to rate how stressful this experience was for him on a scale of 1 to 10, he rated it as a 10 and went on to explain,

> You know, you've already been touted as a talented student, you want to sort of keep that expectation up. . . . But then I think you are also going through that middle school age where you're finding yourself, you're finding girls, and you're going through all of these kind of life issues all at the same time. So, it could be stressful, but I think it's doable.

At very young ages, respondents were taught that achievement and extracur‑ricular activities brought certain sacrifices like recreational time with friends but were necessary in order to become successful. While this situation may have been "doable" for Will, it may not be for every child. It should also be noted that his claim that the experience was manageable may be a show of male bravado and a reluctance to acknowledge and admit personal difficul‑ties. However, because he still rated it as a 10, it is clear that the experience was stressful.

Balancing schoolwork with activities was a significant challenge for many respondents. Alexis was involved in nine different activities between the ages of nine and seventeen. When I asked her if it was difficult to be so involved, she replied,

> It was. Because my thing was school, and that was the most important thing to me. And I didn't really see everything else as important. My dad kinda understood that, but him and my mom always joined forces. . . . So, we would always be fighting over some of my extracurricular activities that they thought were really important.

She went on to report sleepless nights and waking up many mornings around 5:00 a.m. to finish her homework before traveling multiple freeways to get to school. Because Alexis's father was a college counselor, he understood that involvement in activities would help her appear well rounded to colleges and might give her an edge over White students. In many cases like hers, activities were parent initiated for that reason. For instance, when I asked Ariel whether her participation in fifteen different extracurricular activities was at her parents' behest or something she chose to do, she replied,

> Well, I felt like it wasn't what I wanted to do. And [my mother] just wanted us to be on top, especially when it comes to White kids because they're always having the opportunity to do this and that. And she was just like, "You have to be one on top of them if you want to stay ahead."

The strain on the Cosby Cohort to maintain these activities in addition to a high level of academic proficiency was also evident in Ariel's interview when she said, "Sometimes there were days when it was like, oh it's too much! But you sucked it up, and you dealt with it. Sometimes you stayed up later than normal and then just did your work." While these are stories that could easily be told by White middle-class children, the difference is that Black children may be pushed even harder to achieve in response to racism, where parents are attempting to prepare their children to compete more successfully with White peers. These stories cast doubt on Lareau's (2003) claim that the process of "concerted cultivation" (as described by respondents in this study) isn't racialized.

In some part, it seems that extracurricular activities are also part of the politics of respectability and the "keeping up of appearances" (Boyd-Franklin 2003) practiced by middle-class Blacks. Danyelle said that in the summer, she was always in an academic program, as opposed to the day camps in which many children are enrolled during the summer hiatus. She was also pushed into summer activities that would "look good." She gave the example that she had to learn how to play golf in the summer "because that was considered acceptable." In other words, it was an activity that would reflect well on her and her family in front of both the White and Black middle class. It also seemed to be an activity that her parents took very seriously and wanted her to master because, according to Danyelle, "We'd be out there at night with glow-in-the-dark balls!"

The playing of golf is particularly salient, as it is a popular sport played by powerful members of corporate America. Light and Gold (2000) indicate that, "studies of minority men and women have consistently found that competence in the folkways of the male white Protestant upper middle class are vital to success, even if such skills are unrelated to actual job performance" (107; see also Cose 1993, 58).[15] I discovered this firsthand during my short stint at a major telecommunications company when I had lunch with one of the Black female vice presidents who had offered to mentor me. When I asked her what I would need to do in order to ascend the corporate ladder, she paused thoughtfully for a second and said, "You need to learn how to play golf." Stunned at her response, I asked why, and she replied, "Because that's where all of the big deals are made and where the promotions are given out." Given that the only golf that I could play was on a course with windmills and clowns' mouths (and even then I couldn't keep the ball out of the pond), I knew that I wouldn't make it in corporate America. It seems that Danyelle's parents also knew about the importance of golf as cultural and social capital, which is why golf lessons and nighttime practice sessions became so important. Essentially, parents believe that their kids should take advantage of any opportunity to excel in extracurricular activities and in other ways broaden their horizons.

The "Right" Opportunities: Broadening Horizons

Blacks who are able to master the nuances and idiosyncrasies of White society and have familiarity with White cultural knowledge have a better chance of gaining entrance to and succeeding in White workplaces and social spaces. In recognition of this, first-generation Black middle-class parents provided opportunities for their children to broaden their horizons and learn cultural capital through travel, cultural trips, and immersing them in spaces with White elites. These were opportunities that were largely unavailable to them when they were growing up. Access to these opportunities represents one of the many advantages to growing up under the Black middle-class culture of mobility. While parents' ability to provide these opportunities is clearly a function of social class, it usually comes at a greater cost for Black middle-class parents than for White middle-class parents given the differences in wealth and income. Nevertheless, because of the white-collar occupations of the Cosby Cohort's parents, they were able to provide these opportunities for their children and thus a lifestyle similar to what White middle-class children experience. However, it was also very different from what other Black children were experiencing, particularly those consigned to working-class and low-income areas; this leaves both groups with little in common. Nonetheless, access to these opportunities was another vital part of the culture of mobility and the effort to achieve successful assimilation.

One opportunity that the vast majority of respondents reported having was the ability to travel. While travel is certainly intrinsically enjoyable, for the Cosby Cohort it was an aspect of the culture of mobility that endowed them with an urbane sensibility through exposure to different places and cultures. Some trips were school sponsored (another measure of privilege), while others were family vacations. In terms of family vacations, Debra said, "When kids went to, say Orlando, for the summer or some other state, I was going to England, or I was going to Jamaica." Alexis's family also went to Jamaica one year and Hawaii another year. Iyana took family vacations to Sweden, Denmark, London, Paris, and Amsterdam. When the trips were school sponsored, children were able to go to places like Spain and Mexico. Regardless of destination, having the opportunity to travel indicates that these families had financial resources and access to leisure time that most Blacks did not have. In these ways, it created a worldview for the Cosby Cohort as children that was dissimilar to their working-class and low-income counterparts yet exposed them to the cultural knowledge of the White middle class and elite, thereby facilitating their eventual success.

Often, in reflecting on their experience, respondents directly acknowledged the advantage that access to White cultural knowledge gave them. For example, several respondents recalled taking day trips to museums, plays, and the like. One respondent, Camille, clearly recognized how her exposure to these things made it "easier to understand or have conversations with White people about other things that some probably lower-class Black people weren't exposed to or didn't have the advantage of seeing." Likewise, Langston said, "I was just a little bit more exposed to a lot of things as opposed to a lot of my other friends or peers that weren't as fortunate to be exposed to the things that I was exposed to." Debra perhaps contextualized this experience best when she said,

> I think growing up in a middle-class family afforded me opportunity—opportunities that allowed me to be more open minded than those with less money. So, we were able to travel, which opens your mind. We were able to go to

plays, which opens your mind. We were able to live in neighborhoods where other people have done those things as well, so even if you haven't, they'll talk to you about it. So, I think that growing up middle class offered me the opportunity to think on broader levels and experience and tolerate more things than people who didn't have as much.

Debra's statement well reflects the privilege that facilitated these respondent's entrance and acceptance into White society. Yet these experiences can confuse racial identity, as these opportunities are common among White middle-class peers but uncommon to poorer Black counterparts.

As Debra alluded to above, exposure to enriching experiences and elite White culture was simply part and parcel of the middle-class experience for the Cosby Cohort. For example, Marissa recalled attending parties with White middle- and upper-class adults as a result of her mother's employment with a news organization. She said this improved her conversational skills and taught her how to "hang out and talk to and socialize with *anybody* because I was exposed to them." Similarly, Will's stint at a boarding school helped him learn about sailing and other leisure activities of the White elite. As a result of their exposure to White social circles at an early age as well as their exposure to cultural activities, these respondents had an easier time navigating the White world as children, which later served them well as they ascended the class ladder in adulthood. However, as will become evident in subsequent chapters, it further distanced them from the worlds of other Blacks. Language became yet another way in which this distance was magnified.

The "Right" Impression: The Use of Standard English

Despite the controversy over the Black English Vernacular (BEV) versus Standard English, it is still the case that fluency in "Standard English" is required for Blacks hoping to accomplish successful assimilation. As Delpit (1995) indicates, "To imply to children or adults . . . that it doesn't matter how you talk or how you write is to ensure their ultimate failure" (39). She goes on to say that while non–Standard English is unique and wonderful, "there is a political power game that is being played, and if [young people] want to be in on that game, there are certain games that they too must play" (40). Even as far back as 1945, Drake and Cayton's (1962) *Black Metropolis* spoke of the importance of Standard English: "Persons who wish to circulate near the 'top' whatever they lack in money or job, must have enough education to avoid grammatical blunders, and to allow them to converse intelligently. Ignorant 'breaks' and inability to cite evidence of education—formal and informal—can bar a person permanently from the top" (515; cited also in Lacy 2007). Certainly, first-generation parents battling racial prejudice in White workplaces understood the importance of Standard English.

Nearly all respondents reported that Standard English was required in their households. Upwardly mobile Blacks' preference for Standard English has been well documented in previous studies (Doss and Gross 1992; Feagin and Sikes 1994; Neckerman et al. 1999). In most cases, respondents merely mimicked their parents' speech patterns. If they mispronounced or mangled a word or phrase, correction from parents was immediate. Danyelle once said the word "worser" to her parents, which she said was "worse than cursing" in their eyes. Her parents reacted by yelling and threatening to go down to the school to complain to her teachers. Instead, they ended up placing conjugations of "worse" on the failure wall and made her write it repeatedly.

Michael offered his take on why his parents enforced Standard English, which mostly seemed to be about impressing others:

> I think they were just making sure you were able to express yourself. Like my parents had a big thing about breaking verbs like, "I be doing this" or when people say "ax" instead of "ask." You weren't allowed. They instilled being grammatically correct. That's the way we had to talk around the house, so when you went out in public, it was just automatic. So, the point I think was so you don't sound ignorant—so you don't sound like you have less or that there's some deficiency there.

His statement well illustrated middle-class parents' concern over how their children presented themselves in public. In the White spaces and places in which they interact and inhabit, "public" is proxy for "White people," where his parents wanted him to be able to impress White people. The statement also suggests that his parents purposely wanted to set him apart from non-middle-class Blacks who are perceived as having "deficiencies." This is another way in which the in-group/out-group comparison is created by parents and internalized by children.

Parents repeatedly indicated to their children that Standard English was integral to school and job success. For example, Camille recalled, "We were not allowed to speak slang in the house. [My parents] were just really like, 'You will not get a job speaking slang and you will not speak it in this house.'" When Zara came home speaking slang she had picked up from her Black friends, her mother told her that was fine for when she was around them but that she could not speak that way at school in front of her teachers, or they would get a "certain perception" of her. Zara did not specify what that perception was but later spoke about how her parents wanted to make sure that her teachers always viewed her as a serious student. She was the only respondent whose parents promoted code-switching or altering their behaviors in order to fit in better with Black peers (for a more extensive discussion, see Celious and Oyserman 2001).

By and large, respondents didn't have frequent access to non-middle-class Blacks and therefore didn't have the ability to code-switch seamlessly. Terrell (1975) finds that the sociocultural reference group with which one associates plays a greater role in dialectical differences than one's race or ethnicity (72). She also finds that the less middle-class Black children associate with poorer Black children, the more unfamiliar they are with BEV (Terrell 1975). Thus, growing up in majority White neighborhoods and attending majority White schools during their early formative years limited the Cosby Cohort's exposure to BEV and therefore their ability to find a point of connection with other Black peers. Some might argue that they *literally* didn't speak the same language.

As a result of their lack of exposure to common Black linguistic styles, more than half of the respondents indicated that their speech pattern became something that immediately marked them as different from other Blacks once they entered Black social spaces. According to Dillard (1972; also cited in Pattilo-McCoy 1999, 230 n. 7), 80 percent of Blacks speak BEV, also known as "Ebonics" or African American Vernacular English. Although a bit dated, this study suggests that the vast majority of Black Americans do *not* speak Standard English, including some middle class Blacks as indicated in more recent studies (see Dyson 2005; Pattillo-McCoy 1999). Therefore, while many of their peers might have been speaking BEV, the only dialect that most of the Cosby Cohort was fluent in was Standard English.

As the Cosby Cohort grew older and began to have more interactions with other Blacks, their Black peers expected them to be fluent in BEV. For example, Gabrielle recounted the following about arriving into middle school:

> I got to middle school, and I was at a predominantly Black middle school, and for whatever reason, the students there did not accept my word choice or how I pronounced words, and that's when I understood the label of "being Black" or "being White" or "acting Black" and "acting White."

For some, their use of Standard English became a source of constant ridicule; Michele noted that it was one of the major reasons she was "tormented from probably all the way through seventh to the end of eighth grade." The use of the BEV is frequently a contributing factor to group solidarity for Black Americans; those who do not speak it appear as if they are rejecting the group in some way (see Peterson-Lewis and Bratton 2004). While the Cosby Cohort was being taught a dialect that would maximize their opportunities for upward mobility and lead to successful assimilation, it simultaneously distanced them from Black peers. This distance was ultimately magnified by parental messages suggesting that Standard English and the people who use it are somehow better than those who don't. Nevertheless, Standard English, among other things, is identified as necessary for successful performances in White spaces.

The "Right" Way to Deal with Whites

In the seemingly postracial world of the Huxtable children, there were no lessons on how to interact with Whites. On the show, racism and racial differences almost didn't exist. There was never a scene where Cliff and Clair sat Denise or Theo down and said, "Here's how you need to act in front of White people." It is safe to say that such a blatant reference to power differences and White hegemony wouldn't have made for appropriate sitcom fodder. However, for real-life Black middle-class children growing up at that time, these became invaluable lessons. For the most part, the Black middle-class culture of mobility is about teaching children how to navigate and become successful in the dominant group's world. As Delpit alluded to above, this is referred to as "learning the rules of the game." In order for one to be successful in the game, one must master particular strategies to advance to the next level. Several of these have been addressed above. However, knowing how to *behave* in front of Whites and *react* toward them also requires mastery, as both middle-class children and adults experience the majority of their interactions in predominantly White settings.

In their parents' perpetual effort to keep up appearances, the respondents in this study experienced intense training on how to interact with Whites. When I asked Marissa, "According to your parents, how were you supposed to act in front of Whites?," she said,

> Better than them, almost. You know, always use correct English and don't make any references to this or to that. Or, don't become too personal with them because they'll take the information and use it against you. It was almost like training, you know? *Don't do this, don't do that. Do this, do that.* Until it could become something that you did naturally.

In her statement, two messages come to light: (1) the importance of impressing Whites and the preparation required to do so and (2) the importance of protecting oneself against them. These messages were echoed many times by other respondents. For instance, Olivia said her mother was "big on not giving White people the wrong impression," and Zara's misbehaving in public prompted this warning from her parents: "You don't want White people thinking you are a clown because they will treat you like that." Michael's mother was so concerned about him behaving properly in front of Whites that she signed him up for etiquette lessons. Impression management (Goffman 1959) and keeping up appearances in front of Whites was a mainstay in the lives of the Cosby Cohort and was a way to prevent mistreatment.

Yet if one is accepted into the major institutions of White America, it doesn't mean that he or she is fully accepted by Whites; narratives of Black middle-class adults in the workplace speak to this reality (see Collins 1997; Cose 1993; Feagin and Sikes 1994). To prepare their children for this, parents offered "protective messages" that seemed to be variations on the same theme: *If you are not careful, Whites will hurt you.* Many times, respondents relayed parental lessons like, "White people are sneaky and can't be trusted" or "some Whites still have the old mentality," meaning that they still harbor racial prejudices against Blacks. Marissa's parents warned her that "[Whites] were evil and backstabbing and cutthroat and you [should] watch out for them and [not] have too many of them as your friends." When I asked her what her parents said might happen if she had them as friends, she replied, "They would do something bad to you. You know, when you thought that they would be there to support you . . . they would be there to support themselves and you'd be left out by yourself."

Although this type of socialization by middle-class parents has been cited in previous research (see Feagin and Sikes 1994; Lacy 2007; Tatum 1999), what has not been discussed is the fact that these messages can be confusing to young children who are functioning in majority White neighborhoods, schools, or classes, where most of their friends and peers are White. The possible confusion was evident in Shayla's statement surrounding her parents' messages about Whites:

> Oh, it was such a contradictory mess because I'm growing up in a White world with these [people]. [They said things like], "I'm not saying anything about your friends, but you know, just be leery, because even though things seem like they are okay [and like they are] accepting Blacks, it may not always be that way. I'm not telling you to look over your shoulder, but do look over your shoulder."

Because of the confusing nature of these messages, several respondents chose to ignore their parents' warnings about Whites because they didn't have another option. Alexis was a good example of this. She said she received messages from her parents about not trusting Whites but stayed friends with them because she spent all day in honors courses with White children: "I don't think I had White friends by choice. It was the kind of situation I was in."

Fearing that their children would become conflicted about how to deal with Whites, some indicated that their parents showed restraint in their messages. Gabrielle said that her parents waited until she was older to give her messages about Whites because "[they thought], okay, well here's the dream. Gabrielle is in school with White people. Maybe she'll make friends with them . . . so we aren't going to curb that for her." As her story indicates, some parents made an effort not to color code their messages about their children's behavior or influence their friendship circles. This may be beneficial to a Black middle-class child who is then left with an unbiased view of their White friends. However, it can also be detrimental and leave children unprepared for possible incidents of discrimination or rejection. To borrow Shayla's phrase, the situation can indeed be "a contradictory mess."

For respondents who weren't given protective messages about Whites earlier in their childhood, the messages seemed to change as the child got older (see Hughes and Chen 1997). Later in her interview, Gabrielle said that as she got older, her parents wanted her to understand how race worked in America and cautioned her to "be careful and watch your back" around Whites. Similarly, Alexis said that once she started to have an awareness about race, her parents said, "Okay, so we can talk now." In most cases, these talks occurred when the child was in middle school. Racial grouping begins as early as middle school and therefore becomes a time when children begin to recognize race as a salient factor in interpersonal relationships (Tatum 1999). In some middle-class families, messages about Whites are not given until around this age, when it becomes necessary.

Several respondents reported receiving absolutely no messages about White people from their parents during their childhood years and were forced to come to conclusions about them on their own. While some may argue that this a positive strategy, the remaining chapters illustrate how this is detrimental to racial identity development for Black middle-class children, particularly those of the Cosby Cohort. Essentially, whether or not they are adequately prepared to deal with Whites, the specter of racial discrimination is ever present, particularly in White-dominated spaces.

When the "Right" Life Isn't Enough:
The Unyielding Nature of Racial Discrimination

In the White places and spaces in which the Cosby Cohort interacted as children, they quickly discovered that they wouldn't be considered as good as Whites. Olivia's experience of being called a "nigger" in her new neighborhood, for example, illustrates what Cross (1991) might refer to as an "encounter" experience, or a personally salient life event that brings awareness that being a full-fledged member of the White world is not possible. Although Cross claims that encounter experiences happen later for middle-class Blacks (e.g., in college or in the workplace, see p. 199 of Cross), most respondents reported that their encounter experiences happened much earlier. This is in part because most grew up in White neighborhoods and schools where they were exposed to more overt prejudice and discrimination than a child growing up in Black spaces.

For these respondents, encounter experiences usually occurred in school. When I asked Layla about her first encounter experience, she discussed her first day at her new elementary school in the new White neighborhood to which she had recently moved:

> The first [encounter experience] was the very first day at St. Matthew's at school, the secretary taking me to my homeroom and overhearing the teacher announce that "we're going to get a new student and she's [long pause] . . . different." And then, the secretary knocked on the door and the [teacher] said, "Oh well, you'll see what I mean."

This experience at Layla's school indicated to her very early on that she was unlike the White children and might be rejected by them. It also made her feel uncomfortable overhearing the teacher refer to her as "different." Yet residential segregation (both then and now) means that better schools are located in White neighborhoods, thus yielding more frequent encounter experiences like Layla's.

Zara offered another example of an encounter experience—one that she found particularly disturbing as a child. A White girl in her chemistry class had her purse stolen. Zara was immediately called to the principal's office, something that shocked her classmates because "my father kept me under lock-and-key, so I didn't do anything." The principal began asking her about the purse, and when Zara asked why *she* specifically was being questioned, the principal said, "Weeellll, a person overheard another person say [it was] someone by the name of Zara. There are 500 other Zara's in the school, and I'm asking all." The principal's hyperbolic statement of there being "500 other Zara's" began to raise a red flag for her that she was being treated in discriminatory fashion. Harnessing her cultural capital, she said to the administrator, "My Dad is a judge. Do I need a lawyer? . . . When you ask people if they committed a criminal act, don't they usually have a lawyer? If you're going to start accusing me of something, I'm going to have representation." The principal was stunned by her response and had clearly forgotten her father's occupation. She attempted to settle Zara down and assure her that she meant nothing by the accusation. Zara was furious, noting that her parents made just as much money if not more than her White accuser, so she didn't need to steal anything. She later discovered that there was a White girl in the school who was also named "Zara," but she wasn't questioned by the principal. In these ways, it was clear that she had been targeted because of her race, but her class status and cultural capital ultimately allowed her to be cleared as a suspect in the stolen-purse mystery. When I asked Zara what she took away from that childhood event, she said, "It just kind of reinforced what my parents had said—[to] know who you are, be sure of what you're doing, be thorough in what you're doing so that when people come at you with stuff like that, you can just stop them." At an early age, she had to learn how to defend herself against racist accusations.

In most cases, the encounter experiences were far more subtle than Layla's and Zara's. In Belinda's case, for instance, the encounter experiences began in middle school, where she was first confronted with discrimination during cheerleader tryouts. As discussed earlier, extracurriculars play a key role in the culture of mobility, but this is yet another place where Black middle-class children first realize the significance of being Black. For four consecutive years, Belinda tried out for the cheerleading squad and was rejected every year. She noted that this "devastated" her mom, who finally said to her, "Quit trying out! They don't want any 'spots'[16] on the team! I don't want you to try out anymore because you're going to get hurt." Prior to her mother's statement, Belinda did not perceive these as discriminatory incidents, in part because she grew up as a military child who didn't receive any racial socialization except for the military's color-blind socialization (more on this in the next chapter). As a result, her encounter experience was fairly jarring.

In desegregating White spaces in the 1980s and 1990s, these types of discriminatory experiences were common for the Cosby Cohort. For example, Melanie recalled a family vacation to Hilton Head, South Carolina, when she was twelve, where she and her family were the only Blacks at the resort. She remembered that when they got in the pool, "all the White people would get out." Other members of the resort even pulled the fire alarms next to their suite in the middle of the night. Melanie also recalled that a White woman at the resort asked her where the maid was because she hadn't gotten the towels she had requested; she assumed Melanie worked there because she was Black. In a similar example, during a limousine tour to Niagara Falls that Michael took at seven years old, a White family got on board, and Michael reported that the little boys in the family froze and said, "Daddy, do you want us to get in this car with these darkies?" In White spaces like these where respondents traveled as children in an effort to broaden their worldview, they were frequently sent the message that they were outsiders who didn't belong.

There were still other contexts that prompted encounter experiences where respondents first began to realize the significance of being Black. For example, despite the strict culture of mobility, as children, respondents sometimes tested these boundaries, resulting in swift parental correction that served as an encounter experience. Debra remembered getting into trouble as a child for talking in class and her mother's deep embarrassment over this situation:

> There might have also been some embarrassment because my mother is a very, very, VERY, proud person. And I think race had something to do with it because I may have been the only Black person in class, or one of two or three, so my mom was big on, "You are NOT going to be the only Black child and be the child who is disrupting the class. *You will not.*" . . . Kinda like, "You will not embarrass us by being the talkative one, and you're the only Black child surrounded by all these White students who appear to be doing well. . . . You're Black. You have to do better than everyone else."

Zara recalled a similar experience where she received correction after clowning around in class. When her father picked her up from school, he pulled down the rearview mirror and began yelling, "Look in the mirror! . . . Do you see someone there with blonde hair and blue eyes?! Whether you like it or not, being African American has its pluses and it has its minuses. You're going to have to work harder, and you're going to have to prove yourself, and this is where it starts!" In cases like these, discipline was harsh and swift for stepping out of line, especially in front of Whites. Parents perceived these behaviors as running counter to the culture of mobility that they were trying so hard to impart to their children. Situations like these served as a constant reminder of the salience of race in the Cosby Cohort's lives. They may also reinforce the salience of gender as well, where Zara's parents noted that her "double-jeopardy" status as Black *and* female (Hill 1999; St. Jean and Feagin 1998) would further complicate her efforts toward upward mobility.

Although these types of messages appear to be messages about what it means to have a minority status in the United States, they are also infused with a message about what it means to be Black middle class. They are messages that are part of the culture of mobility and promote proper public behavior as an avenue to achievement and success. While all children step out of line, there is more at risk for Black middle-class children who are negotiating the trials of integration and assimilation. Cosby Cohort parents were quick to remind them of this fact. However, while these messages promoted achievement and success, they also primarily emphasized Blackness as a liability. The next chapter looks at the impact of this mode of socialization.

Conclusion

The stories of the Cosby Cohort suggest an intense culture of mobility where the pursuit of class goals was of primary importance. The major emphasis was on long-term academic success that would eventually yield occupational and financial success. The intensity of the culture of mobility was a function of the parents' understanding that in a society dominated by the White racial frame, their children would need every available advantage. As children, the cohort was not allowed to lose sight of these goals. Parents went to great lengths to ensure their future success by raising them in racially isolated yet safe neighborhoods and providing them with a stable family life, superior education, and access to myriad extracurricular activities. These are the distinct advantages of growing up Black middle class. Within the context of a capitalist society and given the decreasing fortunes of the middle class, it is easy to argue that this type of socialization is inherently positive and that, as children, these respondents experienced more blessings than burdens. Nevertheless, this view is shortsighted and ignores the substantial challenges that accompanied this experience and that were difficult for them to shoulder.

As the data indicate, for the Cosby Cohort, there were two major costs of growing up in this racial class. The first is that, as children, most experienced rushed, stressful, and/or overloaded childhoods. They spent their days in hostile White neighborhoods and schools, their afternoons and evenings in extracurricular activities, and their late nights completing homework from accelerated courses. Always present was the pressure to succeed with the knowledge (1) that parents were demanding that success, particularly after having structured their entire lives in pursuit of class goals, and (2) that this level of hard work would be necessary to counteract the harsher levels of discrimination directed at Blacks. This type of pressure made for stressful childhoods for most respondents.

Given the intense pressures and challenges of adhering to the culture of mobility, it would not be surprising if some children rejected this socialization and chose a different albeit less rewarding path—one that required fewer sacrifices of time, energy, and contact with Black peers. For instance, a few teens profiled in Pattillo-McCoy's (1999) ethnography opted out of the culture of mobility. Neisha, for example, refused to go to the magnet school her mother had selected because the commute was too long and she wanted to go to school with some of her neighborhood friends (Pattillo-McCoy 1999, 97). In the end, she attended the less advanced neighborhood school and ended up pregnant by a drug dealer. This suggests that, left to their own devices, some young middle-class Blacks might choose a less rewarding path, one that leads to downward mobility in adulthood. Indeed, a good deal of research details the difficulties Black middle-class parents have in passing on their class status to their children (see Anderson 1990; Attewell et al. 2004; Pattillo-McCoy 1999; Shapiro et al. 2010). Yet the parents of the respondents in this study seemed to "pull out all the stops" to prevent their kids from falling off the path.

A second cost of growing up Black middle class for the Cosby Cohort was the isolation from other Blacks that many experienced. While maintaining meaningful interclass relationships and interactions with other Blacks is part of the minority culture of mobility (see Neckerman et al. 1999), for parents of the Cosby Cohort this appeared to be of secondary concern. Distance from other Blacks, especially low-income Blacks, was intentionally and unintentionally encouraged by parents in both obvious and subtle ways. Certainly, moving to racially isolated neighborhoods and enrolling children in mostly White schools and honors courses results in this outcome. Moreover, involving their children in several time-consuming extracurricular activities severely limited their free time and any potential interactions with Black peers. In these ways, children can lose an important reference group as many in the Cosby Cohort did.

Finally, and relatedly, the subtle yet negative messages about other Blacks, particularly non-middle-class Blacks, presented a formidable challenge to the cohort's racial identity development. Essentially, parents set up an in-group/out-group comparison, always with the underlying message that the out-group was not as smart, capable, or worthy. It was perhaps the parents' own class insecurities as first-generation Black middle class combined with their worries over their children's future financial security that caused them to physically and psychically distance their children from Black counterparts. This distance was particularly problematic because the "legitimate" culture of Black America lies with the lower classes (Patterson 1972, 30; see also Collins 2005; Lacy 2007). Distance from this group of Blacks meant that, as children, many respondents were unfamiliar with popular aspects of Black culture, such as BEV and other behaviors and characteristics needed to enact a successful Black performance. As a result, while the Cosby Cohort was learning everything they need to know to be successful in White social circles and a White-dominated society, they weren't necessarily learning how to be successful in Black social circles. As the next chapter shows, their racial identity development was further challenged by inadequate racial, cultural, and intraracial socialization. As such, the stage was set for the rise of a group of post–civil rights Blacks who had stronger attachments to their class identity than their racial identity.

CHAPTER THREE

~

Race Lessons: What the Cosby Cohort *Really* Learned about Blacks and Blackness

By the 1990s, economic hardship and spatial segregation—key pillars of racial inequality, but also black identity in the twentieth century—were beginning to weaken, leading some to question whether suburbanization might herald the denouement of "African American culture" altogether. (Wiese 2004, 257–58)

As Andrew Wiese alludes to above, the movement of Blacks to the suburbs represented a shift in racial, cultural, and intraracial dynamics. In addition to navigating White surroundings, these mostly first-generation middle-class Blacks had to maintain connections with working-class and low-income members of the community. Much of their connection with those members was based on having grown up with them in Black areas and a shared experience of racial discrimination, particularly during the Jim Crow era. It was also based on shared personal connections between family and friends, where cultural foods, music, slang, and the like were passed down. But when, in pursuit of upward mobility, some members of the first generation moved their children to White neighborhoods and schools and often away from extended family members and friends, these dynamics shifted, necessitating new understandings of race, culture, and intraracial relationships.

In chapter 1, I likened *The Cosby Show* to a mirror reflecting the lives of middle-class Blacks in the 1980s and 1990s but a mirror where the likeness is sometimes distorted much like a funhouse mirror. In matters of race and culture, the similarities between the "reel" life Huxtables and real-life middle-class Blacks intersect and diverge in meaningful ways. Race, culture, and the implications of both were minimized on the show, save for some strategically placed symbols of Blackness, such as Black art, Black magazines, and HBCU sweatshirts. A key part of the show's discourse was its emphasis on achievement, but race was never mentioned as a reason for why achievement was so important. However, as chapter 2 shows, for the Cosby Cohort, accomplishing successful assimilation required a series of elaborate class strategies designed for the expressed purpose of compensating for the racism that first-generation parents knew their children would face. As a result, class and matters of social reproduction gained a sort of primacy in these respondents' lives. Moreover, from early childhood, these respondents grew up in mostly White surroundings without a great deal of access to other Blacks. How do Black children develop a racial identity in this context? Does one develop an identity based on being a member of a racial minority group and a sense of shared experiences even though he or she shares few experiences with other Blacks? Or does their class status pull them toward Whites and White middle-class culture and ideology?

In a third option, it might be the case that the individual must find a way to integrate both race and class into their identity and forge a definition of what it means to be both Black *and* middle class (see Lacy 2007). This is a formidable challenge considering that Blackness is usually conflated with poverty and the behaviors and characteristics associated with low-income Blacks. For first-generation middle-class Blacks, integrating both race and class has meant code-switching between Standard English and Black English Vernacular (BEV) (Jackson 2001; Pattillo-McCoy 1999), living in a White neighborhood but belonging to a Black church (Tatum 1999), or having a birthday party consisting of one's "peops" (e.g., Black friends from childhood) and another consisting of one's "peers" (e.g., colleagues from work) (Jackson 2001). But given the unique childhood experiences of the Cosby Cohort who grew up in White spaces, are these strategies possible or even desirable? As indicated in the above quote by Wiese, growing up in White suburbs and away from Black people and culture may have made it difficult for them to feel rooted in the community. How close does the Cosby Cohort feel to Black people and culture, and what drives their attachments or the lack thereof? Examining the racial, intraracial, and cultural socialization they received as children helps us begin to answer these questions. In essence, in addition to negotiating the attendant challenges of assimilation, as children, the Cosby Cohort had to also figure out what Blackness means not only in terms of racial minority status but also as a historical, cultural, and group identity. As the interviews in this chapter and subsequent chapters show, these were realizations and discoveries that left an indelible impact on their racial understandings and racial identities.

Family socialization plays a key role in a child's racial identity development.[1] Behind closed doors, Black parents must impart to their children a sense of self-worth and reframe the damaging narrative of Blackness perpetuated by the larger society. In other words, parents are frequently charged with providing children with an antiracist counterframe designed to "effectively counter [the] recurring white hostility and discrimination" that is part and parcel of the White racial frame (Feagin 2010, 159). The counterframe must be constantly reinforced in the home. Lessons taught under the Black counterframe include (1) passive and active strategies for dealing with White discrimination, (2) the ability to detect and challenge racist stereotypes and actions when they appear, and (3) an emphasis on the positive aspects of Black humanity, achievements, and traditions (Feagin 2010, 172–73). The knowledge and information contained within the counterframe essentially form a context for racial identity development. In chapter 1, I addressed the passive and active strategies for dealing with White discrimination that are part of Feagin's counterframe. This chapter focuses on the remaining two aspects of the counterframe: (1) giving children the tools to recognize racist behavior and (2) emphasizing positive aspects of Black humanity, achievement, and traditions. It also focuses on intraracial socialization in Black middle-class families and how that shapes children's racialized worldview.

Developing a Black child's racial identity is difficult but perhaps is even more so for middle-class parents whose children spend the majority of their time in White spaces. In *Blue Chip Black*, Lacy (2007) argues that these parents "want their children to be successful members of the White world, but fear immersion in this world will expose children to racial discrimination, alienate them from the larger community, and lead to nagging doubts about their racial identity and black authenticity" (225). In other words, parents hope that their children will still be able to understand the norms and values of the Black world and feel comfortable navigating that world while also developing an affinity for other Blacks (Lacy 2007, 156; see also Wiese 2004, 156–57). Parents in Tatum's (1999) ethnography *Assimilation Blues* echoed the same, where they claimed that they wanted their children to have access to and positive feelings toward Black children of all class backgrounds because "they don't want their children to become 'oreos'" (Tatum 1999, 126), or, phenotypically Black on the outside but culturally "White" on the inside. Hence, Black middle-class parents must strike a balance between teaching the child to navigate the White world (and the racism inherent within) while making sure that they always have a foothold in the Black world by teaching them to appreciate Black culture and their Black brothers and sisters (see also Boykin and Toms 1985; DuBois 1903b; Hill 1999; Neckerman et al. 1999; Peters 1985; Tatum 1999; Willie 2001). Providing children with a Black identity and the ability to relate to other Blacks is also considered to be a critical part of the Black middle-class culture of mobility (Neckerman et al. 1999). In these ways, it is of the utmost importance that parents help their children develop a positive racial identity, particularly while assimilating into a White-dominated world replete with racism and discrimination.

Racial and cultural socialization in Black families has long been a topic of psychological and sociological research, where researchers have devised a variety of models explaining the process (e.g., Bowman and Howard 1985; Boykin and Toms 1985; Demo and Hughes 1990; Hughes and Chen 1997; Marshall 1995; Phinney and Chavira 1995; Stevenson 1994; Stevenson et al. 2002; Thompson 1994; Thornton et al. 1990). Some have asserted that the external conditions dictated by social class have little or no impact on racial identity formation; rather, it is the interpretation of the individual's socialization experiences and their own personal development that determine this process (Carter and Helms 1988). However, such an analysis minimizes the power of class socialization and the ways in which it influences racial identity development. Other researchers who acknowledge social class as a factor in this process don't offer a thorough explanation of its role in racial identity development, and the nuances of the process are frequently obscured by quantitative measures (e.g., Broman et al. 1988; Demo and Hughes 1990; Harris 1995).

While previous research claims that racial and cultural socialization are an integral part of Black family socialization, other research implies that these modes of socialization are less robust in middle-class families. For example, in the last four pages of *Assimilation Blues*, Tatum (1999) details her interviews with two second-generation women who grew up in a White neighborhood in the 1980s and 1990s, thus making them part of the Cosby Cohort. Both reported that their parents offered largely negative messages about Black people and culture that significantly shaped their racial identity. One related the following:

> I asked my mother why there weren't many Blacks in our neighborhood and why many Blacks lived in one area of the city. She then told me that she had worked hard all her life to give us a nice house, car, nice clothes, money to have treats, etc. She said that those other Black people hadn't worked as hard as she had to overcome the many barriers and boundaries that other Black people were confined to. (Tatum 1999, 129)

The young woman went on to say,

At this time, I also found myself hating me as a Black individual and also my culture. . . . I feel that I wouldn't have undergone such severe identity problems if my mother had encouraged Blackness in our house. I think my mother just wanted to evade the whole issue of race and racism. She put and kept us in all-White schools and neighborhoods. Even after busing, she didn't encourage us to interact with our own people. (Tatum 1999, 129)

Comparing and contrasting parental narratives with the story of this young woman leads to a pivotal question: Is there a discrepancy between the messages parents *believe* they are sending children about Blackness and Black people and the messages children are actually receiving and internalizing? Parental self-reports that dominate the literature (e.g., Hill 1999; Lacy 2007; Tatum 1999) lead us to believe that racial and cultural socialization and the development of a positive Black identity for their children are of great importance to Black middle-class parents. Yet the reports from members of the Cosby Cohort, like Tatum's respondent and the respondents in this study, raise questions about whether this is the case. What are the messages about Black people and culture that middle-class children receive from their parents, and how do children internalize and make meaning of these messages?

In this chapter, I explore the content, quality, and extent of racial and cultural messages in the Cosby Cohort's families in order to understand how Black middle-class children acquire a racialized worldview. The previous chapter exposed some of the subtler, often inadvertent messages that "may or may not be directed at children, but nevertheless, transmit information to them regarding their parents' attitudes, values, or views about race or race relations" (Hughes and Chen 2003, 471). These messages are a type of informal socialization. However, this chapter looks at the more deliberate and formally socialized messages regarding Blacks and Blackness that are transmitted in Black middle-class families. In this chapter, I use the interviews with the Cosby Cohort to address three important questions: What are the more intentional messages that some Black middle-class children learn about what it means to be Black, what are the messages that they learn about other Blacks who *aren't* middle class, and, perhaps most important, is the same level of care that is devoted to class socialization and social reproduction also devoted to racial and cultural socialization? Clearly, Cosby Cohort parents spent a great deal of time and energy crafting a rather elaborate culture of mobility that would ensure their children's ultimate success. Were matters of racial and cultural identity treated with as much care, or did these matters take a backseat to the intense class socialization that transpired as a response to the realities of systemic racism and the challenges of assimilation?

Previous accounts of Black middle-class families that focus on parental intentionality cannot fully capture the extent to which racial, intraracial, and cultural socialization occur in these families or the content of such messages, the ways in which children make meaning of them, or the ways in which all of these form a context for racial identity. The personal narratives of the Cosby Cohort that are presented here can help articulate a framework in which to understand how second-generation middle-class Blacks (now in their thirties and forties) have forged a racial identity in the context of their struggle for successful assimilation and integration. The implications are important because the Black middle class presently composes a larger proportion of the Black community than ever before (Pattillo-McCoy 1999) and the Cosby Cohort in particular is now in a position to be of service to the larger Black community. But the extent to which they will be willing to do so will depend on how connected they feel to Black people and Black culture, where the roots of their present connections are, to some extent, located in their racialized childhood socialization. Understanding their journey toward racial identity development is also important because the population of Black middle-class families in White suburbs is expected to grow (Wiese 2004) and become more normative over time (Lacy 2007), which may make for future generations with similar experiences and challenges regarding racial identity development.

In this chapter, I find that when racial, intraracial, and cultural socialization happened in the Cosby Cohort's families, it was frequently *class specific* and occurred in a way that has not been accounted for in previous models and descriptions. While we often conceptualize racial identity and class identity as separate entities, the interviews in this chapter suggest that the two are in fact deeply intertwined for middle-class Blacks. Specifically, what emerged from the interviews were three major types of socialization mentioned in previous research—racial socialization (i.e., minority status socialization), intraracial socialization, and cultural socialization—*but each with a specialized class component*. In other words, these three modes not only were about Blackness as an individual and social identity but also were imbued with a sense of what it means to be *middle-class* Black specifically. In this way, social class played a pivotal role in the race lessons offered to the Cosby Cohort.

Each of the descriptions below includes the influence of class (indicated in italics) on each type of race-related socialization:

1. Racial socialization: In this study, "racial socialization" refers mostly to Boykin and Toms's (1985) description of minority status socialization, which entails a process of providing children with reactions and coping styles for combating racial prejudice and discrimination from the dominant group. This type of socialization is perhaps most important for Black middle-class children growing up in White spaces (see also Thornton et al. 1990), who will need to be prepared for the discrimination that likely awaits them. *However, the stories of these respondents indicate that there was a distinctive class component to these messages in their families where messages about minority status were used to reinforce the strict standards of the culture of mobility while simultaneously encouraging children to internalize and adopt these values as their own.* Essentially, messages about minority status made children acutely aware of what was at stake if they didn't follow the culture of mobility laid out by their parents and thus became a powerful tool in motivating them to achieve and compete successfully with peers of other races. There were also positive types of racial socialization messages where children were taught to be proud of being Black despite having minority status; these messages, however, were few and far between.

2. Intraracial socialization: In previous research, intraracial socialization, or the process of shaping children's feelings about other Blacks, is largely included under the umbrella of racial socialization (Lesane-Brown 2006). However, I separate it from racial socialization (i.e., minority status socialization), as there is a subtle yet salient difference between teaching children about what it means to have a minority status and teaching them how to care about same-race others. While it may be assumed that the former naturally begets the latter (i.e., understanding a shared history of racial oppression naturally leads to feelings of connectedness toward same-race others; see Sears 2008), the increasing class chasm in Black America destabilizes this relationship. Aspects of intraracial socialization have been touched on in the previous chapter with regard to messages about having the "right" friends. In that chapter, parents transmitted covert messages suggesting that working-class or low-income Blacks couldn't so much as be trusted in their children's bedrooms and would ultimately derail their children's success. *In most cases, the overt intraracial socialization also included negative messages about non-middle-class Blacks that mostly cast them as inferior and also tended to*

serve the culture of mobility by providing Black middle-class children with a cautionary subtext that read, "If you don't follow the culture of mobility, you could end up like them."

3. Cultural socialization: This mode of socialization refers to the teaching of Black history, culture, and heritage, which has been detailed in previous research (e.g., Hughes and Chen 1997; Stevenson et al. 2002). For the respondents, this often involved the transmission of Black history and exposure to Black-themed cultural places and events (e.g., festivals, museums, music, and so on). These served as a way of instilling a sort of cultural memory. Mainly, this mode of socialization allowed the Cosby Cohort to feel proud of themselves as Black and to have a greater understanding of what Black culture is about, apart from the hip-hop culture that was so pervasive in their lives and the lives of subsequent generations as well. *However, under the Black middle-class culture of mobility, cultural socialization is also used to show the level of achievement that is possible through hard work. Respondents recalled being exposed to information about Black cultural heroes who had ascended to the top of their respective fields, with hopes that they might aspire toward the same.*

In addition to these findings, several other important patterns appeared. First, the interviews suggest that racial socialization and intraracial socialization occurred with more frequency than cultural socialization. In other words, the sum of these respondents' stories indicate that they received more messages about the problematic nature of Blacks and Blackness[2] than the more positive cultural and historical aspects contained in cultural socialization. Regarding racial socialization specifically, respondents received quite a few messages from their parents that suggested that Blackness was inherently problematic and something from which their class did not exempt them—messages that proved discouraging for some. However, a good portion of respondents received very little or *no* explicit racial socialization, which appears to have been even more detrimental than receiving negative messages, as it left them with little understanding of their minority status. In terms of intraracial socialization, the Cosby Cohort frequently heard the message that working-class and low-income Blacks were inferior and worthy of disdain. Thus, the takeaway message regarding both Blacks and Blackness seems to have been that *being Black is hard, and other Blacks only make it harder by making us all look bad.*

As stated above, cultural socialization was provided less often than the other two modes of socialization, but when it occurred, it focused mostly on Black history. Still, quite a few respondents received little or no form of parental cultural socialization ($N = 16$; 48 percent), which left them without a firm rooting in Black culture and community. Noticeably absent from the accounts of cultural socialization was any socialization or exposure to the more stylized aspects of Black culture that both then and now includes a hip-hop aesthetic and an oppositional culture. This left many respondents with little familiarity with Black culture as it was and is presently constructed and without a way to connect with Black peers when they eventually came in contact with them.

Finally, in comparison to the level of class socialization provided under the culture of mobility, far less racial and cultural socialization was provided in these families. Unlike class socialization, these modes of socialization didn't appear to be part of the daily lives of the Cosby Cohort, and when they did occur, they most often appeared to participate in the service of the culture of mobility than anything else. One could argue that racial and cultural messages are the subtext of the culture of mobility, and that is true. After all, in order to motivate children toward high achievement, parents explained how their children's minority status could impede their success. In addition, as this chapter will show, they were taught that they owed it to the Blacks who came before them to live up to their full potential. In these ways, racial and cultural messages are the subtext of the culture of mobility. However, while nearly every respondent spoke about how important class reproduction was to their parents, 40 percent of respondents reported receiving very little to no racial socialization, and 48 percent reported receiving little to no cultural socialization. In these ways, it appears that matters of class trumped matters of race and racial identity in the Cosby Cohort's families. First, we turn to racial socialization and the ways in which this cohort was made aware of their minority status.

The Racial Socialization of the Cosby Cohort

The racial socialization of the Cosby Cohort included many messages about having a minority status—messages that were much more prevalent than the more positive messages about the richness of Black culture and heritage. These messages were rooted largely in the first generation's experience with discrimination in White workplaces. By way of example, in Cose's (1993) *The Rage of a Privileged Class*, he interviews a friend who had gone to Harvard and worked hard at his elite law firm but still ran into discrimination regularly from those on the job, thus leading to his conclusion that "you do have to work harder, every step of the way, and you have got more obstacles than a white person" (49). Given this reality, it is no great surprise that parental socialization from the first generation included messages about what it means to be middle class but still have a minority status. As their children embarked on their own journeys of integration and assimilation, racial socialization would give them a sense of the discriminatory treatment they might receive at the hands of Whites. Many parents also used these messages to motivate their children's achievement. During a time period where there was a great deal of resentment toward affirmative action and Black advancement in general, parents might have felt that the doors of opportunity were going to close for their children and that academic excellence and high achievement would be their only way to compete. As such, they felt the need to provide them with some measure of racial socialization to ensure that achievement. Analyzing these messages received by the respondents offers additional insight into some of the pressures the Cosby Cohort faced.

When asked, "What did your parents and/or family teach you about what it means to be Black?," overwhelmingly the first messages respondents mentioned were those that had more to do with race (i.e., having a minority status) than culture (i.e., more positive messages about African and African American heritage). As the statement from Cose's respondent above suggests, the most common message cited was that, as minorities, they would have to work harder and achieve more than Whites in order to be considered equal. The overall sentiment is not new and is certainly one frequently expressed during the civil rights era when Blacks were trying to prove their equality with Whites. Nevertheless, these messages emphasize Blackness as a liability, an unfortunate reality for most Black Americans.

Blackness as a Liability in the Past and Present
One way in which family attempts to instill a sense of racial identity in their children is through recounting stories of what Blacks have endured throughout their tenure in America as a result of their minority status. Because parents and grandparents grew up in the age of Jim Crow, unsurprisingly the family stories passed onto the Cosby Cohort recounted the hardships of the segregation era. For instance, Jamika recounted some of her grandparents' stories about the hostile treatment they received from Whites when they lived in Mississippi. Camille's parents conveyed their sadness over not being able to drink at "WHITES ONLY" water fountains as children. Chuck's father told him about the racial slights he experienced as the first Black man in a high-profile military position in the South—a story that highlighted the costs associated with upward mobility for Blacks. Elisa's father attempted

to do much the same when he told her about being hit with spitballs on a school bus while integrating a school in Georgia. According to Elisa, he told her the story in order to help her understand the struggle he went through to provide her with a better life and that she could endure the discriminatory treatment she received in her majority White school because it was "nothing" compared to his experience.

Through these stories, parents and grandparents[3] are attempting to transmit a racial wisdom that will (1) give Black middle-class children roots and a heritage to which they may be able to attach and identify themselves, (2) provide examples of how other Blacks have experienced and ultimately overcome racial discrimination, (3) imbue them with a cultural memory (see Zhou et al. 2008)[4] that will motivate them to achieve in light of the past (and present) struggles Blacks have faced, and (4), much like with immigrant families (Barajas and Pierce 2001; Vallejo and Lee 2009; Zhou et al. 2008), underscore the sacrifices various family members have made so that the next generation could prosper. This type of racial socialization served as motivation for the Cosby Cohort and served as a way of ensuring their compliance with the blueprint provided by the culture of mobility. However, they can also be experienced negatively in that they paint Blackness as a liability that may prove exceedingly difficult to surmount.

For example, messages that positioned Blackness as a liability were often given in the context of lessons on the importance of hard work. The cohort received lots of messages about the work ethic, with the accompanying message that this was of the utmost importance given their minority status as Blacks. For instance, Michael's parents conveyed this message to him as a child:

> They told me that you definitely have to work hard. And I remember them always saying, "Because you're Black, you're going to have to work twice as hard to get half as far. And then when you get there, you're going to have to work twice as hard, again. You work, and everything you do is going to be overanalyzed. And, if you succeed when everybody else fails, they're going to wonder if you did it honestly." So, you have to continually set this pattern in motion that you're going to be successful.

At a young age, the Cosby Cohort was taught that their Blackness meant that they have been consigned to a life of hard labor where everything they do will be subject to intense scrutiny and even discreditation. To be sure, *the parents weren't wrong.* In the context of White racism, this is indeed a reality for middle-class Blacks (e.g., Collins 1997; Cose 1993; Feagin and Sikes 1994). Moreover, it is a message parents likely felt they must relay, particularly given their own experiences in White-dominated work spaces

(Hughes and Chen 1997). Nevertheless, it is still a message that emphasizes the negatives of being Black and requires counterbalancing with more positive messages.

Michael's story offers insight into how messages about the perils of discrimination can be experienced as intimidating or frightening for children. When I asked Michael how these messages made him feel when he began receiving them at age nine, he replied,

> Well, you feel kinda like you're just working for no benefit at all. It's like you never really get a break to relax, but you keep working hard. . . . And the point is to keep you always working hard so you don't ever like get to a point where you want to relax and sit back. 'Cause that's when everybody catches up with you, when you start sitting back.

As a child, Michael experienced this message as not only intimidating but also discouraging because it suggested that hard work may not pay off in the end. The second half of his quote reflects the ways in which the Cosby Cohort experienced a somewhat truncated childhood where there was little opportunity to rest from the intense training they received in an attempt to triumph over a racist structure. In these ways, they were likely forced to mature much quicker than their White counterparts through their constant exposure to the realities of racial discrimination. Additionally, a message like this impacts racial identity formation by presenting Blackness as an undesirable characteristic and indeed one from which an individual might want to distance him- or herself.

Regardless, parents believed it was important to convey to children the grim realities of race and that middle-class status doesn't present an escape from racial discrimination. For example, Vivian's father told her a story about how he applied for a job and was asked to schedule an interview over the phone. When he showed up in person, he was immediately informed that the position was filled, thus suggesting to her father that, on the phone, the employer thought he was White. This story became an illustration of the inescapability of Blackness—a point that was reinforced again when her father eventually opened up his own auto shop. He told Vivian about how White patrons would often come in and ask to speak to the owner, and when they found out that he was the same, they would react with disbelief. In fact, some didn't believe him and would simply keep asking for the owner. Entrepreneurship is a challenging avenue for Black Americans (Butler 2005; Walker 2009; Woodard 1997), but undoubtedly, one of its benefits is the ability to become one's own boss and not be immediately beholden to a White patriarchal power structure. Yet even entrepreneurship didn't offer an escape from racism for Vivian's father.

Stories like the ones above have been relayed in books like Feagin and Sikes's (1994) *Living with Racism*, Cose's (1993) *The Rage of a Privileged Class*, and Lacy's (2007) *Blue Chip Black*. However, what is often not discussed is the fact that children either witness these slights or hear about them from their parents and may be left with a sense of despair in knowing that this is their destiny as well. In many ways, this knowledge is beneficial because it prepares them for what they can expect in a world where they will always be judged by their race. Certainly, these stories had enough impact on Vivian that she was able to recount them in detail many years later. Hearing these stories at a young age again forces Black middle-class children to grow up faster and face racial realities and pressures that many of their White counterparts do not have to face. Moreover, this type of socialization reinforces the notion that being Black is mostly a liability. If the negative aspects of being Black are emphasized to the exclusion of more positive messages, then it becomes more difficult for the child to develop a strong racial identity that isn't entirely predicated on victimization. Additionally, the stigma of victimization may prompt a physical and psychological distancing from all things Black, thus creating a fractured personal identity and a nonexistent group identity. As chapter 5 indicates, this was indeed the case for some members of the Cosby Cohort, Vivian included. However, perhaps even more detrimental than receiving messages about Blackness as a liability is receiving *no* messages about what it means to be Black.

Not Getting the Message

Silence about race leaves Black children ill prepared to deal with racial prejudice and discrimination and also results in them feeling uncomfortable around Black counterparts (Boykin and Toms 1985; Murray et al. 1999; Ogbu 1982; Phinney and Rotheram 1987; Spencer 1983; Thornton et al. 1990, all cited in Lesane-Brown 2006). It may further render them vulnerable to internalizing negative images and messages about Blacks disseminated by the larger culture, thus hindering their psychological functioning (Semaj 1985; Thornton et al. 1990). An example of the vulnerability born out of receiving no messages about race was evident in Belinda's story about her unsuccessful tryouts for the cheerleading squad, detailed in the previous chapter. Belinda said that she never grew up with any preconceived notions of what it meant to be Black, which meant that she had little understanding of the implications of America's color line. As a result, it came as a complete shock to her that she wasn't being accepted onto the squad even though she believed she was as good as the White girls who had also tried out. Her story illustrates the implications of providing children with little or no racial socialization.

Thirteen respondents reported receiving very little or no racial socialization. It is notable that of these thirteen, seven were military children. (There were eleven respondents total who had a parent in the military.) Blacks, particularly those in the South (Stewart 2009), have often used military service as an avenue for upward mobility. The American military is a unique institution because it stresses a philosophy of racial equality where supposedly no racial group is important than another (Moore and Webb 2000; Moskos and Butler 1996; Stewart 2009). This is a philosophy that runs counter to the dominant civilian culture where race is a salient factor in everyday life. Nevertheless, military parents tended to offer no messages about what it means to be Black to their children or any messages about what to expect from White people. By way of example, Ariel grew up as the child of a military officer, and although she mostly lived in the South during her middle and high school years, she spent her early years growing up in Europe. As she explained in our conversation, she was not taught a great deal about race, which she attributed this way:

> I guess it's this military thing. I know we knew we were brown or dark brown or whatever you wanna call it. But I didn't really know that there were such classifications as White or Black. I mean we saw like peach people and brown people, you know what I'm saying? And so, it wasn't until we moved to [the South] and this boy called my sister a "nigger," and we told my dad, and he got really angry. And that's when we knew that "nigger" was a bad word. Yeah, I kinda wish my parents woulda told us [about race] instead of keeping us in this military frame of mind that everybody loves each other.

Ariel's statement illustrates the complications brought on by not providing children with racial socialization. Until she moved to the South in the second grade, she had little concept of race. Before this, she spent some formative years outside the context of American race relations. Although her parents may have avoided the topic because they were overseas, they did not make an attempt to discuss it when she was older and they were stateside. In addition, race was not something that was talked about on the base that Ariel referred to as "a little bubble community" where "once you move outside the base, the bubble pops."[5] Thus, while many Blacks are forced to use the military as an avenue to upward mobility, there is a price to be paid for this as well where military children may walk out into the world unprepared for the implications of their race and experience a sort of shock when they realize that their race matters quite a bit in how others perceive or treat them.

To be sure, it was not just the military children who received few explicit messages about minority status. Six other respondents *without* parents in the military also reported the same experience. In the context of systemic racism, not having an understanding of what it means to have a minority status also makes it difficult for Black middle-class children to understand why they are being pushed so hard under the culture of mobility and why they need to overachieve. In this way, the culture of mobility might seem silly or unnecessary, in which case keeping children on track proves more difficult. Additionally, Black middle-class children raised in White environments with lifestyles similar to White peers may begin to see themselves as no different than their White peers. When racial discrimination occurs, they may find themselves wholly unprepared for the realities of race crashing in on them; this is indicated in Belinda's cheerleading story and Ariel's story about the first time she heard the word "nigger." When these incidents arise, it might be helpful for children to feel like they have a community with whom they have shared experiences or things in common. This makes some measure of positive intraracial socialization necessary.

The Intraracial Socialization of the Cosby Cohort

Important to racial identity development and a sense of rooting in the community is the feeling that one shares the same interests and experiences as similar others. For middle-class Black children in White spaces, this may prove important in the moments when they are interacting with other Blacks and looking to feel a sense of connection. Because the middle class still represent a small portion of Blacks (Attewell et al. 2004; Pinkney 2000; Sue and Sue 2003), their interactions with other Blacks will often be with non-middle-class Blacks. In these ways, the parental messages that middle-class children receive about other Blacks are extremely important and shape their attitudes and behaviors toward Black counterparts throughout the life course.

To gauge the more overt parental messages that the Cosby Cohort received about Black counterparts, I asked a simple question: "What did your parents tell you or teach you about Black people?" The answers that came up immediately were answers regarding *non-middle-class* Blacks. This suggests that some parents saw themselves as having an unusual status within the Black community, where Blacks counterparts are simultaneously conceptualized as the norm but also "the Other." In some cases, it was clear that the Other referred to working-class or low-income Blacks; in other cases, it was unclear if it referred to this group or merely to Blacks with values different from their own. Nonetheless, according to the respondents' accounts, parents saw themselves as belonging to one distinct and unique group, while other Blacks belonged to some different group.

Many parental messages communicated embarrassment over the behaviors or characteristics of other Blacks. Layla recalled the following about her parents:

> And I think in regards to Blacks, the message was never overt but was kind of covert in regards to "trust" and "worthiness" maybe. And they're always, I think, really creating harsh judgments of other Blacks living up to some standard they made up. . . . So, you know, it's just a very critical kind of perspective.

While Layla says these messages were covert, it seems they might have been more obvious than that and were messages she either overheard or were subtly communicated. In her parents' eyes, it seemed other Blacks could not be counted on. Messages from Olivia's parents communicated the same. Her father taught her that Black people are always late, while her mother would designate other Blacks as undesirable by saying things like, "I don't want Black people moving into my community because the community tears down." Olivia said she was put off by this message from her mother and once said to her, "Mom, you're Black . . . that's what they were saying when *you* came." In this way, she reminded her mother about her own vulnerable status as first-generation middle class (see Hill 1999, 44). Perhaps feeling this vulnerability, her mother quickly responded, "But I keep my yard up." As Olivia said, "Because she does things this way and somebody would do it another way, that would put them in another class."

The conversation between Olivia and her mom bring two important points to light. First, while previous research indicates that Black children are sometimes taught to distrust and be wary of Whites (Hughes and Chen 1997), it often doesn't focus on the ways in which Black children are taught to be suspicious of other Blacks,[6] particularly in the direction of the middle class toward poorer counterparts as indicated in Olivia's and Layla's stories. Second, this conversation illustrates that while social class is based on objective characteristics like occupation, income, and wealth, it is also based on class distinctions that "reflect values and behavior related to work, education, leisure, consumption, and place of residence" (Wiese 2004, 159).

Essentially, Olivia's mother was alluding to Bourdieu's theory of *habitus*. As mentioned earlier, habitus is a fluid and constantly reformulated set of dispositions that are created through personal and social history and compose a particular lifestyle (Bourdieu 1984). These dispositions structure individuals' actions in the social world and operate at every moment as a matrix of perceptions, tastes, and behaviors (Bourdieu 1984). Indeed, the tastes and behaviors indicated by the culture of mobility compose a Black middle-class habitus, which becomes a lens for all of their interactions with working-class or low-income counterparts. Of particular note is that habitus "operates at a conscious and subconscious level, as individuals reproduce practices and ideas about themselves and the world around them without complete cognizance of actually doing so" (Young 1999, 203). As such, Black middle-class habitus manifests itself almost unintentionally and becomes a reflex response in which they compare their worldview to that of other Blacks and judge them unworthy by comparison. As John L. Jackson (2001) says in *Harlemworld: Doing Race and Class in Contemporary Black America*, "Connected to any one person's assertion of class superiority is often a complementary accusation of 'failure' for another" (151). Given this type of negative intraracial socialization that many received in childhood, a psychic distance was created between these respondents and their non-middle-class counterparts.

The manifestation of this interclass dynamic was evident in several interviewees' recollections of parental conversations about "ghetto" Black people. Even respondents like Camille who said that her parents didn't really give her any messages about Black people and culture said that the one message she received was that there were "ghetto Black people." When I pressed for further explanation on this term, respondents did not seem to have a solid definition about what made someone "ghetto." Perhaps as children, they didn't know exactly what the term meant but knew it was "bad" or an undesirable designation. However, it seems unlikely that in adulthood, they still didn't know what the term meant. The phrase frequently refers to a mentality that has its origins in the social conditions of the ghetto. Among other things, the mentality involves an acceptance of unfavorable behaviors like chronic unemployment, defaulting on bills, acting out in public, having children out of wedlock, preoccupation with material items, or a fixation with the present with no vision for the future (see Anderson 1990; Pattillo-McCoy 1999; Wilson 1987). And so, when Chuck's father, for instance, taught him that there are "different mentalities in the race," it is likely that he was referring to this "ghetto mentality" and that this was the meaning that other respondents had attributed and internalized as well.

Nevertheless, there was some sense of embarrassment or shame over defining the term "ghetto" out loud even when respondents were specifically asked for a definition; most seemed reluctant to overtly defame poorer

Blacks.[7] When Elisa inadvertently did so in her description of "ghetto-fabulous" Black women (which she described as being heavily tattooed with lots of jewelry and cleavage showing and often with blonde streaks in their hair), she quickly said with embarrassment, "Oh, I just did a stereotype!" Her shame over this description and others' reluctance to provide a description at all suggests that, in adulthood, respondents wanted to steer clear of openly judging poorer Blacks perhaps in the same way that their parents did before them. Nevertheless, it was clear to them as children that their parents wanted them to avoid Blacks who possessed characteristics that ran counter to the culture of mobility.

Still, the fact remains that not every working-class or low-income Black person is "ghetto." Elijah Anderson's (1990) work speaks quite convincingly to the existence of "decent" parents in low-income areas who subscribe to the same values as middle-class Blacks. Even if this weren't the case, parental messages implied that lower-income Blacks—who represent a majority of the Black population—weren't worth their children's consideration and time. The fact that parents voiced negative comments so freely suggests that either (1) they were deliberately trying to set up an in-group/out-group comparison that cast lower-income Blacks as inherently inferior in order to keep their children away from them and on the path to mobility or (2) they were unaware of how detrimental these messages could be, particularly to a child's burgeoning racial identity.

Indeed, some parental assessments of other Blacks were rather harsh. For example, Shayla's father said that he couldn't stand "niggers" and that they have no common sense. After they witnessed a fight between a Black couple at a gas station whom he perceived as being low income, he turned to Shayla and said, "Sometimes you just wish you could just disown them for a good ten minutes."[8] It is perhaps significant that Shayla's father said he wished he could disown them for only ten minutes. Such a short window of time suggests that he wishes he could get away from them long enough that non-Blacks don't associate him with them but not long enough that he is divorced from them forever. This reflects the ambivalence of middle-class Blacks who on some level desire associations with other Blacks but on *their* terms. This is an ambivalence passed down from parents to children, where parents differentiate between "good" Blacks and "bad" Blacks and communicate the idea that bad Blacks make life difficult for good Blacks because Whites judge all Blacks the same. While it is true that Blacks are often judged as a group and individual failures translate into group failures in the eyes of the dominant group, this can be a difficult message for children to reconcile and leads to questions about who they are as a Black person and whether they want to associate themselves with other Blacks. As a result, Black middle-class children may rapidly come to the conclusion that other Blacks are inherently bad people, and, as a corollary, their middle-class status makes them the exception to that particular rule. The negative messages about poorer Blacks may also serve as a cautionary tale for Black middle-class children that reads, *If you don't follow the culture of mobility that we have laid out for you, you might end up like them.*

Given Mary Waters's (2001) work on Caribbean families, it is unsurprising that some of the harshest critiques of other Blacks came from parents with Caribbean heritage.[9] These negative messages about African Americans[10] may be due to the fact that when Caribbean immigrants first arrive, they often believe that America is a meritocracy and that, with proper education and skills, much success is possible. This notion was reflected in several interviews, like my interview with Felicia, who said of her Jamaican parents,

> We're talking about parents who are not African American. We are talking about West Indians, so you have to factor that in. We're talking about people who came here because they believed that America was a land of opportunity. And so, of course, they couldn't understand why these Blacks weren't making it. They couldn't understand that . . . they certainly had more positive things to say about White folks than Black people.

Similarly, Marissa said that even though her parents chose not to make negative statements about African Americans because they recognized that most of her friends would be native-born Blacks, her extended family frequently characterized African Americans as "lazy" and unwilling to work as hard as West Indians: "[They often said], 'Well, [as] West Indians, we may look Black, but we're not because we're better than Black Americans."

As Felicia's and Marissa's stories indicate, for Caribbean families, if conventional notions of success (e.g., professional achievement and financial well-being) aren't achieved, it must be through some fault of their own (see also Waters 2001), which casts most African Americans as failures in the minds of Caribbean parents. Previous ethnographic research also confirms that Caribbean parents encourage their children to keep their distance from native-born Blacks (African Americans) because of their low social status in the larger society (Pessar 1995; Waters 2001; see also Jackson 2010). In this way, distancing from native-born Blacks also represents a distancing from racial stigma and the history of racial oppression in the United States (Waters 2001; see also Noguera 2003a).

In her essay "On the Backs of Blacks," Toni Morrison notes that accepting the dominant group's view of Blacks is in fact an integral part of successful assimilation for immigrants:

> Only when the lesson of racial estrangement is learned is assimilation complete. Whatever the lived experience of immigrants with African Americans—pleasant, beneficial or bruising—a hostile posture toward resident blacks must be struck at the Americanizing door before it will open. (cited in Jackson 2010, 193)

While disavowing Blacks may be a requirement for Caribbean immigrants' successful assimilation, it could be argued that it is likewise a requirement for African Americans' successful assimilation. To some extent, the culture of mobility under which African American middle-class children are raised is predicated on distinguishing (and to some extent distancing) oneself from other Blacks and Black stereotypes. Thus, it might be the case that a "hostile posture" toward Blacks is an unfortunate requirement for *all* Blacks who desire successful upward mobility.

Regardless, the stories of Caribbean respondents indicate that while African American middle-class children must negotiate being Black in a White-dominated world and middle-class status in a Black world where most Blacks are lower income, Caribbean middle-class children have to negotiate an additional status—being Caribbean American in the context of an African American community. Children like Marissa and Felicia must negotiate the White world, the African American world, and the Caribbean world all at once. Since the performative expectations differ by which world they are functioning in at the time, Caribbean middle-class children may have an even more difficult time developing a racial identity. However, there is potential for the racial identity of Caribbean children to be stronger than that of African American children because their parents imbue them with a strong sense of pride in that heritage (see Jackson 2010). These children may also return to the islands to visit, which gives them the opportunity to experience life in a place where Blacks are well represented in positions of power and authority. For these reasons, they may be more immune to the internalized racism that African American children must negotiate.

Lest it appear that Caribbean and African American middle-class children receive only negative messages about Blacks and Blackness from parents and family, there were some positive parental messages also offered to the Cosby Cohort that tended to emphasize unity and group solidarity. For instance, in contrast to the messages given by her Jamaican mother, Debra's father, who is African American, told her that she should always speak to and acknowledge a Black person if she saw them on the street. Langston's parents taught him not to be judgmental of Blacks who have less than him—a message also sent by Jensen's father:

> He worked a lot in the community, so he would always tell me that, "You respect everybody. I don't care if it's the president or if it's the person taking out the trash can. You respect everybody and treat them with respect because as humans we all have a commonality, and you just find that commonality and you relate it."

In a similar vein, Michael was taught that if he ever saw a Black person who needed help, it was his responsibility to help them simply because they are Black. He was also taught to help them because White people help their own and Blacks should do the same. In addition, Michael's parents constantly reminded him to "remember where you came from"—a phrase frequently used among Blacks. As most middle-class Blacks are only a generation or two out of poverty, the phrase means that one should always remember their humble beginnings and not forget those who are still in that position.

Chuck's father also offered positive messages about other Blacks when he cautioned Chuck not to be a "sellout" or "oreo" who "turns the corner to get out, keeps going, and never goes back." However, his father offered a caveat. Drawing on his own experience in the workplace in a high-profile army position, he told Chuck:

> "You've got to be very fair [when dealing with other Blacks]. Because you're not helping [them] by letting [them] 'get over.' But two, if they're not going to do anything for you, they're going to pull you down. If I recommended this particular person because he's Black and they don't do a good job, then that reflects on me." So, [Dad said] you have to be very, very careful of that.

Statements like these reveal the class insecurities of middle-class Blacks and their social and psychological ambivalence toward Black counterparts. They also reveal the extent of their class-based concerns and the desire to protect themselves from the gravitational pull of downward mobility in the context of White racism. While the above stories indicate that some positive racial and intraracial socialization exists in Black middle-class families, the vast majority of messages around being Black were largely negative for the Cosby Cohort and cast Blackness and Black people as inherently problematic.

Before moving to the next section, it bears mention that there were fourteen respondents who reported receiving no intraracial socialization. Eight of these were military children. Given the military's colorblind paradigm, it is unsurprising that most of them received no intraracial socialization. But it is somewhat unclear why the six nonmilitary respondents also didn't receive this type of socialization that might help them understand how to think about and treat other Blacks. Perhaps they adopted the same color-blind paradigm as the military parents, or maybe there were other reasons. In all likelihood, some parents probably thought that their children would naturally be able to relate to and understand other Blacks and therefore didn't need formal socialization in this area. Perhaps they looked at the interclass relationships they had developed in the areas in which they grew up or within their own families and couldn't foresee that raising their children in White areas might complicate these relationships for their children. Alternatively, some may have simply decided to let their children figure out how to deal with their fellow brothers and sisters on their own. Another more cynical possibility is that some parents didn't feel they had positive things to say about other Blacks, so they said nothing at all. This isn't completely outside the realm of possibility given some of the harsh parental assessments of other Blacks recalled by respondents in this section, in which case it was perhaps better that some parents offered no messages. However, this missing component of socialization opens the door to strained or nonexistent intraracial relationships, where chapter 5 shows that those members of the cohort who received positive intraracial socialization developed stronger attachments to Blacks in adulthood. Frequent and positive cultural socialization that emphasized to children the rich, varied, and extraordinary characteristics of Black history and culture also served to strengthen attachments to Black people and culture in adulthood.

The Cultural Socialization of the Cosby Cohort

Cultural socialization involves providing specific teachings about Black/African history or culture, transmitting messages about racial pride, taking children to Black cultural events or activities, or supplying them with Black dolls or books featuring Black characters (see Boykin and Toms 1985; Coard et al. 2004; Demo and Hughes 1990; Hughes and Chen 1997; Phinney and Shavira 1995; Stevenson et al. 2002). Certainly, knowledge of Black history and culture has a great impact on the way middle-class Blacks think about their identity and group interests (Neckerman et al. 1999; see also Hochschild 1995; Peterson-Lewis and Bratton 2004; Price

2009). Thus, providing Black middle-class children with sufficient cultural socialization is of great importance and proved to be fairly beneficial to members of the Cosby Cohort.

In many ways, effective cultural socialization serves as a counteractive strategy designed to refute messages about Blacks disseminated in mainstream culture in hopes of creating positive self-esteem for Black children (Constantine and Blackmon 2002; see also Feagin 2010). In this way, it is an important part of the Black counterframe (Feagin 2010). One respondent, Zara, explicitly said that her parents wanted to provide her with positive cultural socialization so that she could get a more balanced view of being Black and understand that the stereotypes about Blacks that she saw in the mass media weren't true. In these ways, providing a child with cultural socialization may (1) imbue a sense of pride in Black culture, which acts as a barrier against deleterious mainstream messages in the mass media and public discourse; (2) act as a shield against racism directed at middle-class children in the White spaces in which they function; and (3) serve as a defense against assaults on their racial identity from Blacks who have adopted essentialist and oppositional notions of Blackness that suggest that "authentic" Blackness lies in hip-hop language, music, and culture. In these ways, understanding how cultural socialization occurs in these families offers a basis for understanding the racial identity development of Black middle-class children.

The fourteen respondents who reported receiving regular cultural socialization described how their parents tried to instill a sense of Black pride by buying them Black-themed books and dolls, showing them Black movies and television shows, or celebrating Black holidays like Kwanzaa and Juneteenth. They also reported attending Black cultural events and activities. For example, a few discussed attending the Sweet Auburn Festival in Atlanta, Georgia—an annual event designed to revitalize the historic district where Blacks owned businesses during Jim Crow. The buildings that stand on Auburn Avenue today "honor the determination and tenacity of Black Americans operating within the confines of extreme social and economic segregation between 1880 and 1965 to create a thriving community" ("Sweet Auburn" n.d.). They also visited various Black or African museum exhibits and frequented the Martin Luther King Jr. National Historic Site designed to honor the late civil rights leader and his struggle for integration. These outings were intended to celebrate the accomplishments of Blacks who were able to overcome oppressive and extreme levels of racial discrimination. In addition to providing children with a generalized appreciation for their cultural heritage, these activities and excursions reinforced the culture of mobility by suggesting that success is possible even under the most confining social structures.

Michael made these connections explicit in his childhood recollection of a performance given by the world-renowned Black dancer, Alvin Ailey:

> I remember seeing Alvin Ailey dance, and that was like so cool because [my parents] kept telling me that the significance wasn't so much the dance [but that] he was recognized as being at another level. So, even if I didn't want to take ballet . . . [for my parents], it was just that this was a Black person that was recognized as being at the top of what they were doing.

Ailey formed his own company of other Black dancers in 1958 during a climate of overt racial hostility. The company has survived long after his death and continues his legacy of expressing Black culture through ballet and modern dance. As Michael indicates, trips to see accomplished Blacks like Ailey served as more than entertainment value or a way to instill cultural pride. In showcasing Black excellence, these outings were part of the Black middle-class culture of mobility where parents provided children with examples of how hard work brings ultimate success.

Still, even aspects of Black culture that were representative of Black achievement were subject to scrutiny from respondents' parents. For instance, rather than recognize or even celebrate the laudable history and accomplishments of HBCUs, Olivia's mother did quite the opposite. One day, when she needed to see a doctor, she told Olivia, "I'm not going to any Black doctor." When I asked Olivia what her mother thought would happen if she sought help from a Black doctor, she said, "I don't know. She feels like if Black people go to a Black doctor, they might—because they went to a Black school—they might not have gotten the same type of education as a Black doctor who went to a White school." Surprisingly, in spite of this negative assessment of HBCUs, Olivia went on to receive her master's degree from a historically Black college. This didn't escape her mother's scrutiny, either, as Olivia explained, "On one instance, she was really proud of that, but on the other instance, kind of like not, you know what I'm saying? She wants a Black person to come out of an Emory [University, a prestigious predominantly White college in Atlanta] or someplace like that." Even though Olivia seems to have given little weight to her mother's point of view, some may internalize negative messages sent by their parents and develop a perspective on Blacks and Blackness that reflects these views.

A large portion ($N = 16$; 48%) of respondents received very few cultural messages or none at all.[11] If these members of the Cosby Cohort had any exposure to Black culture as children, it was church or school sponsored, but their parents never initiated the exposure, nor was it regular. For example, Vivian said that her parents never took her to any cultural events and that she had to "initiate a Black cultural experience on my own." Dana said that she got exposure to Black cultural events only through the church during events like trips to the Heritage Museum or to Black colleges and universities. Ariel claimed that she never went to any Black events unless sponsored by her church or the military base where she lived. The fact that all respondents indicated a great deal of class socialization in their families but so many reported low levels of racial, intraracial, and cultural socialization suggests that racial identity development took a backseat to the Black middle-class culture of mobility and matters of social reproduction for this cohort.

A good portion of the sixteen who received little or no cultural socialization were military children ($N = 7$), but a substantial proportion ($N = 9$) were not. Receiving little or no cultural socialization may lead children to take their cues about Black culture and Black people from pernicious media messages or their peers rather than their parents or family who might offer more positive messages. Without positive and frequent cultural socialization, they are vulnerable to internalizing stereotypical and destructive definitions of Blackness, which makes positive cultural socialization integral to racial identity development.

Noticeably absent from the accounts of cultural socialization was another dimension of this type of socialization that proves much more challenging to teach but whose mastery is essential for moving comfortably amongst other Blacks: the cultural norms and values of the Black social world. Black children are expected to "act Black" around Blacks by speaking Black English, perfecting certain styles of dance, and exhibiting athletic prowess and can be penalized for not doing so (Hill 1999, 44). They must be able to approximate a kind of "mood," or a form of cultural expression where they "adopt the language, clothing, and gait associated with poor black children in a dramatic show of symbolic allegiance to the poor," as racial identity is based largely on "a demonstrable awareness of the culture of the black lower class" (Lacy 2007, 174). Those who don't have adequate knowledge of the lifestyle, culture, and idiosyncrasies become outsiders to the rest of the Black world. However, generally, these things are not overtly or formally socialized with explicit instruction. Instead, informal socialization usually takes place where Black cultural motifs (e.g., dialects, dress, foods, and styles of behavior) are observed through daily encounters with family and peers and ultimately become a reference point for Blackness (Boykin and Toms 1985).

Yet the class realities of the Cosby Cohort proved to be an impediment to the formal or informal transmission of Black cultural norms and styles. Daily or frequent encounters with extended family like same-age cousins weren't very common, and in growing up in predominantly White spaces,[12] they often lacked regular contact with a Black reference group. Moreover, had one been available, the time constraints of the culture of mobility may have offered little time or opportunity for these interactions. In these ways, the cohort had limited access to the stylistic elements of Black culture. Furthermore, parents tended to find these stylistic elements to be negatively evaluated by Whites and therefore an obstacle to their child's success (see Hill 1999).

It also bears repeating that these were parents of the first generation who, in order to survive and thrive in their jobs and communities, had to successfully master White interactional styles, including ways of talking, acting, and dressing. Their lives included a playing down of cultural Blackness and group affinity (Cose 1993; Feagin and Sikes 1994; Stewart 2009). For instance, Cose (1993) tells the story of a first-generation middle-class man who had ascended to vice president of personnel for one of America's largest companies. Cose says, "He had acquired the requisite symbols of success: a huge office, a generous compensation package, a summer home away from home. But he had paid a price. He had decided along the way, he said matter-of-factly, that he could no longer afford to be black" (65). Cose goes on to explain that this man had been "moderately outspoken" about racism within and outside his company, but "his moderate attempts at advocacy got him typecast as undesirable" (66). As a result, when he changed jobs, he distanced himself from any suggestion of a racial agenda (66). While Cose explained that this decision meant that his respondent was labeled as an Uncle Tom by other Blacks at the job, he felt he had no other options.

Similarly, Feagin and Sikes (1994) tell the story of a college-educated secretary and civil rights activist who was working at a large corporation in the 1980s and was a delegate for Jesse Jackson during the Democratic Convention in Atlanta. As she put it, "Many companies would have been proud to know they had somebody [who was a delegate]; and my company would have too, except that I was a delegate for a black person, Jesse Jackson. Then they call me in the office and say, 'Okay, we don't want any NAACP work done on the job. We don't want any democratic [political activity]'" (Feagin and Sikes 1994, 165). She then went on to suggest that these types of activities may have played a role in her review, even though others were engaging in "political activity" on the job, but, notably, they received no such scrutiny. In these ways, middle-class Blacks in the 1980s and 1990s learned early on that silence and invisibility around issues of race and culture were the only way to achieve upward mobility and, as a result, passed this sentiment on to their children.[13] The cumulative impact of these factors is a segment of the Cosby Cohort who were physically distanced from a Black reference group, were unable to learn or had little access to Black cultural norms and styles, and, as a result, have found it very difficult to feel a sense of connection to Black culture and community.

Debra indicated the sense of frustration these respondents experienced in lacking the cultural knowledge necessary to interact successfully with other Blacks as children:

> I didn't know. I mean, I didn't know what game you had to play, or how you had to talk, or what you had to do, how you have to dress to be liked by [other Blacks]. And so I was just being me. I was just being Debra, which unfortunately was not what they expected from another Black person. And so, that did affect my interaction with them.

As her statement indicates, as children, many didn't know the latest dance moves or hip-hop artists or even the phrases and slang used by other Blacks and were punished by Black peers for not having this knowledge (see chapter 4). This is knowledge that parents often don't have because of the generational gap; the second-generation Black middle class was/is the "hip-hop generation," which means it has been defined largely by this aesthetic (i.e., dress, lifestyle, and form of political expression) (Kitwana 2002; Ogbar 2007; see also Dyson 2005). These elements were rather foreign to the parents' civil rights generation. Also of note is that it would have been difficult for the Cosby Cohort to get access to this knowledge even from the media, as hip-hop culture was just gaining momentum in the 1980s and 1990s. At that time, it was confined largely to a single show on MTV (i.e., Yo' MTV Raps) or most of the programming on BET; both channels were cable channels at a period when many households didn't have cable.[14] Even with access to cable, there appeared to be little leisure time available for this group and thus little time for watching television. Therefore, access to 1980s and 1990s styles of Blackness was limited for the Cosby Cohort.

Moreover, as alluded to above, a good portion of what constitutes "authentic Blackness" are qualities and characteristics that run counter to the culture of mobility and are actually part of the Black oppositional culture. The oppositional culture that has existed since desegregation suggests that speaking BEV, listening to "Black" music, and/or avoiding academic achievement (among other things) are all part of being "authentically Black" (see

Fordham and Ogbu 1986; Ogbar 2007;[15] Tatum 1997). Peterson-Lewis and Bratton's (2004) content analysis of fifty-six Black teens' descriptions of what constitutes acting Black or acting White offers further insight into the expectations for Black performativity. The authors identified five dimensions on which authenticity is judged:

1. *Academic/scholastic*, such as not going to class, not doing schoolwork, or acting "street smart" rather than "school smart"
2. *Aesthetic/stylistic*, such as listening to rap music, dressing in hip-hop clothes, or wearing expensive name-brand clothing
3. *Behavioral*, such as using Ebonics or slang or being violent
4. *Dispositional*, such as being disrespectful, having a negative attitude, being loud in public, or having an "I-don't-care" attitude
5. *Impressionistic*, such as giving the impression of being wild, ill mannered, or rude

Nearly every characteristic mentioned by Peterson-Lewis and Bratton (2004) runs counter to the Black middle-class culture of mobility. As the stories in the previous chapter indicate, the culture strictly prohibits the academic/scholastic, aesthetic/stylistic, dispositional, and impressionistic dimensions. Even if they weren't prohibited, the Cosby Cohort's knowledge of it would be very limited considering the distance they experienced from other Blacks. Furthermore, if parents wanted to provide cultural socialization for them along these lines, it is unclear what such socialization would look like. How does a parent teach a child to speak BEV (or "Ebonics") when that isn't the language primarily spoken by the parents or even by others (i.e., Whites) in the neighborhood? Why would a mother or father buy their children baggy clothes or pants that sag when they believe these things to be antithetical to their children's assimilation and ultimate success? In these ways, it is difficult to understand how such socialization would come about. Nonetheless, the result is that this cohort received limited exposure to 1980s/1990s constructions of Blackness, which significantly impeded their ability to enact a successful Black performance and raised questions and doubts for them about their racial identity. The implications of these are presented in the next chapter.

Conclusion

In Shayla Nunnally's (2010) article "Learning Race, Socializing Blackness: A Cross-Generational Analysis of Black Americans' Racial Socialization

Experiences," Nunnally firmly maintains that "the finger-pointing [toward] post-civil rights/hip-hop generation Black Americans cannot occur without reflection upon the role that prior generations of Black Americans had in socializing them about being Black in America and the politics related to being Black in America" (212). In this way, the accounts of the racial, intraracial, and cultural socialization of second-generation middle-class Blacks go a long way toward helping us understand this generation's present connections to Black people and Black culture. Essentially, this is a group of Blacks more likely to have received socialization that emphasized how difficult it is to be Black and be lumped in with less successful Blacks and the importance of using achievement and class resources to compensate for these obstacles. They are also a group of Blacks who grew up in households where *historical* Blackness (e.g., stories of Black struggle during slavery and Jim Crow) was emphasized over more current constructions and manifestations. Perhaps even more detrimental was the lack of racial and cultural socialization for so many respondents, which resulted in a rather feeble understanding of the sociopolitical and cultural implications of being Black in America (more on this in remaining chapters).

Explicit racial, intraracial, and cultural socialization are necessary in order for Black middle-class children to understand what it means to be Black, what their relationships are to other Blacks, and what Blackness means as a historical, cultural, and group identity. Children who sit on the racial and social margins of society need to feel a sense of belonging and rooting to a common culture and community in order to feel a personal sense of affirmation, particularly within the context of racially hostile spaces (see Dalmage 2000; Harris and Khanna 2010; Lacy 2004). Furthermore, having a strong racial identity acts as protection against psychological distress (Kaslow et al. 2004), increases self-esteem (Constantine and Blackmon 2002), and offers refuge and consolation in the midst of discrimination (Miller 1999; Sellers and Shelton 2003). In essence, to provide children with racial and cultural socialization is to provide them with a Black identity that can potentially resist attack. In this way, the process is important for *all* Black children but seems particularly important for middle-class children who (1) grow up in White spaces that are distant from other Black children and Black relatives and (2) experience lives that are qualitatively very different from the rest of the community.

Ultimately, the stories from the Cosby Cohort suggest that what Black middle-class children (and indeed *all* Black children) need is an explicit socialization that not only explains the difficulties of minority status but also emphasizes the rich and varied nature of African/African American history, including the long tradition of African/Black intellectualism and communalism. With this type of socialization, they would be more prepared for racial slights but could also find themselves rooted in a culture, community, and tradition in which they feel they belong, thus minimizing feelings of ambivalence and uncertainty.

The potential ambivalence toward other Blacks and Blackness is no small matter for either the individual or the community at large. The impact to the individual is made obvious in Lacy's quote regarding the "nagging doubts" that parents fear their children will have about their racial identity. But the group impact of this ambivalence has important sociopolitical implications (for a recent discussion, see Price 2009), particularly considering that in the not-too-distant past, Blacks were much more likely to conceptualize themselves as a large, extended, nonbiologically related family whose fates were tied—a sort of "fictive family."[16] The idea dates back to slavery where enslaved Africans shared their paltry allotments of food, cared for newly arriving slaves, looked after children whose parents had been sold away, and covered for each other with the overseer, master, and mistress (Blassingame 1979; Mellon 1988). During Jim Crow, segregation relegated all Blacks to the same neighborhoods, which created more organic ties between the middle class and lower classes, particularly as the middle class provided services for the Black masses (Drake and Cayton 1962; Frazier 1957; Watkins 2005). Additional examples of cooperative relationships abound in the present day, like the "other-mothering" tradition—the practice of women sharing mothering responsibilities and/or raising children in the absence of biological mothers (Collins 2000)—which remains an important and necessary tradition in Black America. Furthermore, Blacks have frequently taken in distant relatives in need (Collins 2000; McAdoo 1975; Pinkney 2000), and historically, wealthier Blacks have given money to support poorer friends and relations (Cose 1993; Jackson 2001; McAdoo 1975; Pattillo-McCoy 1999; Pinkney 2000; see also Neckerman et al. 1999). As if all of this weren't evidence enough, for centuries, Blacks have referred to each other as "brother" or "sister," thereby invoking familial labels whether biologically related or not. These examples indicate that throughout history, Blacks have often conceptualized themselves as a symbolic or fictive family whose fates are tied (see also Dawson 1994). The question, of course, is whether Blacks—particularly recent generations of middle-class Blacks—feel that same sense of attachment to the Black community today.

While various race scholars have bristled over the notion of a monolithic "Black community" or a singular Blackness (Brunsma and Rockquemore 2002; Higginbotham 1992; Jackson 2001), it may be in Blacks' best interest to conceptualize themselves as a community, particularly in the context of the struggle for social justice and advancement (Dalmage 2000; Klor de Alva et al. 1997; Stubblefield 2005). Moreover, political ideology and activity is shaped by racial ideology (Price 2009; Stewart et al. 1998). Therefore, combating the strongholds of institutional discrimination that threaten Black sociopolitical progress requires a sense of group unity and a shared identity based on common racial struggle.[17] A remarkable amount of scholarly literature suggests that Black parents strive to impart these feelings to their children through racial and cultural socialization. Indeed, research shows that middle-class Black parents in particular, because they live and work in more racially integrated settings, anticipate that their children will do the same and may focus more on racial/ cultural socialization than other Black parents (Thornton et al. 1990; see also Marshall 1995; Tatum 1999). However, the stories presented in this chapter cast significant doubt on whether this is actually the case.

Still, we are left with one major question: why did so many respondents receive negligible levels of racial, cultural, and intraracial socialization from their parents? There are myriad reasons why parents may not have imparted or emphasized these messages. For instance, family communication about race is largely influenced by the sociohistorical conditions and values of that particular period in time (Nunnally 2010; Parke 2004; see also Lesane-Brown 2006). It might be the case that first-generation parents didn't feel a great need to formally socialize Blackness into their children because they didn't receive such explicit socialization from their parents while growing up during Jim Crow and the civil rights era. Growing up in the context of such blatant and overt racism, including the ubiquitous presence of "Colored Only" signs, was likely all that was necessary for children growing up under Jim Crow to understand Blackness as a minority status. As a result, some parents may not have realized that this type of socialization was necessary for their children who were growing up absent this context.

On the other hand, Nunnally's (2010) research shows that the parents' civil rights generation actually received quite a bit of racial socialization. As such, it could be the case that given the 1980s and 1990s era of increased opportunity, they didn't feel that their children required the same level of intense racial, cultural, and intraracial socialization. When comparing their formative social worlds to their children's, they might have perceived there to be less overt racial hostilities and as a result passed on fewer messages about minority status to their children (Schuman et al. 1997 cited in Nunnally 2010). The discourse of the 1980s and 1990s could have also led parents to believe that it would be better to minimize the implications of

Blackness for their children. At that time, the discourse increasingly leaned toward "color blindness" where (1) racism was perceived as a thing of the past or mostly the result of a few prejudiced individuals, (2) achievement was perceived as being rooted in merit and character, and (3) race-conscious policies were believed to be unnecessary and in fact discriminatory toward Whites (Bonilla-Silva 2001, 2010; Brown et al. 2003; Carr 1997; Doane 2003; Feagin 2001; see also Bobo et al. 1997; Sears 1988). If parents adopted these attitudes in earnest, they might have felt that racial and cultural socialization was unnecessary or even harmful. Moreover, parents knew from their own experience that the White racial frame (Feagin 2010) demands silence on race and the downplaying of cultural markers in lieu of marketplace success, where those who violate this mandated are subject to sanction (Cose 1993; Feagin and Sikes 1994; Jones and Shorter-Gooden 2003; Rooks 1996). This represents another possible reason why racial and cultural socialization was lacking in these families. Furthermore, the 1980s and 1990s were characterized by a strong anti-Black discourse where poor Blacks were routinely demonized, which perhaps led some parents to discourage identification and relationships with poorer Blacks. In these ways, the lack of racial, cultural, and intraracial socialization in these families may have reflected the racial discourse and sociopolitical patterns of this particular era, thereby leading parents to minimize the implications of Blackness and instead focus their children on matters of social class and achievement.

There is perhaps another important reason why respondents' parents provided little racial and cultural socialization, which is that they may have internalized negative messages about Blacks from the larger society (Thornton et al. 1990). Certainly, the messages transmitted to children about Blacks and Blackness indicate that, to some extent, these parents were fighting their own internalized racism. Many of them were native Southerners growing up under Jim Crow who would have been constantly exposed to negative messages about Blacks and Blackness. Also, in growing up under such intense levels of racism and discrimination and succeeding in spite of it, they may not have understood why many of their counterparts hadn't converted on the gains of the civil rights movement (Dyson 2005; see also Nunnally 2010) and as a result harbored negative feelings toward these Blacks. It is entirely possible that their own internalized racism made them reluctant to provide racial and cultural socialization for their children. It may also have led to the negative intraracial socialization respondents discussed in their interviews.

The lack of explicit positive intraracial socialization could also likely be the result of an important generational difference: the parents' generation was more likely to have felt natural and organic connections to other

Blacks as a result of growing up in segregated neighborhoods. This leant a certain similarity to the experiences and histories of Blacks at that time. Consequently, it might not have occurred to some parents that providing an explicit and positive guide to interactions with (non-middle-class) Blacks was necessary for their children. The parents' proximity to non-middle-class Blacks during their own formative years probably facilitated their ability to pick up the more stylized aspects of Blackness and "code-switch," or alter their linguistic and interactional style for the purposes of fitting in better with other Blacks (Anderson 1990; Neckerman et al. 1999; Pattillo-McCoy 1999). However, in being removed from this context of Black people and Black spaces, members of the Cosby Cohort lost the opportunity to learn code-switching behaviors and in other ways create and nurture connections with other Blacks—the consequences of which may have been underestimated by their parents and the Black community at large.

For the third generation and beyond, racial and cultural socialization might be altogether nonexistent because the present racial climate is one increasingly being billed as "postracial," where many believe that the barriers surrounding race have decreased to the point of allowing for the election of a Black president as well as the embracing of cultural markers of Blackness, such as hip-hop culture. The ubiquitous nature of hip-hop and stylized Blackness also means that there is greater exposure to Black culture as it is presently defined, which therefore makes it far easier to emulate. Moreover, there are a greater number of Black suburbs (Lacy 2007; Wiese 2004), which means that third-generation middle-class Blacks may have more access to other Blacks who perform stylized Blackness, even if they don't know how to enact the performance themselves. On the other hand, if these suburbs are mostly middle class where there is a culture of mobility present, the children would find themselves in good company with other like-minded Black peers. In these ways, third-generation Black middle-class children (and beyond) may have an easier time finding a sense of Blackness.

Yet, because Black middle-class children are still integrating White areas (Lacy 2007), it is quite possible that we will see the second generation's experience play out all over again. The lessons learned from the Cosby Cohort tell us that it is necessary for future generations to receive some explicit and positive racial, cultural, and intraracial socialization from their parents to help them negotiate these challenges. Indeed, this may be the only way for them to reconcile the status inconsistency of being Black middle class, where they are situated at the lower end of America's racial hierarchy yet somewhere near the middle of its class hierarchy. (This, of course, assumes that such a reconciliation is possible.) However, when racial, cultural, and intraracial socialization is minimal or nonexistent, it may close the door to reconciling these identities and negatively impact Black middle-class children's understanding of having a racial minority status as well as their ability to relate to and connect with other Blacks.

~

CHAPTER FOUR

Cast Out of the Race: The Reality of Childhood Intraracial Rejection

In a society continuously shaped by a White racial frame that relegates Blacks to particular stereotypes, it is difficult to recognize and understand Blackness outside the confines of poverty. Whiteness is automatically conflated with middle-class status, and Blackness is automatically conflated with poverty (Collins 2005; Jhally and Lewis 1992; see also Cole and Omari 2003; Lacy 2007; Ogbar 2007; Patterson 1972). Whites seem not to know what to do with Blacks who fall outside of these expectations, which leaves them in a sort of "racial vertigo" (Joseph 2010) where they are forced to reconcile contrasting, contradictory, and even "dizzying" ideas about race. This process proves difficult for many, where many Whites appear unable to place Blacks in any other boxes but the narrow boxes that they have already defined for them. In large part, this is why the election of the nation's first Black president continues to baffle many and lead to peculiar incidents where Barack Obama appears to be the only American president in recent memory to be heckled during a congressional address (and later during a presidential press conference) or to be repeatedly asked by "birthers" for proof of American citizenship much like a freed slave being asked to show manumission papers.

This is a type of discrimination that everyday upwardly mobile Blacks continue to face—a type of discrimination that casts them as outsiders or intruders who are trespassing in areas of social life that are usually reserved for Whites. Researchers have well documented this particular brand of discrimination (e.g., Feagin and McKinney 2003; Feagin and Sikes 1994; Lacy 2007). It is a type of discrimination that I have faced in my own life as well. For example, I have apparently worked at Target, Walgreens, Payless Shoes, Kinko's/FedEx, and a few other stores as well despite never having drawn a paycheck from any of them. Still, I must have worked there because at each one of them I have been asked by White customers where they can find various items and which items are on sale, even when I look like any other shopper strolling the store holding my purse and keys. (Wearing professional clothing doesn't seem to stop these queries either.) In the eyes of these shoppers, I can be only "the help"; I can't be a fellow shopper and certainly can't be a professor of sociology.

Several of these encounters have been particularly hurtful. For example, on a chilly Chicago morning, I bounced down to my local Walgreens, clad in my black windbreaker and keys in hand, to pick up several copies of the *Chicago Tribune*, where I had been quoted as an expert in one of their articles. As I was picking up the extra copies that my mother had requested, a customer asked me if the lotion was on sale and where he could find it. On another occasion, I was at the Kinko's/FedEx, finally and elatedly mailing a 300-page completed book manuscript to my editor, when I was asked by a customer where she could find a particular kind of decorative paper. And even while on the job, a White adjunct professor, assuming I was the administrative assistant, threw his papers at me one evening and asked if I could copy, collate, and staple thirty copies before his class started in twenty minutes. When I explained to him that I was actually tenure-track faculty, he sheepishly scurried away, only to return in ten minutes when he thought I had left the office. Horrified that I was still there, he nervously said to me, "Forget what I said earlier. Besides, I'm sure you've been insulted worse than that before."

So goes the inescapability of Blackness—Blacks are rarely allowed to forget their minority group status among Whites or even their group membership among Blacks. When one appears to have lost sight of Blackness in either of these contexts, there are usually people in line who are anxious to remind them and put them in their "place." In this way, racial boxes, while socially constructed, are simultaneously real and matter. When they are upended, racial vertigo occurs, leaving victims in its wake. We see it, for instance, in the narratives of biracial Americans (e.g., Garrod et al. 1999; Harris and Khanna 2010; Khanna 2011; Rockquemore and Brunsma 2007) who are frequently forced to choose between a Black or White identity or in the narratives of Blacks who lack a phenotypically Black appearance and are able to "pass" as White (Derricotte 1999; Scales-Trent 1995). We also see it in the narratives of middle-class Blacks.

As stated above, it isn't just Whites who have trouble reconciling the existence of middle-class Blacks. Blacks are also prone to this type of racial vertigo. Yet, because Whites are the dominant group who make and define the rules of racial engagement, people of color take their cues from the racial order as they have defined and enforce it (Feagin 2010). For example, when Whites define one group as "the model minority" or another group as "illegal immigrants" or even another group as "thugs" and "welfare queens," it becomes the basis for most social interactions even among and between people of color. When a member of a racial group exhibits characteristics or behaviors that fall outside these expectations, people of color may experience the same racial vertigo that Whites do. As such, Blacks who appears to be living in the valley between America's prescribed racial lines are often met with distrust and suspicion by other Blacks. In addition, because Americans lack the language to understand and conceptualize complex race-class intersections, when a Black person exhibits middle-class qualities, some Blacks (and also Whites) race those qualities as "White," which by extension means that the Black person in question is "acting White" and thus inauthentically Black.

Even during the iconic *Cosby Show*'s run, viewers had trouble understanding the Huxtables as Black because of their class status. Earlier, I discussed Jhally and Lewis's (1992) findings where White audience members identified with the Huxtables along the basis of class lines and really didn't think about them as Black, except perhaps to use them as evidence of a postracial world and one where policies like affirmative action were no longer necessary. However, it wasn't only Whites who had difficulties reconciling the Huxtables' race and class:

> Just as most white respondents found it difficult to talk about class issues, so did black respondents. Though this difficulty led both sets of respondents to similar understandings or misunderstanding about the world, some of its consequences are quite specific. Among blacks, it appears to have created a form of displacement. The absence of a notion of class results in the substitution of the notion of race: "upper middle class" became "white" (82).

Essentially, some of Jhally and Lewis's Black respondents thought that the Huxtables were acting White. Even Innis and Feagin's (1995) Black middle-class respondents referred to the Huxtables as "White people in blackface" who weren't "a true representation of the Black experience in America" (700). All of this points to the conflation of race and class where there is little room for Blackness to exist in tandem with middle-class characteristics and tendencies: "The idea that the Huxtables have adopted upper middle class cultural norms has been displaced by the notion that they have become 'like white people.' Without reference to a relevant discourse, class differences become racial differences" (Jhally and Lewis 1992, 83).

The show itself also had difficulty reconciling the Huxtables' Blackness with their class status. The closest the show ever came to tackling the issue was an episode titled "Vanessa's Rich" (season 3, episode 8 originally aired November 13, 1986; Hatch 1986). In it, Vanessa invites over some members of the cheerleading squad. They begin to take notice of all of the fancy items in the Huxtable brownstone, and Vanessa proceeds to tell them that one of their paintings cost $11,000. The next day, she goes to school and is peppered with taunts of "rich girl," which leads to her first physical fight. Her disheveled appearance at home causes Cliff and Clair to question what happened to her. When Vanessa tells them the story, they chastise her for having told the cheerleaders how much the painting cost. And much like the parents of the respondents in this study would have explained to their own children, Cliff is quick to tell her, "Your mother and I are rich. You have nothing" (Hatch 1986). Nevertheless, those fictional cheerleaders understood Vanessa as someone with privilege, which sparked jealously. But *The Cosby Show*, in its bid for universalism and generalizability, couldn't handle the racialized aspect of this. For real-life Black middle-class children growing up in the 1980s and 1990s and entangled in America's racial vertigo, having privileged status or exhibiting any other behaviors perceived as middle class drew taunts of "oreo" or "wannabe" as well as the dreaded acting-White accusation.

For children, racial vertigo hits especially hard because nuance is difficult for many children to comprehend. Literally and figuratively, for children, the social world works in black and white. In this way, children (and also many adults) become fixated on identity performance, or socially constructed expressions and manifestations of Blackness or Whiteness. Essentially, much like the concept of "doing gender," there is such a thing as "doing race." According to West and Zimmerman (1987), doing gender involves "a complex of socially guided perceptual, interactional, and micropolitical activities that cast particular pursuits as expressions of masculine and feminine 'natures'" (126). Extrapolating from this definition, "doing race" involves a complex of socially guided perceptual, interactional, and micropolitical activities that cast particular pursuits as expressions of one's race and/or culture. When one fails to perform these behaviors, they have not accomplished race correctly (see Hill 1999; Lacy 2007). As Omi and Winant (1994) claim, "We expect people to act out their apparent racial identities; indeed we become disoriented when they do not" (59).

There was perhaps less emphasis on performativity in the past when nearly all Blacks shared the same socioeconomic standing and therefore the same neighborhoods, churches, and schools. A cooperative history and shared traditions arose from that proximity to the point where, by 1980, John

Langston Gwaltney claimed that there was a "core Black culture" to which all Blacks subscribed. Based on his interviews with Blacks in the 1970s, Gwaltney (1980, xxv–xxvi) argued that the core Black culture emphasized truthfulness in speech and deed, sacrificing for kin, and a belief in the natural sequence of cause and effect. However, shortly after the writing of his book, Black culture changed as Blacks were no longer definitively tied to the lower classes and feelings of an organic connection based on shared experiences began to dissipate.

The rise of the Black middle class that began shortly after desegregation but that perhaps hit its apex in the 1980s saw Black middle-class families moving out of Black areas and into White suburbs and a handful of Black suburbs (Wiese 2004; Wilson 1980). Their increased exposure to Whites in neighborhoods, schools, and places of employment likely made it so that honesty in speech and deed were not always possible, as a good degree of pretense is often involved in making Whites comfortable (Cose 1993; Feagin and Sikes 1994; Jones and Shorter-Gooden 2003). Additionally, because of the precariousness of Black middle-class status, values like sacrificing for kin became increasingly difficult for middle-class Blacks trying desperately to maintain their mortgages and pay for their children's education (Cole and Omari 2003; Conley 1999; Oliver and Shapiro 1995). While they undoubtedly felt the pull to help poorer counterparts (Higginbotham and Weber 1992; Jackson 2001; Neckerman et al. 1999), the extent to which they were able to do so was likely compromised by their delicate financial status and lack of family wealth.

In their new neighborhoods and spaces, a Black middle-class culture of mobility flourished where children were taught values and behaviors suited for successful assimilation—striving for academic/professional excellence speaking Standard English, wearing conservative styles of dress and hair, and subscribing to the values of hard work, sacrifice, and delayed gratification. However, for Black Americans left in ghettoes and urban areas, life became progressively worse, where poorer Blacks developed a collective identity *in opposition to* the mainstream and in response to discriminatory treatment in economic, political, social, and psychological domains (Fordham and Ogbu 1986, 181).[1] This newly formed oppositional culture suggested that the behaviors under the culture of mobility constituted "acting White," while speaking Black English Vernacular, listening to "Black" music, or avoiding academic achievement (among other things) were all part of acting or being "authentically Black." A cultural war of sorts was born and the "core Black culture" described by Gwaltney (1980) began to deteriorate with the growing class fissure. As such, there is greater emphasis on performativity and affectation, where middle-class

Blacks must know how to "do Blackness" correctly in order to prove group loy-alty (Lacy 2007). Failure to enact the proper racial script brings censure from other Blacks, including the acting-White accusation. For the Cosby Cohort who (1) grew up under a strict culture of mobility that placed the pursuit of class goals at the center of their lives and (2) had little access to other Blacks, performing Blackness in a way that was socially accepted by Black peers proved quite difficult.

A good deal of research examines the acting White accusation, where scholars have focused almost exclusively on its relationship to academic achievement. This research finds that children who are confronted with the accusation underperform academically in order to avoid this label (see Ford-ham and Ogbu 1986; Tatum 1997). Other research, however, convincingly refutes these findings (Carter 2005; Chavous et al. 2003; Cook and Ludwig 1998; Datnow and Cooper 1996; Horvat and Lewis 2003; Tyson et al. 2005). Certainly, for the Cosby Cohort who were raised under the culture of mobil-ity, underperforming academically was not an option, as their parents placed a premium on academic achievement. As such, this chapter does not focus on alleged academic underachievement in response to the acting White accusation. Indeed, Peterson-Lewis and Bratton (2004) find that academic/scholastic performance was the dimension least likely to be identified by their teenage respondents as representative of authentic Blackness. Instead, it was the other performative aspects of Blackness that their respondents most focused on as indicators of authenticity: the aesthetic/stylistic (e.g., listening to rap or hip-hop or wearing brand-name clothes), behavioral (e.g., speaking BEV or being violent), dispositional (e.g., being disrespectful or having an "I-don't-care" attitude), and impressionistic dimensions (e.g., giv-ing the impression of being wild, ill mannered, or rude). Of particular note is that these characteristics identified by Peterson-Lewis and Bratton in 2004 are the same ones identified by the Cosby Cohort who grew up twenty years before their research was conducted, which indicates the enduring nature of these norms and their crystallization over time, even before researchers had the language and concepts with which to describe them.

In this chapter, I move the conversation about acting White past its implications for academic achievement and focus on the other performative aspects of Blackness that are necessary for proving authenticity and gain-ing acceptance into the Black fictive family. As is consistent with previous research (Neal-Barnett et al. 2010; Peterson-Lewis and Bratton 2004), the accusation played a pivotal role in this cohort's lives largely because of the vast array of other behaviors construed as acting White that *didn't* pertain to academic achievement. I also focus on the consequences of "bad performances" and the impact they had on the Cosby Cohort's sense of racial identity and thus their sense of self. Bad performances carried the immediate consequence of being cast out of the Black adolescent peer circles. However, for these respondents, they also carried the more long-range consequence of feeling permanently excluded from the Black fictive family.

Feelings of ostracism are further magnified by the ways in which social class has become inextricably tied to authentic Blackness. For the last thirty years, part of what it has meant to be authentically Black is to have a working-class or low-income background. The media, in particular, have played a crucial role in the process of conflating authenticity with poverty:

> In the 1980s and 1990s, historical images of Black people as poor and working class became supplemented by and often contrasted with representations of Black respectability used to portray a growing Black middle class. Poor and working-class Black culture was routinely depicted as being "authentically" Black whereas middle- and upper-middle class culture was seen as less so. Poor and working-class Black characters were portrayed as the ones who walked, talked, and acted "Black." (Collins 2005, 122; see also Cole and Omari 2003; Lacy 2007; Ogbar 2007; Patterson 1972)

As a result, presently, "authentic" Blackness is more likely to emphasize stylized ways of talking, walking, acting, and thinking exhibited by poorer Blacks as the root of Blackness rather than the characteristics that Gwaltney mentioned in 1980. This was problematic for the Cosby Cohort, who had little access to Black people and stylized aspects of Black culture—the salience of which became obvious when the racial composition of their schools began to change. While their early schooling was spent in majority White schools, the diversity of their schools increased in middle school and high school (see Tatum 1997), where they came into contact with larger numbers of working-class and low-income Blacks. As this chapter shows, when that occurred, they found their Blackness under scrutiny and found themselves having to successfully negotiate both White and Black social circles, where negotiating Black circles appeared to be the more challenging of the two. The subsequent rejection from Blacks in particular frequently haunted them and (as the next chapter shows) was an experience they brought to interactions with Blacks thereafter.

In large part, the Cosby Cohort's adolescent interactions with other Blacks were unpleasant because it seemed to their Black peers as if these were rejecting their "true natures." This highlights the essentialist nature of racial performativity: the perception is that all Blacks automatically know how to enact a "Black performance." Indeed, it is often conceptualized not as a performance but simply as "natural" behavior that all Blacks exhibit. Children, in particular, are susceptible to subscribing to this ideology, as they lack full understanding of the socially constructed nature of race and culture and have no knowledge of the historical shifts in cultural Blackness and racial scripts. It is difficult for them to understand that what they witness now is merely the most recent incarnation of Blackness.[2] As a result, it appears as if Blacks, particularly those who are middle class and have adopted the habitus of the culture of mobility, are rejecting their "true natures" and therefore cannot truly be considered part of the extended Black family. As Dalmage (2000) says,

> When more than one identity or set of experiences is recognized, community boundaries begin to blur, and a sense of unity becomes difficult to achieve. . . . Unfortunately, essentialism creates alienation by ignoring (or degrading) some experiences while privileging others. Those who don't quite fit into the prevailing notions of community are often jettisoned to the margins. (12)

In this chapter, I discuss how the inability of respondents to perform Blackness to their peers' satisfaction left them feeling cast out of Black circles, which led to deep feelings of isolation and loneliness that they would ultimately carry with them for the rest of their lives. To be sure, their class status alone could have been enough for them to earn the acting-White label (Martin 2010), as the White racial frame that is enforced on people of color (see Feagin 2010) suggests that Blacks are not capable of ascending to middle-class status, and thus doing so is construed as outside the realm of Blackness. However, their lack of convincing performances seemed to further indicate to their Black peers their lack of authenticity. And, while they had frequent contact with Whites because they were in majority White spaces much of the time, they didn't find great acceptance among Whites either as they grew older. In these ways, the Cosby Cohort was without a place where they belonged and had difficulty finding someone who related to their predicament. When they told their parents about feeling cast out and being accused of acting White, some parents offered very effective responses (as defined by the respondents) that reaffirmed the child's self-esteem, while others appeared not to have a helpful response. The experiences detailed in this chapter point to the personal salience of race in the lives of all Blacks regardless of class status and the ways in which performativity plays a key role in racial identity development and feelings of attachment to Black people and culture over the life course.

When first looking for acceptance, the Cosby Cohort initially turned to White social circles, as many of their interactions were still with Whites in their neighborhoods and schools, and it was also a group with whom they had become familiar. Yet this option proved complicated because of the negative messages their parents transmitted about Whites and also the subsequent rejection from them that they experienced as time went on. This, along with the changing racial compositions of their schools, ultimately forced them out of White spaces and into hostile Black spaces. Still, life inside White spaces proved complicated as well.

Childhood Relationships with Whites

Constant interactions with Whites become unavoidable when living in majority White neighborhoods or spending most of the day enrolled in advanced courses with White children. For some members of the Cosby Cohort, this led to a social gravitational pull toward befriending Whites. The reality of having no choice but to befriend Whites prompted a generalized acceptance of White friends with little critical analysis of the nature of the friendship. For example, Genevieve said, "Before nine years [old], [I was] at a private school which was predominantly White. So, being the only Black child in class from kindergarten up to second grade, I accepted White people just because they were the only ones around." For this reason, most of her friends were White, including her best friends. Ariel, Alexis, and Scott likewise said that most of their interactions were with Whites because they were the students with whom they were in the advanced courses, and in Scott's case his membership on sports teams at predominantly White schools led to more friendships with Whites. Essentially, these friendships were by default, as respondents had little other choice but to befriend those closest to them, in terms of both physical space and lifestyle.

When parents hinted that they needed to be careful about their interactions with Whites (see chapter 2), some chose to ignore those warnings because they didn't have another option. Some reported very good interactions with White friends and acquaintances despite these warnings. For instance, Camille said that even though she had received messages from her parents about not trusting Whites, she still had very satisfying friendships with them that met her social needs. Langston said that even though he was the only Black child at birthday parties, he didn't feel uncomfortable because "I didn't even notice." Shayla indicated that for most of her life, her friendship circle was anywhere from 95 to 98 percent White but believed this "worked out well" for her. In these ways, White friendships were sometimes very productive where, even with racial differences, the similarities in social class and childhood experiences were enough to create a sense of belonging among Whites. As such, race isn't always a factor in middle-class Blacks' relationships with Whites.

By and large, however, there were more reports of negative than positive interactions with and feelings toward White peers. Sometimes, the negative feelings were over having less money than them. While the Cosby Cohort had more privilege and opportunity than Black counterparts, they typically had less than their White counterparts. This is but one of the ways in which this cohort spent their childhood betwixt and between White and Black America. As a result, they had to learn to interact successfully in both social worlds, where interactions in the White world were complicated by having fewer resources than their White friends. Thus, in addition to feelings of insecurity surrounding race, for the Cosby Cohort, there were also feelings of insecurity regarding income and wealth.

Respondents reported other painful interactions with Whites that evoked feelings of exclusion and loneliness. Iyana recalled the events surrounding a classmate's birthday party where she was the only child in the class not invited to the party. The birthday girl explained that this was because her father did not like Black people. Iyana's mother felt like this required an effective, hands-on response:

> Iyana: At the time . . . I don't think I thought too much of it until my mother sat down and we talked about it. And then, we also talked to that family about it and what that meant because their children couldn't understand why I couldn't come to the party. So then, it ended up being kind of a learning experience for everybody.
>
> Author: So, she actually talked to the parents?
>
> Iyana: Oh yeah. Oh yeah. We nipped it in the bud. And did a little educational process about it—you know, teaching them about race and stuff like that as well.
>
> Author: Okay. Do you approve of the way your mom handled it?
>
> Iyana: Yeah. I thought she did a great job, considering.

Incidents like these become difficult to negotiate for Black middle-class children. However, her mother's advocacy and her attention to the identity issues that her daughter was experiencing by being outcast by a White member of her social circle turned out to be extremely helpful in Iyana's ability to make sense of and navigate the situation. Her mother's attention to this detail is even more impressive considering the fact that she was a single parent with limited time but still made Iyana's concerns a priority.

Other respondents also reported negative interactions with White peers. For example, Belinda discussed how, in fifth grade, she befriended two White girls in her school with whom she and her parents eventually established a carpool. They had become so close that Belinda thought that they were all best friends. To confirm her assumption, she playfully said to them one day, "Let's tell each other who our best friends are!" She already had her answer prepared and was going to name both of them as her best friends. But to her astonishment, when she asked the question, the two White girls named each other their best friends, which left Belinda out in the cold. The girls explained that their rationale for having chosen each other was that they had known each other longer. Belinda didn't buy this: "In my mind, I was like, *Mmm-hmm. Y'all didn't choose me because I'm Black.* It just you know, hit me—hit me in my heart that it was a race thing." Interactions with Whites indeed proved to be a delicate situation for these members of the Cosby Cohort. The examples above, along with those in chapter 2 where respondents describe the hostility of White neighbors, the discrimination from White teachers and school administrators, and the unpleasant interactions in public places, speak to this fact.

In part, these negative interactions reflect the southern roots of many in the study. In the 1980s and 1990s, the South was still immersed in an atmosphere of racial turmoil. By way of example, in 1987, talk-show host Oprah Winfrey aired a show about the exclusion of Blacks from Forsyth County, Georgia. At the time of the show, not a single Black person had lived there in seventy-five years (http://www.oprah.com/oprahshow/Race-on-The-Oprah-Show-A-25-Year-Look-Back) because of the strong racial prejudices of its inhabitants.[3] As such, growing up in this southern context might be partially to blame for some of these respondents' negative experiences with Whites. Still, these experiences weren't unique to Southerners, as respondents who grew up in California, Maryland, Ohio, and Illinois reported similar interactions; it would be a mistake to conclude that this is merely the result of Black middle-class children growing up in White southern spaces. Nevertheless, the respondents' experiences of being cast out of the White world in which they were raised and perhaps even felt most comfortable was yet another cost of upward mobility and made them vulnerable to loneliness and isolation. This was only exacerbated by feeling like they had no home in the Black community either. Indeed, when they were thrust into Black social spaces, they found them even more difficult to negotiate.

Identity Events and the "Acting-White" Accusation

Armed with the worldview they had acquired under the culture of mobility and the often inconsistent and negative racial, cultural, and intraracial socialization provided by their parents, members of the Cosby Cohort were eventually forced to leave predominantly White spaces and enter spaces where other Blacks were present. Negotiating such treacherous racial terrain was difficult for these respondents. Often, their ordeal began when a Black peer pointed out that they hadn't mastered the correct Black performance.

Acting Black: Matters of Performativity and Social Location

> People have responded to my use of English as though I were an impostor, a usurper, as if I were puttin' on airs, stubbornly willing myself to speak in a way that wasn't natural to "my kind," and by doing so have marked myself as an adopted (or at least adoptable) member of the ruling class. (McKnight 1993, 109)

As indicated in the above quotation from Reginald McKnight's essay "Confessions of a Wannabe Negro," identity is a precarious issue for Blacks striving for upward mobility. Inability to enact a credible Black performance seems to place one automatically outside commonly held notions of Blackness. This puts Black middle-class youth, in particular, in a difficult situation where some try to ignore their Blackness while others embrace essentialist notions and still others try to walk somewhere in between, constantly fearful of eminent discreditation (Tarpley 1995). This is the dilemma that awaited members of the Cosby Cohort when they finally encountered more Black peers—many of whom were not middle class. The narratives detailed in this section illustrate the various difficulties of this experience and the ways in which unconvincing performances bring a variety of repercussions for middle-class Blacks.

Michele ran into trouble when she transferred to a school she estimated to be 75 percent Black from her former school that was mostly White and Latino. Very quickly, she realized the importance of performance:

> And, there was like a housing project area right behind the school, and a lot of kids that lived in the housing project area went to that school, and from the second I walked in the door, just because I dressed differently, I looked differently, I talked differently. . . . I was tormented from probably all the way through seventh to the end of eighth grade.

Genevieve endured a similar ordeal when she transferred from a mostly White private school to a multiracial public school because her mother could not afford the tuition after her father's untimely death:[4] "When I got to public school, I was teased for talking White supposedly by the Black kids and teased for the clothes I wore. Because I came from private school, I still wore dresses and skirts, and I didn't wear tennis shoes." As if the transition to a new school wasn't difficult enough, these respondents were suddenly forced to confront their racial identity upon increased contact with other Black children. Unexpectedly, they were left standing on their own in a place where peers who looked like them didn't accept them.

By the standards of the oppositional culture, these respondents were acting White, where there were a multitude of ways in which they acquired this dubious distinction. In every case, the reason harkened back to their socialization into the Black middle-class culture of mobility. For instance, in this study, the characteristic most identified as "White" is speaking Standard English.[5] In addition, like Genevieve indicated in her story about the change from private school to public school, dress was also mentioned several times as a behavior that might provoke the acting White accusation. For example, in the early 1990s, when most respondents were growing up, an expensive urban clothing line called "Cross Colors" was born, consisting of bright and sometimes mismatched colors on T-shirts, baggy pants, and jackets. Several respondents reported that their parents would not buy them clothing from this line because it was so expensive, yet this became another reason why they were accused of acting White. Avoiding the purchase of pricey items is part of the culture of mobility and the values of sacrifice and delayed gratification. Therefore, buying flashy and expensive clothes so that their child fit in wasn't top priority for these parents. Some respondents also mentioned that they were not allowed to wear the same trendy clothes as their Black peers because their parents wanted them to be perceived by authority figures as being "different" from other Black children.[6] Lacy (2007) refers to this as "social differentiation" (76), a form of exclusionary boundary work where middle-class Blacks make a concerted effort to differentiate themselves from the Black poor. This further reinforced the negative in-group/out-group comparison between middle-class Blacks and working-class and low-income Blacks. Nevertheless, not conforming to these peers' standards ultimately led to respondents feeling outcast from a community in which they desired to belong as children.

There were other behaviors that respondents failed to perform that also earned them the acting-White label. Several respondents talked about how being well behaved and not getting into trouble was cast as acting White by Black peers. Gabrielle elaborated on this and other behaviors that earned members of the cohort this distinction:

> And then how you presented yourself—how you handled yourself in certain situations, probably I think determined acting Black or acting White. Maybe for their definition of acting Black, you were a little bit more aggressive in handling a situation . . . versus wanting to talk about it. Or, the way you were aggressive. So, maybe [their] words were like, "Well, let's fight then—let's handle it," versus, "Well, we need to talk about this as soon as possible." That's aggressive also but going about it in different ways.

She went on to say,

> And then how you react to certain situations. Maybe like if there's a certain song playing, and so if it's a song that most Black people resonate with, you get excited about it and dance to it or jump up and down. And if you don't, then maybe you aren't acting Black or something. I would say things like that would be a definition of acting Black.

Gabrielle's statements well illustrate the behavioral and impressionistic dimensions of acting Black (Peterson-Lewis and Bratton 2004), where things as trivial as word choice or song preference to something as significant as one's problem-solving technique were indicators of acting White and thus enough to be cast out of Black peer circles. This was particularly frustrating for respondents in the study who felt like there was nothing they could do as children to sufficiently prove to their Black peers that they were "Black enough."

In addition to issues of performativity, as alluded to earlier, class membership alone was enough to be considered acting White. Zara said that she thinks she received the "oreo" label because of her class status, where both of her parents held graduate degrees and prestigious jobs:

> I had some of the oreo stuff. I think that some of it was class. . . . I think [the] whole perception of my family [being] from a class status really came from other people who would say, "What does your mother do?" And I would say, "Well she does this." And, "What does your dad do?" And then they would say, "Oh you must be rich!" . . . But I think that's where a lot of it came from. . . . I think a lot of it had to do with class. And, I think some of the comments I would get from the Black students were more related to class than anything.

Likewise, Jamika said that she was harassed by Blacks who attended a public school next to her private magnet school, where her attendance at that school served as an indicator of her class membership:

> And that was more so the problem that we had was dealing with the people who were from the neighborhood who resented us coming into their neighborhood with all of our expensive things and then getting this "special" education, and then they thought that we thought that we were better than them. . . . I think people thought that I was kind of like out of my place, and I didn't realize who I was supposed to be, and I was trying to act White.

In these cases, it appears that simply having more money caused other Blacks to think that the respondents were putting on airs and/or being standoffish. While adults may have difficulty dealing with this perception from their peers, it means a lot more to children who lack the resources and experience to understand what is occurring and desperately want to fit in, as children of all races do. Still, there is a specifically racialized component to this: Black Americans' racial minority status means that it becomes even more important for them to feel that they have a home in their own racial community because they often feel that they lack one in the larger White society. For the Cosby Cohort, feeling "homeless" in the Black community created a kind of trauma[7] in childhood that lingered for many into adulthood, as also evidenced by the respondents' efficient recall of the feelings and particulars around these events many years later.

To be sure, it is important to note that the working-class and low-income Blacks mentioned in these stories are more than just antagonists to the respondents. Their frustration toward the class status of their middle-class counterparts was real albeit perhaps misdirected. The frustration is born out of a structure that relegates most Blacks to impoverished areas or existences where families are barely making ends meet. As some of the respondents mention, their tormentors were less privileged than them and from less wealthy sections of town. For these lesser-privileged children, going to school with Blacks who have more privilege and who have also managed to get into honors courses and maintain a presence in extracurricular activities can be painful for children who feel like they don't have these opportunities. They must bear witness to a life in which they see someone who looks like them begin to accumulate the cultural, social, and (eventually) economic capital that they know will make a difference in that other child's life chances and wish they could have access to the same. Yet the difficulties that these middle-class children were having remained invisible to them, and perhaps all that was visible was their privilege. Also invisible to them were the structural roots of race-class inequalities, particularly in the context of the 1980s and 1990s color-blind discourse that obscured the nature of these inequalities and instead emphasized meritocracy and personal responsibility. For working-class and low-income children feeling powerless at the time, perhaps the only place to safely direct their anger and frustration was toward wealthier counterparts. Moreover, these identity-related insults were fairly easy to come by because of the ways in which Blackness has been narrowly constructed by the dominant society and the ways in which middle-class Blacks fall outside these parameters.

Just as gender is a process of social interaction that can be "done unto" an individual by others (Hollander and Howard 1996), these stories show that race is a similar process where racialized conventions of behavior can also be forced on the individual. However, what is being imposed is a uniform, narrow, stereotypical notion of Blackness that is resistant to heterogeneity and change but nevertheless is the benchmark for "authenticity." According to Dyson (2005),

> The question of black authenticity gathers all the intersections of black life in miniature; it portrays the relation between identity and class, culture, gender, ideology, sexual orientation, region, religion, age and the like. Some blacks think that "real" blacks don't vote Republican, marry outside the race, adopt gay lifestyles, support abortion, bungee jump, climb mountains, attend the opera, or love country music. These views reveal the tribalism that can trump complex views of black life. Proud of their roots, some blacks worship them. But roots should nourish, not strangle, black identity. (40)

In this statement, Dyson argues for a more expansive view of cultural Blackness and Black authenticity—one that isn't as narrowly defined thereby forcing Blacks into constricting boxes.

Of some note is that his list of items in which Black people supposedly don't participate includes many behaviors or opportunities from which Blacks have been systematically barred from participation, thus leading them to be defined as "White people's terrain." For instance, the gay liberation movement and lesbian/gay/bisexual/transgender/queer community in general have largely shut out its members of color (Collins 2005; Han 2010; Rust 2009). Moreover, where Blacks in country music are concerned, Darius Rucker has spoken about the challenges of breaking into country music and Nashville's White-dominated and exclusionary music scene (Harris 2010; see also Wiltz 2009). And activities like mountain climbing, bungee jumping, and attending the opera have traditionally required disposable income that many Whites have but that many Blacks do not have. As a result, these activities have become defined as "White," where Blacks who participate in them have been subjected to other Blacks' judgments about their identity and authenticity.

The question becomes, how do we move away from narrow construc-tions of Blackness and move to a more expansive and inclusive definition that embraces all Blacks? In *Ethics along the Color Line*, philosopher Anna Stubblefield (2005) advocates for such a definition. Stubblefield argues for a notion of unconditional acceptance into the Black fictive family, much like what happens in biological families.[8] This conceptualization would include an appreciation and unconditional acceptance of all members regardless of differences (including differences in gender, sexual orientation, age, disabil-ity, etc.), as well as an obligation to care for all members unconditionally (166). As she puts it, "Family are precisely those people about whom we do often care simply because they are our family and for no other reason" (156). In this way, all members could be included, whether gay, biracial, or middle class. To be clear, Stubblefield's assertion is highly idealistic for it would be difficult for even blood relatives to live up to such lofty standards, let alone an entire population of unrelated Black Americans. Moreover, in a Black community rapidly diversifying along class lines and that includes members with varying degrees of privilege (by skin tone, sexuality, social class, and so on), unconditional acceptance of all members proves difficult. In these ways, promoting an inclusive "family"-based definition is challenging but perhaps necessary for group cohesion.

Another solution might be to extend the definition of cultural Blackness beyond the oppositional culture and hip-hop aesthetic to include the gran-deur of African/African American history, cultures, languages, and traditions (including the long tradition of African/Black intellectualism). In large part, this cultural knowledge has been lost because of the legacy of slavery and institutional racism, which have played a key role in systematically erasing or minimizing Black and African culture and achievements. Hence, there is a knowledge gap where this kind of information has been largely absent in the community and thus is difficult to pass down to children despite the fact that these histories and traditions exist. A more expansive definition of Blackness that includes a recognition and appreciation of the African/African Ameri-can history and culture, along with a more inclusive definition of community membership, might aid middle-class children and indeed *all* Black children in locating themselves in the context of a more comprehensive, progressive, and inspirational conceptualization of Blackness than what currently exists. It may also foster a greater sense of unity and group identity that could be mobilized in pursuit of Black advancement. Yet, for now, the definition of Blackness is narrow, which appeared to cause the Cosby Cohort a great deal of difficulty and distress.

Taking a Closer Look at Identity Events

When told by other Black peers that they aren't doing race correctly or aren't "Black enough," the feeling is devastating for a number of reasons. First, at the adolescent stage in particular, children are in the midst of a critical point of development, marked by the key questions of "Who am I?" and "Who do others think I am?" (Erikson 1968). These questions are at the forefront of their consciousness. Second, the desire to conform to peers' expectations is common during adolescence (Clasen and Brown 1985; Heaven 2001) and is something to which most adolescents aspire; falling short of peer expectations becomes a source of distress. Third, Black adolescents, specifically, are more likely to compare themselves to those who are most like them rather than to the dominant culture (see Tatum 1997), which means that Black peer attitudes and behaviors become the benchmark for their own. For all of these reasons, the accusation had great impact on the Cosby Cohort.

In order to understand the impact fully, we must also understand how much emphasis younger generations of Black Americans put on their peers' assessment of their Blackness. Journalist and political analyst Bakari Kitwana (2002) discusses this in his book *The Hip Hop Generation: Young Blacks and the Crisis in African-American Culture.* Speaking as a member of Generation X (Blacks born between 1965 and 1984, who are well represented in this study), he argues the following:

> For our parent's [sic] generation, the political ideals of civil rights and Black power are central to their worldview. Our parents' generation placed family, spirituality, social responsibility, and Black pride at the center of their identity as Black Americans. They, like their parents before them, looked to their elders for values and identity. The core set of values shared by a large segment of the hip-hop generation—Black America's generation X—stands in contrast to our parents' worldview. For the most part, we have turned to ourselves, our peers, global images and products, and the new realities we face for guidance. . . . Today, more and more Black youth are turning to rap music, music videos, designer clothing, popular Black films, and television programs for values and identity. (7–8)

As Kitwana astutely states and as the narratives in this chapter show, recent generations of Black Americans have been more likely to look to their peers to validate their Blackness, where Blackness has come to be defined by the hip-hop aesthetic and the variety of images, products, and attitudes associated with it. Not adopting these qualities and subsequently being rejected by peers carries a lot of weight and caused some respondents to feel like outsiders who didn't belong. The rejection is devastating because children's social worlds often feel very small to them, and thus, when Black peers weren't accepting of the Cosby Cohort, it often felt like the whole of Black America didn't accept them and perhaps never would.

In the section of the interviews where I asked about identity events, I was frequently taken aback by some of the emotion that arose from the respondents. Heads were cast down as if embarrassed or ashamed, while others sat with tears in their eyes. Some recounted their stories while sadly shaking their heads and looking away. In the middle of one woman's story, she stopped the interview, paused for a minute, and said, "Wow, this is like therapy." These reactions to events that happened well over ten years ago suggest that the emotional scars of the experience run deep and made an indelible impact on respondents' racial identity development. The stories these interviewees recount and the emotion they evoke suggest that we need to pay more attention to the emotional lives of privileged Blacks. They also indicate the continuing significance of race in the lives of the Cosby Cohort despite a life spent focused on class goals.

As children, these respondents endured various forms of ridicule and taunting over their racial identities. The most often used tool of ridicule was verbal taunting. In several cases, the term "oreo" or "ice cream sandwich" was used to indicate that although the person was Black on the outside, they accepted White values, culture, and lifestyles.[9] For example, Langston was called an "oreo" by other Black children because he was a good student involved in a variety of clubs and organizations. Scott and Alexis were called "ice cream sandwiches" for having White friends. The verbal taunting appeared to be very painful for these children. For at least one respondent, Layla, the verbal taunting could not be avoided because it was actually coming from extended family members who weren't as well off as her family:

> If we were with relatives, someone would make a remark about the way I spoke or make a joke about it. . . . Rather than say, "Oh well, don't say that to my daughter," [my mom] would join in. I mean she would laugh, too. . . . And so you know, 'til this day, I do keep my family at arm's length now. And I don't avoid a relationship with them, but I'm not looking forward to relationships with them.

She later divulged that the resentment she harbors over her family's having treated her this way as a child continues to affect her in the present to the point where she now limits her children's contact with her extended family for fear that they may be subject to ridicule as well. In Layla's case, her strategy for dealing with identity issues necessitated distance from her own family in order to feel comfortable with who she is and with who she is raising her children to be. However, the fact that she is distancing her children from other Blacks suggests that the social gap between middle-class and non-middle-class Blacks (even within the same family) may widen as time goes on, in part because of issues of performativity and privilege.

Perhaps more difficult than the verbal abuse many respondents received was the physical abuse some endured as children as a result of their failure to give a convincing Black performance. In some cases, physical abuse was threatened but not actually carried out. Fear and anxiety appeared to be normal fixtures in the lives of these respondents who faced the looming threat. Aubrey talked about being afraid of some of the Black girls who wanted to beat her up because she had more money than them. Debra said that she avoided a certain part of the school because lower-income Blacks who had a problem with her hung out there. Marissa said that she never ate breakfast in middle school and high school because her stomach was in knots as she would think to herself, "Lord, what is this day going to have in store for me?" As if the pressures presented by the culture of mobility and the everyday pressures of simply growing up weren't enough, these respondents had to negotiate identity issues as well that felt insurmountable and frightening to them as children.

In some cases, the physical abuse *actually* occurred, like for Shayla, who frequently had Cheetos thrown at her and had gum stuck in her hair that her mother had to keep cutting out. The most extreme case of physical abuse reported came from Michele. She was teased mercilessly by other Black children because of the way she talked and dressed. A few girls in particular began bullying her by touching, hitting, pushing, and tripping her. The situation deteriorated to the point where teachers had to escort her to and from class. However, on a day when she was not being escorted, Michele recounted the following occurrence:

> One particular day, I was walking down the hallways and I didn't have my teacher. And a girl, she just walked up on me and snatched my earring out of my ear. She tore my ear lobe. And at that point like, I tried to kill her. . . . They tried to kick me out of school, and my Dad was like, "No, I've been coming up here for two years trying to get y'all to do something about these girls . . . this is ridiculous. And if you try to kick [my daughter] out, I'm going to sue you."

While Michele's case is on the extreme end of the spectrum, it illustrates the consequences of not doing race "correctly." Michele grew up existing in spaces that were predominantly White, was fairly sheltered, and hadn't mastered Black performativity. Children like her appear to Black peers as out of touch and as if they are trying to be something that they are not. Not only was she denied admission into the Black fictive family, but she was violently banished from it.

The reaction from most respondents on receiving verbal and physical abuse in childhood ranged from anger, fear or anxiety, sadness, bewilderment, and sometimes indifference. Those who were angry were reacting to the fact that they had always thought of themselves as Black and were not trying to be anything other than what they were. A common refrain throughout many interviews was, "I knew I was Black!," which suggested that *they* recognized their Blackness and identified as Black, but because they weren't doing Blackness the way other children were, it wasn't accepted. The anger and frustration is particularly salient because it is a function of structure; in response to systemic racism born out of the White racial frame, these children were forced to adopt a culture of mobility that distanced them both spatially and experientially from other Blacks and somehow deracinated them in the eyes of Black peers. Their parents' efforts to help them get ahead in a White-dominated society became the same reason why they were rejected by other Blacks. This seemed nonsensical to many of the Cosby Cohort respondents and appeared to be a recurrent source of frustration.

Perhaps the most common emotion was sadness, where respondents recalled frequently coming home crying after school. Genevieve even begged her mother to transfer schools, while Camille became increasingly dejected over other kids saying that her parents must be White because of the way she talked. Debra best described the deep sorrow many children felt over this situation:

> There was sadness, okay. There was sadness. . . . Sadness in that I'm alone. I felt like I was alone. And sadness in that I'd finally come to a school where there were more people who looked like me than [just] my sister. . . . So, I was finally at a school where I could have Black friends because I wanted that. I didn't have it, but I wanted it. And I was finally at a place where I could have Black friends, and no one wanted to have me.

Debra's statement reflects the deep desire that Black middle-class children have to connect with other Black children, socialize with them, and be accepted by them. Many like her spoke about their time in all-White schools and how excited they were to go to a school where there were other Black children. Their expectancies were high; they thought they were coming "home" (see Evans 1993). As a result, when they were rejected, it was a long fall down from their high expectations.

Debra's dilemma was further complicated by the fact that her father taught her that her White friends might also hurt her, which then led to her avoiding them as well. Consequently, when she was rejected by Black peers, she was left on her own with no peer group with which to socialize. When I asked about how this experience made her feel at the time, she simply said, "I felt like I was alone. I felt like I was in this space that no one could really share with me." This is an elegant description of the feelings of displacement some Black middle-class children may feel as they sit either on the periphery or completely outside of both White and Black peer circles. This can lead to a palpable sadness or in cases like Michele's, a sense of dumbfoundedness and confusion:

> At some points, I wondered where I belonged, but it was never really a sadness. I'm too Black for the White people or too White for the Black people, you know what I'm saying? Where do I fit in in all of this? It was never a sadness. It was never an anxiousness. It was just a question of, where do I go?

Indeed, the feeling that interviewees reported most in their formative years was a generalized sense of being "stuck," where they were caught between the White and Black social worlds and fit into neither to some extent. Her statement indicates the importance of belonging and feeling connected for these children and the disorientation that not belonging presents.

As children, when respondents attempted to dislodge themselves from being stuck, even White members of their social circles sometimes noticed their struggle. For instance, Chuck was in marching band, and during football games, he would visit with Black kids in the rival high school's band. He reported that this did not escape the scrutiny of his White friends who wondered aloud why he kept disappearing from their stands during football games. Scott's story was particularly moving and another good example of the racial dilemmas these children face. In high school, Scott had one group of White friends and another group of Black friends. On the weekends, he was at social functions with his White friends, but during the day and during the week, he hung out with Black friends. However, there were times when he had to choose which group he was going to be with. This was especially the case every day during lunchtime:

> I would stand at the door with my tray and be nervous of where I was going to sit at. . . . I could remember instances where I would say, "Where am I going to sit at this week?" At some point, I thought maybe I'd have to rotate. . . . Sit with [the Black kids] two days and then sit with [the White kids] three days or something, or every other day.

These kinds of issues came up often for Scott, to the point where it became obvious to his peers that he was having an identity crisis. He discussed another incident where the Black and White kids decided to have a basketball game with the Black kids on one team and the White kids on another. While it was clear to the other children who was going to be on which team, the Black kids asked, "Which team is Scottie going to play on?" They knew that Scott was friends with many of the White kids because they played on a travel basketball team together; as a result, the Black kids would taunt him for hanging out with his White friends. Recollections like Debra's, Michelle's, Chuck's, and Scott's reveal the anxieties surrounding identity for the Cosby Cohort where there was an underlying assumption that they needed to make a choice between the two worlds.

While the temptation might be to cast these challenges as "just another part of growing up," where many children feel as if they do not fit in because they have acne or because they are too tall, this is a false comparison. Having acne or being too tall may be monumental for children at this age but are usually temporary or rectifiable or are perceived as being beyond the individual's control (see also Tatum 1997). This is not the case for Black middle-class children being teased over identity; they are perceived by other Black children as having made a conscious choice to be something they "naturally" aren't. Their speech patterns, mannerisms, and other traits evolving from the culture of mobility are perceived by other Black children as intentional, inauthentic, and worthy of derision and rejection. Nevertheless, they are qualities they were forced to adopt in order to ensure their upward mobility. As such, the problems the Cosby Cohort experienced around identity evolved out of a structure that rewards White middle-class norms, values, and characteristics and punishes those who don't conform to these prescriptions.

Despite the stories above, not all respondents had such strong reactions to being rejected by Black peers. Some reported feeling indifferent toward it and tried to ignore it. Zara said that because most of the people who accused her of acting White were not very close to her, she was not hurt as much by what they were saying. Others like Shayla developed an attitude of resignation. She said she still kept trying to be friends with other Black kids, but said, "I just knew that there's probably going to be a good, you know, hour or two, maybe three hours, of people asking me stuff, talking about me, throwing jokes, you know." However, not all respondents had Shayla's resolve.

For some respondents, altering their behaviors in order to fit in became a better coping mechanism. This is referred to as "identity work," where people "engage in a range of activities to create, present, or sustain identities that are congruent with or supportive of their self-concept" (Snow and Anderson 1987, 1348). Notably, none of the respondents in this study resorted to academic underachievement in response to the acting-White accusation, as several studies have previously indicated. However, in order to minimize feelings of uncertainty about their Blackness, they found ways to reaffirm it to themselves and others. Typically, as children, the Cosby Cohort employed two different types of identity work: (1) *selective association*, where they associated only with other Black children or disassociated with Whites, and/ or (2) *cultural symbolic*, which involves the highlighting of cultural symbols that they perceived as authentically Black, such as clothing, music, hair, and language/way of speaking (see Snow and Anderson 1987; Storrs 1999).

Alexis was one of those respondents who employed the selective association strategy in order to gain acceptance:

> When I went to middle school it got a little more difficult because there were more Black people at my school, and I came from a predominantly White school, so most of my friends went to elementary school and to junior high with me. And we still continued to be friends and Black folks were like, "Why are you hanging with these White folks?" [I was] trying to get out of hanging out with my White friends and move to the Black friends to fit in more with my Black friends.

Here, Alexis leaves behind her White friends to prove her Blackness to other Black children. Her strategy ended up failing, as it didn't gain her admission to the "Black table" in the cafeteria, or the table where Black kids often sit that in many ways serves to reinforce their burgeoning racial identities.[10] Later in the interview, Alexis confessed to feeling "really bad leaving my [White] friends behind" but said that she "didn't want to be looked at as an oreo."

Cultural symbolic identity work appeared to be more typical than the selective association strategy. Felicia actually employed both strategies where she tried to distance herself from her White friends in order to avoid being called an "oreo" but then doubled down on her efforts by participating in the cultural symbolic identity work of emulating the way her Black friends spoke. She reasoned to herself that it would be "one less thing to worry about" if she could but said that she was only moderately successful at doing so because she didn't have enough familiarity with Black English Vernacular. Genevieve similarly tried to change her characteristics and behaviors by convincing her mother to take her shopping for the clothes the other Black kids were wearing so that she could fit in more. After she received the new clothes, she said it helped her feel more like the other Black kids and eased a lot of her anxiety. It also seemed to lessen the teasing. This was one of the few times that identity work proved a successful strategy. While this seemed to have worked for her, it is a rather temporary solution to a much larger problem: the way in which Blackness is so narrowly (and often negatively) constructed.

From the stories of respondents in this section, it appears as though the Cosby Cohort faced a great deal of difficulty when they emerged from their all-White neighborhoods and schools and came into contact with other Black children. While they anticipated that they would have no problems fitting in with Black peers, they were shocked and dismayed when this turned out not to be the case and they were rejected out of hand for the characteristics they had acquired under the culture of mobility. When this occurred, parental support became extremely important.

Parental Responses to Identity Events

As children, perhaps the only thing worse for these respondents than feeling rejected by fellow Blacks was failing to get positive parental reinforcement when the situation occurred. The parental response is very important in how Black middle-class children define the situation and subsequently how they react to it. Generally, when parents responded with empathy and concern to their son's or daughter's identity events and in a way where their self-esteem was reaffirmed, the child tended to feel better and not react as strongly to the accusation. However, if the parent was dismissive toward the child or in some way suggested that their concern was trivial, the child tended to react more negatively toward the assaults on their identity. In this section, I discuss the effective and ineffective approaches parents used to deal with the Cosby Cohort's identity issues. Effectiveness of the approach is simply measured by whether the respondent said that their parents' response helped them better deal with the identity challenges at hand.

Effective Parental Responses

For the Cosby Cohort, the most effective parental responses empowered the child and recontextualized the ridicule the child received from other Black children. For example, both Camille's and Genevieve's parents explained to them that the children teasing them were doing so because they were jealous that they did not have as many material items or in some other way were unhappy with their lives. In contextualizing the situation this way, the child does not feel like what is happening to them is their fault or that they are doing something wrong. Both women said this approach was helpful to them as children. Langston's parents attempted to recontextualize the situation by explaining to him that some people were just cruel and mean, but "you couldn't physically beat up every person who called you a name." These effective parental responses appeared to entail a "shifting-the-blame" technique and/or an emphasis on pragmatism.

There were other ways in which parents attempted to recontextualize their child's identity events as well. For example, Alexis's father tried to reframe the situation by emphasizing that what she was going through was temporary and would soon change:

> [I'd] been called an oreo before, [like] I'm not down with Black people over whatever else. I think that was more middle school than high school. And so, I think that was a difficult period. And my dad really helped me out and was like, "Screw that!" So, I was like, "Okay.". . . And he was like, "When you go to college, it's going to be different. You're going to meet more people like you that are Black and are educated." And most of what he said was pretty true.

She said that, overall, her father's approach was very helpful. First, his utter defiance of what the other children were saying empowered her and made her feel that what was happening was through no fault of her own. Second, explaining to her that this experience was transitory served to minimize the magnitude of the events in question.

Gabrielle's parents also tried to recontextualize the acting White accusation but instead framed it in a sociological context:

> They [explained] to me that there is no such thing as acting Black or acting White, but it has been socially created that there is this *idea* of acting Black or acting White. . . . And so once I understood that, I think I felt a little bit more comfortable with who I was. . . . I think my parents helped me to understand what the differences were and how it was just a perceived type attitude or action. There is no definition, there are no set steps and you follow step 1 through step 10 and you will be Black. You know, I felt that it was okay to be me.

Here, her parents explain how subjective and arbitrary assessments of Blackness can be. In Gabrielle's case and even in Alexis's case, these type of sophisticated explanations were surprisingly helpful, even though they were only of middle school age at the time. It would appear on the surface that they would escape a young child's understanding, but both said that their parents' explanations were very helpful to them as children. In each case, the parents shifted the blame away from the child and did not make her feel as if there were something inherently wrong with her.

It is important to note that parental responses that either shift the blame to the accusers or suggest that children ignore accusers altogether may serve as a protective mechanism designed to justify the choice to raise their children in White-dominated social spaces and socialize them into a culture of mobility. However, the extent to which parents actually had a "choice" is debatable given the limits of residential segregation in the 1980s and 1990s that forced them to seek out White neighborhoods and schools for their children. Furthermore, in the parents' eyes, the realities of systemic racism necessitated a stringent culture of mobility. Even while recognizing the structural constraints that guided their "choices," it is quite possible that parents internalized a sense of guilt that these decisions and strategies complicated their children's lives. As a result, their attempts to shift the blame to their children's attackers might be an effort to defend to themselves against attacks on their child-rearing choices.

Another extremely effective response to children's identity issues was when parents became advocates for their child. For example, when Iyana was taunted by the other Black children in her neighborhood for not going to the neighborhood public school, her mother forced her to invite those children to their house and made her get involved in community activities. This was an attempt to make her feel less isolated and also to help the other children get to know her better in order to decrease the likelihood of teasing. In another example, earlier in this chapter, I told the story of Michele, who was bullied mercilessly to the point where she had teachers escorting her from class to class and eventually was assaulted by Black girls who were teasing her. She reported that her parents were frequently at the school to address the bullying, which is how the teacher escort system came to be. When the school threatened to expel Michele for fighting back against the girl who tore her earlobe, her father threatened to sue the school. Michele said of her parents' advocacy, "They did everything they could besides sit in the classroom with me." In cases like this, the parental response proved necessary in preventing further physical altercations. It also reaffirmed to their child that they shouldn't have to endure this treatment.

The above stories indicate the need for effective responses to children's racial identity issues. They also indicate the need to provide children with racial and cultural socialization that also stresses that Blackness doesn't lie in how one walks, talks, or handles confrontations. Internalizing a sense of Blackness that was independent of their peers' definition might have made these respondents' identity events less jarring. Nevertheless, their parents offered responses that helped them make sense of the intraracial rejection they experienced as children. Their responses stood in stark contrast to the ineffective approaches offered by other parents.

Ineffective Parental Responses

Dealing with a child's racial identity issues is an extremely difficult challenge for parents. For several respondents, the challenge perhaps proved too great for their parents who offered approaches that were less than helpful. In general, these responses were characterized by a lack of understanding of how serious the issue was to the child or by simply encouraging him or her to ignore the problem altogether. The less effective responses offer insight into how some middle-class parents are unprepared to deal with issues of identity and therefore have great difficulty in assisting their children when the need arises. This seemed to be the case for several of the Cosby Cohort respondents in this study.

One of the most peculiar parental responses to identity events came from Debra's parents. As she recounts in the story below, her father's response to her being teased by other Black children was rather odd:

> I remember going home and telling my dad, you know, oh, "They don't think I'm Black," and my dad telling me, "Go back to school and tell them that they are QUASI-Black!" [laughs] I'm in second grade and I'm like, "You're quasi-Black!" [When I said it], they were just looking at me like, "What does quasi mean?" Understandably so. I didn't know what quasi meant till last night!

Her father's response, while valid and understandable perhaps to an adult, seems to be far beyond a child's comprehension. Moreover, the response did not send the explicit message that she had done nothing wrong and that what was happening was not her fault. For these reasons, the message failed to empower her. When I asked Debra what she thought of her father's reaction, she said,

> My dad probably could have come up with a different word [laughs]. A word that kids would understand. . . . If you're already being made fun of, coming to school with a word that nobody's ever heard of before probably didn't help the situation. But I think my dad tried his best. I think he meant well and I mean . . . technically, he was right.

Debra's story indicates the importance of age-appropriate explanations for Black middle-class children that can bolster their self-esteem in the face of racial identity challenges. But it also indicated the challenges the cohort faced in trying to reaffirm their racial identity as children.

Unfortunately, Debra's mother's response was equally as unhelpful as her father's but illustrated another ineffective parental approach. As discussed earlier, Debra's mother is Jamaican and thought very little of African Americans. As such, her mother's reaction came as little surprise:

> My mom's response was pretty much, "Ignore them they're stupid. Ignore them they're ignorant. Ignore them, that's how Americans are." My mom is very culturally biased . . . it was, "For you to be upset, for you to be nervous, for you to be anything is a waste of your time because they're stupid. You're going to go a lot farther than them." So, my mom's response was putting them down, I guess in an attempt to make me feel better or putting them down, just because she literally did not care about them, because she just thought that they did not matter enough even to talk about.

When I asked Debra what she thought about the way her mother handled it, she said that "it didn't help a whole lot" because her mother belittled the importance of the situation and didn't understand how important being part of the fictive family system is for Black children (Fordham 1988), particularly for Black kids who grow up in hostile White neighborhoods and schools. Essentially, Debra was being denied admission to "the family," and her mother's response amounted to saying that it is unimportant to be a part of this group. Perhaps her mother's Caribbean heritage made it difficult for her to understand how important this was to her. Nevertheless, her mother's suggestion that she ignore them, combined with her father's "quasi-Black" strategy, served as ineffective approaches to her identity issues.

Not only did some parents encourage their children to ignore the troubles they were having over identity, but parents themselves turned a blind eye to the issues their children were having. Shayla's parents never intervened and advocated for her in front of school officials, even when they were constantly cutting gum out of her hair that had been placed there by Black children who accused her of acting White. Will's mother told him that the identity issues he was facing as one of the only Black students at a predominantly White boarding school were not as important as his getting a good education. For these parents, ignoring the problem seemed to be a better solution or the only solution to the problem.

Nowhere was this more evident than in Ariel's case. Ariel had an extreme reaction to feeling rejected by her Black peers in middle school that her parents simply ignored. She discussed several times her experience of being raised and socialized under the military's color-blind paradigm. As a result, the rejection from her fellow Black classmates was a real shock that led to her acting out:

> It was sad. I kept myself really isolated. I would just be by myself. And I think it even was reflected in my clothing . . . I would wear ties and baggy pants. Or, I would do a mixture of gender clothing. I don' t know why I was doing this. . . . Or, I would wear all black, all dark colors. Or, I would wear my hair really plain or just really out there. It would be like two extremes. But [I would] definitely just isolate myself . . . I wasn't accepted among anyone, so I just stayed within myself.

At the time of our interview, her parents had just visited, and they talked about that time in her life when she was acting out. They admitted to her that they did see some differences but did not know what to make of it and thought maybe it would just go away. When I asked her if she wished they handled it differently, she said, "I think I wished they would've asked me [about it] . . . I really do wish that if they'd noticed it, we would've talked about it and maybe we could've done something. Even like bringing me around more of my cousins." Ariel plainly states that parental intervention would have been helpful, as would greater interaction with other Black children like her cousins. Her response suggests the sense of isolation she felt from all other Black children, even those who were a part of her family. As discussed previously in chapter 2, this is often the case for Black middle-class families who frequently live far from their extended family. This again illustrates the impact of social class on racial identity, where the pursuit of class goals leads to racial isolation and alienation. For children, this is emotionally painful but a pain that their parents are sometimes reluctant to acknowledge or act on.

Fearing their parents' response, a few respondents said that they did not tell their parents about the identity events that they were experiencing. When I asked Marissa why she never told her parents what was happening to her, she said,

> I didn't really think that my parents would understand. I felt like . . . especially with the pressure they placed on me to make sure I was doing well in school, I just didn't feel like they would see what was going on with me and these little kids at school as important. So, I just kept it to myself . . . I thought that the response from them would be, "You know what? Just don't worry about it," or "Forget about it." . . . It wasn't worth it [to tell them].

Marissa's response suggests that it would be fruitless to tell her parents because their main concern was her academics. While Marissa's parents were from the Caribbean, which may have been partly to blame for her perception that they would be dismissive of her trouble, it is important to note that this wasn't unique to Caribbean respondents; several African American respondents reported that their parents had the same feelings. Given the strong (and at times overwhelming) socialization into the culture of mobility, identity issues appeared rather insignificant particularly when many of the characteristics and behaviors related to Black authenticity appeared to compromise children's upward mobility in their parents' eyes.

It could also be the case that parents assumed that their children would automatically be accepted among Blacks and therefore were inattentive toward identity issues. For their generation, it was far easier to gain instant admission to the Black fictive family because of the shared oppression of the Jim Crow system. Blackness was less likely to be questioned, as most Blacks were economically disenfranchised and barred from White society, which brought a commonality to the Black experience. Since the 1980s and the growth of the Black middle class and also their exodus to the suburbs, this hasn't been the case.

Yet another reason for the lack of effective parental response was that the acting White/acting Black phenomenon is a postdesegregation phenomenon (Tatum 1997), occurring around the late 1960s to the 1970s, when Black Americans began to emphasize race as a source of pride. Respondents' parents spent their formative years in the 1950s and early 1960s, before the oppositional identity discouraging Black achievement and embracing Black stereotypes began. When their parents were growing up during the age of segregation, the oppositional identity actually *promoted* education and achievement for Blacks (Tatum 1997, 64) and the destruction of negative Black stereotypes. As a result, parents of the Cosby Cohort may have had trouble understanding their children's experiences because the concept of today's oppositional identity was lost on them. For all of these reasons, many parents were ill equipped to handle effectively the identity issues of their children, which made identity development more difficult for their children.

Still, more questions remain. How have the Cosby Cohort's childhood experiences helped or hurt their adult racial identities? Which factors from their childhood ultimately determine who has stronger attachments to Black people and culture in adulthood and who has weaker ones? The answers to these questions are addressed in the next chapter.

Conclusion

In 2006, Dr. Rose Merrell-James, a school counselor in the Rochester, New York, School District, wrote a conference paper titled "Intra-Racial Bullying: An Issue of Multicultural Counseling." In the paper, she focuses on African American children and describes "intraracial bullying" as a form of bullying between Black children which is unique because of the "racial, social, political, and educational factors that this form of bullying embodies" (Merrell-James 2006, 284). A child could be targeted by other Black children for his or her failure to embody phenotypical standards of Blackness (e.g., hair type or skin color) or having atypical social characteristics (e.g., middle-class status). However, as the stories in this chapter indicate and as Merrell-James's paper suggests, the broader issue is the (in)ability to enact a convincing Black performance based on stereotypical notions of "authentic" Blackness and the consequences of such "bad" performances. The interviews in this chapter indicate that this is the major point of separation between Black middle-class children and their working-class and low-income counterparts.

The inability to enact a successful performance yielded a variety of important consequences for the Cosby Cohort, including (1) sadness and frustration over not being able to enact a successful Black performance, (2) ostracism and loneliness from Black peers and the ever-present anxiety over acceptance, (3) the expending of energy on identity work in an attempt to gain acceptance, and (4) a sense that adults in their lives didn't understand the complexities of their experiences and/or weren't going to be responsive to it. The difficulties over not fitting in among Blacks were further compounded by the feeling of displacement among the White community as well, where they were subject to the racism of White peers' parents, rejection from White friends, feelings of insecurity regarding their class background, and yet more isolation. Thus, in addition to the pressures of the culture of mobility, there is the additional discomfort and sadness over not having a home among any of their peers. Furthermore, the sense of displacement comes with a conspicuous sense of shock. As Russell et al. (1993) acknowledge, "While the parents of African American children often prepare them for the possibility that White children may call them 'nigger,' few parents seem to warn them about the hateful name-calling from their 'own people'" (101). The respondents in this study emerged from their White spaces and expected to receive a warm welcome from Black peers and were astonished when the opposite occurred. They were essentially told, "You are not one of us—you are some phony version of Blackness." As a result, there was no point of connection between them and other Black children; there was no sense of shared experience and the negative interactions reified those differences.

To be sure, the point of separation is over what constitutes "authentic" Blackness. When a people's culture has been systematically destroyed with few remnants of the original culture left, a different culture made up of a patchwork of ever-changing ideas and symbols thrives in its place and becomes the new benchmark for authenticity. As such, what existed from the 1980s until now is a Blackness largely conflated with poverty and rooted in oppositional culture and the most sensationalized, reductive elements of hip-hop, often propagated by the White mainstream as "authentic Blackness." It is a Blackness reliant on performativity—e.g., fluency in Ebonics, the wearing of brand-name clothes, the sagging of pants, demonstrating a propensity for violence, and membership in the lower classes, among other things. It is a Blackness that is promoted by the White profiteers of the hip-hop industry while simultaneously reviled among the larger community of Whites as behaviors inconsistent with successful assimilation. Yet it is this version of Blackness that flourishes, and it does so quite nicely in the absence of African cultures stripped away during slavery as well as the knowledge of African history and even African American history that have been stripped away with multiple forms of institutional racism. What remains is a narrowly constructed Blackness that must be mastered by all Blacks, particularly those of the middle class, in order to prove membership in and loyalty to the community at large.

The Cosby Cohort's inability to affect a "successful" Black performance and thus form a connection with Black people and culture was born out of the spatial and experiential distance from other Blacks as dictated by the culture of mobility. Upward mobility in the 1980s and 1990s for Blacks meant moving into White neighborhoods and attending White schools in places that were fairly distant from other Blacks, including family members. Moreover, because they received inconsistent or nonexistent positive racial and cultural socialization from their parents, there was little else to hold onto when identity challenges occurred, which increased their levels of "performance anxiety" and emotional upheaval over bad performances. In these ways, middle-class status played a key role in the racial identity development of the Cosby Cohort, where the singular focus on class mobility came at the expense of stronger connections to Black people and Black culture. As Debra said earlier, the cohort was indeed stuck in a space that no one could share.

Of paramount importance was the parental response when such incidents occurred. While the parents were not interviewed in the study, it appears from the interviews as if many reacted in typical adult fashion to intraracial bullying (see Merrell-James 2006); they were in denial as to how bad the problem was, and they minimized the situation, rationalized it, or avoided it altogether. Others recognized that their children were clearly in pain and took steps to ameliorate their discomfort; these children fared much better. Yet the emotional scarring over the experience of displacement in childhood runs deep enough that some ten to twenty years later, in adulthood, the interviewees still tear up and exhibit a body language that suggests shame or discomfort over feeling displaced among other Blacks. This indicates that when experiences like these occur to Black middle-class children, it is important that parents recognize their import and take steps to protect and nurture their children's racial identities in the face of these challenges. Indeed, when Merrell-James (2006) addresses solutions to intraracial bullying in schools, one of her first suggestions is simple awareness and acknowledgment that this is a legitimate problem that requires a response. She also suggests that Black children who experience this in schools should be encouraged to research their racial heritage, read literature from the Black/African tradition, attend cultural events, and interact with experts on Black history and culture. These are steps that Black parents could take at home as well in order to reinforce a sense of Blackness away from the narrowest, most reductive definition.

CHAPTER FIVE

Losing the Race? Attachment, Ambivalence, and Retreat

Many of us 80s babies came from parents with pasts full of struggle. Our parents fought twice as hard to get the opportunities that were readily available to us, their children, and they pushed us to grab as much of it as we could. Unfortunately, too often, the concept of charity got trampled in the race to the top. It was the 80s: the middle class was rapidly growing. For many families, struggling became a thing of past. People just wanted to wear Jeri curls, listen to Kool and the Gang and Celebrate good times, come on. Forget the Evans family and the Sanfords; we wanted to be the Jeffersons and the Cosbys. And in our haste to be the best and the brightest and have the biggest and the shiniest—our less fortunate brothers and sisters were forgotten. (Donaldson 2010, 154)

In the above quote from her book tracing the complexities of the Black middle-class experience and the tensions between middle-class and low-income Blacks, blogger and media creator Jam Donaldson well encapsulates the struggle for mobility and identity among second-generation middle-class Blacks. While beginning their climb to upward mobility—one fraught with extraordinary challenges—connections to Black culture and Black people were often compromised. Given their socialization into the culture of mobility and their lives spent in White social spaces, it comes as no great surprise that many continue to grapple with issues of race and class. It is a struggle that Beverly Daniel Tatum perhaps predicted in her ethnography *Assimilation Blues* about the experience of Black middle-class parents raising their children in the White California suburb she referred to as "Sun Beach." Prophetically, she opined,

> Surely when it comes to evaluating their lives in Sun Beach, the bottom line for most, if not all, of these [Black middle class] parents is providing a better life for their children. Materially speaking, there is no question that they have been able to do that. The question is, 'At what cost?' Has there been something lost in the process, perhaps a sense of family, a sense of history, that sense of 'Blackness,' of which some of the parents speak? And, if so, of what long-term significance will it be in the lives of their children? (Tatum 1999, 108)

Essentially, what Tatum was asking was, does raising children in mostly White environments impact one's sense of connection to other Blacks and their sense of Blackness as an individual identity over the life course? In many ways, the very lifestyle and worldview of the Cosby Cohort predisposed them to becoming distant from Black culture and Black people in adulthood. Is this what actually happens to these children? Do some have stronger attachments to Black culture and people than we might imagine? What accounts for the difference in who has stronger attachments and who has weaker ones? In sum, as Tatum wondered twenty-five years ago, what actually happens to second-generation Black middle-class children who spent most of their time in White spaces and grew up with spatial, experiential, and psychological distance from Black people and Black culture? Over two decades later, we now have some answers to these questions.

Before addressing the more complex questions of racial identity, it is important to note the class-related outcomes of this experience for the Cosby Cohort. By most standards, they became extremely successful. While the strategies for mobility provided by their parents made for stressful childhoods carefully crafted in response to systemic racism and an insidious White racial frame, these strategies proved effective for the respondents in this study. At the time of the interviews, they were between the ages of twenty-three and thirty-seven and were already professors, doctors, lawyers, teachers, researchers, corporate managers, and master's and doctoral students.[1] They are very accomplished and have succeeded to the levels their parents had hoped. In this way, the childhoods that were marked not only by a great deal of privilege but also by the pressures of achievement and assimilation have brought immeasurable returns on their parents' investments. Yet what price did they pay for this privilege, particularly in terms of racial identity? Do they now seek an escape from Blackness in adulthood? Are they (still) distant from their fellow brothers and sisters, or has this generation found a way to connect with the rest of the community despite their childhood experiences? Finally, what can the stories of these thirty-three interviewees tell us about how social class affects one's racial identity and affinities to culture and community?

Assessing racial identity is a thorny issue because it is difficult for any researcher to truly understand how personally salient race is to a particular individual's identity. However, I believe it is useful to assess how attached middle-class Blacks feel to their culture and community, in part because this group has historically provided a great deal of leadership for the community. As race scholars know, providing leadership for the Black community was the idea behind DuBois's (1903a) "Talented Tenth," where he predicted that a small group of educated Blacks would provide leadership for the rest of the community and advance the Black agenda. However, in later years, DuBois would backpedal on this idea by stating, "I realized that it was quite possible that my plan of training a Talented Tenth might put in control and power, a group of . . . well-to-do men, whose basic interest in solving the Negro problem was personal; personal freedom and unhampered enjoyment and use of the world, without any real care . . . as to what became the mass of American Negroes, or the mass of any people" (DuBois 1948, 3–13). Thus, DuBois realized that Blacks who ascended to wealth and prestige wouldn't necessarily be clamoring to help their less fortunate brothers and sisters. Certainly, in looking at the stories of a second generation of middle-class Blacks raised in White suburbs and under a culture of mobility, we must wonder how connected this group feels to Black people and Black culture now that they have ostensibly become part of DuBois's prophesied talented tenth.

To better understand the depth and degree of the Cosby Cohort's connections to Black people and Black culture, I identify three levels of attachment: strong, ambivalent, and limited. These categorizations are based not simply on one characteristic but on the presence of *several* characteristics in that category. Descriptions of each are detailed below along with the number of respondents in each category:

Strong attachments (N = 7; 21 percent)—Blackness is of high personal salience. The individual

- feels a strong pull toward Black people and Black culture;
- maintains an attachment to Blacks of all class backgrounds;
- pledges to work on behalf of the entire Black community and subscribes strongly to uplift ideology;

- is able to recognize and, for the most part, fully appreciate the role that social structure plays in the problems of the Black community;
- has defined Blackness for him- or herself independent of stereotypes or the notions of the oppositional culture; and
- feels a strong connection to Black/African culture.

Ambivalent attachments (N = 19; 58 percent)—With these types of attachments, the individual may

- demonstrate a "push–pull" feeling toward Black people and culture;
- show support for the entire Black community, at least in theory, but are somewhat hesitant to be in the company of non-middle-class Blacks in particular;
- participate in community service but mostly out of obligation to an organization;
- acknowledge the role of social structure but are more likely to emphasize personal responsibility when discussing the problems in working-class or low-income Black communities;
- be sensitive to the judgments of other Blacks;
- be preoccupied with defining "authentic Blackness";
- be sensitive to the judgments of Whites; and
- have a tentative attitude toward Black or African culture.

Limited attachments (N = 7; 21 percent)—There is little or no realization of the personal and social significance of being Black. Also, the individual may

- consciously and intentionally detach from Black people and culture;
- exhibit anti-Black attitudes and strong disdain for Blacks as a group;
- denigrate Black culture and institutions;
- believe that White culture and norms are superior and be very sensitive to the judgments of Whites;
- indicate extreme sensitivity to being judged by other Blacks, sometimes to the point of avoiding them altogether; and
- have a recently developed awareness of what racism and discrimination mean for their lives.

In part, the above typology owes much to William Cross's (1991) Nigrescence theory.[2] Cross argues that Blacks move through five stages of identity development. In the first stage, *preencounter*, the Black individual seeks White acceptance and often accepts negative Black stereotypes. The second stage, *encounter*, brings awareness that being a part of the White world is not an option and that a new identity must be constructed. During this stage, he or she may experience emotions like anxiety, anger, or hopelessness. In the *immersion/emersion* stage, the individual withdraws into a Black world. He or she may think, feel, and act the way they believe "authentic" Black people should. Additionally, the individual may frequently judge and evaluate others. This is the immersion part of the stage. While in this stage, however, it is possible for the individual to enter the emersion part of the stage, where they join various political groups; develop a more expansive view of Blackness; and acquire the ability to sort out the strengths and weaknesses of Black culture. In the fourth stage, *internalization*, the individual forges a positive, personally relevant Black identity. He or she begins to negotiate his or her position on Whites and no longer judges others by their group membership (Helms 1993, 28). In the final stage, *internalization-commitment*, the individual may devote more time to finding ways to transform their personal sense of Blackness into a plan of action or a general sense of commitment.

The primary strength of Cross's model is its ability to provide a framework for examining the process involved in Black racial identity development. It is also valuable given its underlying premise, which is to determine how an individual forms attachments to Black culture and Black people. Still, the model can be difficult to apply because each stage is defined very specifically and doesn't allow for the fact that individuals may express characteristics of two or more categories simultaneously. As such, it becomes difficult for a researcher to pinpoint a particular individual's stage of racial identity development. Also, where Cross's typology measures mostly cultural affinity (i.e., how much an individual appreciates Black culture and heritage) in the case of Black middle-class individuals raised in White communities, it is necessary to measure not only cultural affiliation but intraracial affiliation as well, or the extent to which they feel connected to other (i.e., non-middle-class) Blacks. In light of these challenges, the proposed typology is broader and more flexible and is driven largely by the patterns that emerged in the data.

In this chapter, I find that most of the Cosby Cohort respondents profiled in this study maintained a sense of attachment to Black people and culture—the extent to which was largely dependent on their racial, cultural, and intraracial cultural socialization in childhood and their childhood relationships with other Blacks. Considering their unique socialization and the struggles with identity that they faced in childhood, it would not be terribly surprising if many of the respondents rejected the Black community and culture altogether. Indeed, some did. However, as adults, most respondents felt some sense of affinity to Black people and culture, although some attachments were significantly stronger than others. Essentially, most respondents arrived at adulthood with ambivalent or limited attachments to Black people and Black culture as a result of (1) the childhood spatial and experiential distance from Black peers; (2) a socialization that problematized Blackness, Black people, and Black culture; and (3) childhood experiences of being outcast from Black social circles. Twenty-six of the thirty-three respondents fell into the ambivalent or limited categories, while only seven indicated much stronger attachments. In these ways, their parents' efforts to compensate for systemic racism and ensure successful assimilation for their children significantly impacted their racial identity over the life course and yielded a segment of second generation of middle-class Blacks who are considerably tentative about their membership in the community.

Before moving on to the data, I would like to offer two important caveats about these categories of identity. First, the analysis of the data may appear as if I am arguing that those in the strongly attached category exhibit qualities that are inherently positive and that somehow they are being judged as "better" than respondents in the ambivalent and limited categories of identity. In reality, the situation is far more complex than this. Racial identity development is an ever-changing process that remains a work in progress for most people. It is also fraught with great complexity in that someone who is willing to sacrifice the bulk of their time, energy, money, and resources in pursuit of community advancement (i.e., strong attachments) may be no "better" or "healthier" than someone who approaches such activities with a greater degree of skepticism and protectiveness over committing these types of scarce resources (i.e., ambivalent attachments). Moreover, categories of identity are rarely discrete because human behavior is very complex; in this study, there are times when the strongly attached sound more like the ambivalents or when the ambivalents sound more like those with limited attachments. In these ways, the boundaries around the categories are somewhat permeable. As such, it is important to recognize and appreciate the multifaceted nature of racial identity and the ways in which individual journeys are bumpy, intricate, and difficult, particularly when one has spent a life on the periphery of Black and White social circles as much of the Cosby Cohort has.

Second, to be clear, it is quite likely that there are factors outside of childhood socialization and intraracial interactions that have shaped the Cosby Cohort's adult racial identities. Perhaps a limitation of this research is that there isn't more "connective tissue" that discusses these other variables. I acknowledge that a multiplicity of other factors, such as one's college experience, their major, whether they have children, their participation in Black clubs or organizations, or even a particular book they may have read, could potentially play key roles in shaping their adult racial identity. However, I chose to center this research on the childhood experiences and socialization of these respondents as well as their childhood intraracial interactions because these haven't been thoroughly researched in the prevailing literature. There is a great deal of information to be mined from these variables alone. They tell us much about the difficulties of reconciling race and class and the ways in which social location have a great impact on one's personal identity and their attitudes toward same-race others.

Below, I describe the adult racial, cultural, and intraracial attachments of the respondents in each category and draw connections to their childhood experiences with both race and class.

The Fiercely Loyal: Strong Attachments to Black Culture and Community

Realizing a strong attachment to Black people and culture proved quite challenging for most of the thirty-three interviewees, yet seven appeared to have reached a place in life where they spoke of a deep and abiding love and appreciation for Black culture and community. Among other things, they had defined Blackness for themselves and felt very attached to Blacks of all class backgrounds. As children, the majority of those in this group received effective parental racial, cultural, and intraracial socialization. While they were socialized to understand the burdens of being Black, this group was most likely to have parents who also heavily emphasized the rich heritage of Black Americans and the connections that Blacks share.

Unsurprisingly, most of the respondents in this category subscribed heavily to "uplift ideology," often as a result of positive intraracial socialization from their parents. Gaines (1996) describes this ideology as promoting "a positive black identity in a deeply racist society, [and] turning the pejorative designation of race into a source of dignity and self-affirmation through an ideology of class differentiation, self-help, and interdependence" (3). Recalling the messages from his childhood, thirty-seven-year-old Michael, who was pursuing a master's degree at the time of the study, discussed his socialization into this mind-set:

> I think the big thing I heard [from my parents] is that you should always, no matter what, try to help other Black people out. In particular, if you realize they are less fortunate than you are, you gotta help them out. That's why you're in that position. You know, if you have something or you have a position, that's why you have it. It's like your duty to pull everyone else up.

Racial uplift was also emphasized in Jensen's childhood, where her family frequently volunteered at homeless shelters where many of the residents were

Black. Her father also pursued community development in Black neighborhoods. Jensen's parents frequently emphasized the connections between poorer Blacks and wealthier Blacks.

Racial uplift was also stressed in Monica's family. At the time of the study, she was thirty-seven, had just finished a stint in corporate America as a data manager, and showed definite signs that her family socialization remained with her many years later:

> Even in the workplace, when you do find a Black person that has made it to the next level, they don't ever seem like they want to come back and help that next person at that next level and say, "This is what I did. Let me help you. Let me mentor you." You know, it's like, "I don't want that competition. I just need for you to stay riiiiiight there. Let me progress on and move forward in corporate America, and I just need you to stay at a distance." . . . I'm not going to say it's a sellout—but I think in order for Black people to prosper, we are going to have to help each other. Bottom line.

In these ways, the intraracial socialization stressing uplift ideology that these respondents received in their childhood had carried over well into adulthood.

However, not all of the respondents in this category received such positive intraracial socialization. Two actually overcame some confusing or nonexistent socialization. For example, while Langston's parents showed some understanding toward poorer Blacks by explaining to him that "not everyone walks at the same pace," they also taught him that low-income Blacks would treat him differently and try to "bring you down" but that you had to "always keep your head up." Jeremy, on the other hand, received no parental messages at all about what it meant to be Black or any messages about relationships with other Blacks; he grew up as a military child. Even with these less-than-ideal levels of racial and intraracial socialization, both expressed strong levels of attachment to all Blacks, which points to the fact that socialization isn't destiny and that agency or other life experiences can play a role in racial identity development.

In part because of their parents' emphasis on uplift ideology, community service was clearly a priority for these seven. Indeed, this group had the highest rates of community service participation compared to the remaining two groups. They were more likely to spend several hours per week performing community service, often without the benefit of organizational affiliation (e.g., fraternity or sorority membership, although some did belong to Greek organizations). For instance, Michael is involved in a grassroots mentoring program for Black boys and girls in elementary to high school that meets every Saturday in order to promote academic preparation, character education, and public speaking. Jensen started her own program for low-income children where she finds fun ways to educate them on the importance of being healthy. At the time, both were graduate students immersed in their studies and familial obligations but still carved out time to help young Black children whom they felt needed the assistance.

Langston, who was thirty-seven years old at the time of the study and working on a graduate degree, spoke passionately about the ways in which he feels obligated to help low-income members of the Black community:

> I owe credit to Black people. And I would be doing a disservice not only to myself, not only to my race, and not only to them if I wasn't able to provide that same discipline and morals[3] and confidence into other Black kids. I think that's real important. . . . A lot of times, I invite [the kids in town] over to have cookouts, to play games with them, play ball with them and just ask them, "Hey, how's school going? What's your favorite subject?" You know, if they're not doing well in it, "Can I help you?" or "Are you seeing your teacher after school?" . . . So, it's just really important to almost be a role model in some aspects to them and try to give back to what was given to you because that's what you're expected to do.

In his interview, Langston also mentioned that several of the children he mentors are being raised by their grandparents, which is "always very difficult to do." This shows not only an understanding of the challenges facing less privileged members of the Black community but also a willingness to be involved.

In terms of cultural socialization, these respondents tended to have parents who went to great lengths to give them an appreciation for Black culture and history. For instance, on their annual vacations, Melanie's mother would scout out a piece of Black history in that area (e.g., a slave plantation) and take the entire family. Others had parents who heavily emphasized Black culture and heritage by forcing them to watch television shows like the miniseries *Roots* or by taking them to Black operas or Black history museums. In chapter 3, I discussed Michael's parents, who took him to see Alvin Ailey and other Black icons, such as Jesse Jackson, when he was growing up. Part of his parents' intention was to show him Black people who were "recognized as being at another level." African American culture was revered and celebrated in these families, which in turn provided these respondents with a greater cultural affinity and appreciation for Black achievement.

Still, growing up as Black middle-class children under the culture of mobility brought about identity events in these respondents' childhoods, but such events tended to be less severe and far less frequent than those with ambivalent or limited attachments. Essentially, they carried fewer emotional scars from not being completely accepted by other Black children. Moreover, during the few times when they were teased or outcast from other Black children, their parents offered more effective approaches to their identity issues. Melanie commented that she was teased for acting White from fourth to eighth grade, but in response, her parents went to the school on several occasions to talk to the parents of the Black children who were bullying her. She noted that her parents' hands-on intervention was helpful to her and let her put those incidents behind her. Similarly, when I asked Monica how she reacted to the acting-White accusation from her peers, she indicated that her response was greatly influenced by her mother's attitude toward the situation:

> "Pssh. Whatever." That's basically what my momma said. She said, "You'll look back fifteen or twenty years and you'll see where you are and you'll see where they are and you'll see that what you're doing is no different than just being who you are and doing the right thing." . . . She said, "It's not even worth you to waste your energy and time trying to figure out how to appease them to make them feel good about themselves." She's like, "It's not even worth it. Go on. Don't even worry about it."

While the "ignore it" strategy didn't work for many respondents, it worked for Monica, perhaps because her mother reaffirmed her self-esteem as part of her response. However, it is also important to note that Monica's mother's response also draws the inevitable in-group/out-group comparison that positions middle-class Blacks as superior. Regardless, in this case, Monica also received a great deal of positive racial, cultural, and intraracial socialization that encouraged strong attachments to other Blacks. She also took several sociology courses in college, which further reinforced a strong racial identity in adulthood. As a result, Monica was clear in saying that the identity events and issues she faced as a child had no impact on her adult racial identity. For respondents like Melanie and Monica, it seemed that their parents' attentiveness toward their identity events in childhood, along with their parents' reassurance, allowed them to put those events behind them in adulthood.

As adults, these seven fiercely loyal respondents expressed the strongest attachments to Black people, particularly non-middle-class Blacks, and talked at length about their connections to them. For instance, in expressing his attitudes toward other Blacks, Langston said,

I never ever like to think of myself as being more of a U.S. citizen because I'm in the middle class and [others] might be in the lower class. So, I never even have a problem in the community identifying or hanging out. You know, but through church and through my fraternity and just the things here on campus, [I have been] able to go into those areas that are in the apartments in [the neighborhood] and take kids to basketball games, football games.

This group was much more likely to associate with Blacks of all class backgrounds and felt more comfortable doing so than respondents in the other two categories. They were also very careful about appearing condescending toward other Blacks or "putting on airs." For example, while talking about his community service, Michael noted,

Like I said, I had that underlying social responsibility thing, and I will go out of my way for [other Blacks] to make sure [they] have what everybody else has. . . . But I try not to do so in a patronizing way because it's important to keep people's feelings. I think some people try to help people and make them feel bad in the process. *I know you don't have nothing to eat, so I'm going to give you this and I want you to enjoy it.* If a person throws it in your face, what did you expect? I think I'm real cognizant of that.

His statement emphasizes his commitment to uplift ideology while speaking to the importance of treating others with dignity regardless of their socioeconomic status. In many ways, respondents like Langston and Michael were striving to bridge the gap between middle-class and non-middle-class Blacks.

Where the two remaining groups were more likely to attribute social problems in the Black community to issues of personal responsibility, the strongly attached group offered rather in-depth, structural explanations for these problems. Monica offered this analysis of poverty in the Black community:

It's almost like, without the resources, what do you do? It's hard to motivate an inner-city child when they really have nothing or no one to look to. I mean they have a lot of mentoring programs, but those mentoring programs are so few and far between to reach all the thousands of kids that need it. I mean [e.g., with welfare reform], now what do you do? These women now coming off of welfare who're barely making minimum wage, how do they take care of their family? When does she have time or when does he have time to be at home with these kids to help them with their schoolwork? Because they're so busy trying to hustle to make the next dollar to put food on the table, let alone pay the rent.

Monica was symbolic of the respondents in this group who were much more likely to subscribe to a more nuanced and structural view of the problems in the Black community. In another example, Jensen, age twenty-six and pursuing a doctorate, also noted,

> The entire [American] culture is set up to beat [low-income Blacks] . . . and I know that you make choices in life, but there's a lot of different factors that go into the reason why this person is acting like "this" or why she chooses to do X,Y, and Z instead of "this" over here, you know. And I'm very cognizant of that, and I think that we all should be more sensitive.

In these ways, this group was particularly adept at recognizing the structural difficulties that other Blacks face and the impact this has on their life chances while also taking wealthier Blacks to task for being critical of low-income counterparts.

In fact, this group was quick to take other middle-class Blacks to task for not being more connected to other Blacks. This was another marked difference from respondents in the other two groups. For example, all respondents were asked which things made them most proud and most ashamed of Black people and Black culture. The strongly attached said they were most proud of Blacks' creativity (according to Jeremy, "We can make anything work. . . . We can take $5 of food and feed fifty people"), the perseverance and strength that Blacks have shown throughout history, and the regal history of African civilizations, among other things. However, when asked what things made them feel ashamed, Jensen said,

> I don't know if I'm more ashamed of the people who can't identify with the people who have the "anti-intellectual" or low-class mentality or if I am ashamed of the people who have these mentalities. I think that I'm actually more ashamed of the people who can't identify with them. . . . And I don't like [for them] to sit up and criticize. Instead, go in and educate, do something if you truly feel that way. . . . Go and look and see where it stems from. It's not just a whole generation was lazy or their whole community is full of lazy people! That's not reality. So, I think I'm ashamed of the people who do not take the time to learn our culture, our history, and where we've been, and where we need to go. Or those that won't go take their hands and reach back and give to the other people. I'm not ashamed of those people; I'm ashamed of those who won't help.

Melanie similarly said that she was ashamed that "more successful Blacks haven't reached back and helped less fortunate members of the community" and began to talk about how she mentors a young girl in the community. The strongly attached were far more likely to criticize middle-class Blacks for their lack of involvement but "walked the walk" and did a great deal of service.

Nevertheless, there were subtle ways in which it was clear that these respondents grew up with class privilege and had been socialized into White middle-class norms that they carried with them into adulthood. When asked what things about Blacks made them feel ashamed, a couple were concerned that poorer Blacks had become "complacent" or were "settling" and weren't taking advantage of every available opportunity. As Michael said, "Even if people don't have anything, there are opportunities that they're not taking advantage of." Langston pointed to slavery and Jim Crow to argue, "Your great-grandfather and your great-grandmother worked sun up to sun down. . . . We can't become complacent. We still need to get out there and sweat to make sure that our future generations are still moving one step further to owning a piece of the U.S., a piece of this world." In a related sentiment, Jeremy said he was most ashamed of Blacks' "lack of knowledge about our buying power," adding,

We spend foolishly. So I don't think we really invest in spending our money wisely or as wisely as we could. Everybody can't ball [i.e., be a "big spender"]. Only a select few can afford to ball and do those things. But we've got to be more about building up our community. And so we shouldn't have to go to a corporate sponsor or White man to always be able to pay our bills or help fund our education. We should be able to fund it out of making good financial decisions. But I think that also some racist laws or the powers that be [prevent] passing [wealth] on to the next generation, and we never get to infiltrate things like real estate and other areas that really make a difference in the world.

In these ways, some of the strongly attached exhibited a slight tendency toward meritocratic values and bootstraps theory even while acknowledging the role of structure in the overall lack of Black advancement.[4] However, unlike those with ambivalent attachments who also attributed Blacks' shortcomings to a combination of personal responsibility and structure, the strongly attached tended to think of themselves as change agents who could make a difference in the Black community through continuous and frequent involvement and maintained strong connections to working-class and low-income Blacks in order to do so. The sum of their statements also revealed a heavier tendency toward structural explanations than individualism and notions of personal responsibility.

In terms of their cultural affinity in adulthood, the strongly attached group had stronger cultural attachments than the other respondents in the study. As mentioned earlier, they noted how proud they were of Black culture and Black accomplishments, emphasizing the fact that Blacks have been able to persevere even through mountainous obstacles. They also discussed their love of poetry readings, live jazz performances, and Black artwork and still frequented Black cultural events like they did as children. In speaking of Black culture, Jeremy, who was in his late twenties and worked for a university at the time of the study, said, "Our culture is one that is lively and people always want to be a part of it. People are always taking from it." This group also talked about how much they felt connected to Africa and how much they liked the term "African American" because it encompasses that connection. For these respondents, Blackness was of great personal salience, and they defined Blackness on their own terms rather than through stereotypes. For instance, Langston said,

> Don't tell me I'm not a Black person because I like the way my jeans fit from The Gap as opposed to FUBUs. . . .You know, people are going to stereotype [me] because I don't wear Mecca or Enyce or Sean John and all that stuff. But what a lot of people don't understand [is] yeah, Black people are [pictured] on the Internet [websites], but White people own those brands!

This is but one example of how respondents in this category eschewed stereotypical notions of Blackness and analyzed the ironies of narrow conceptualizations.

As the stories of the seven members of this group indicate, it is possible for Black middle-class children to develop a very strong racial identity in adulthood. This process was facilitated by positive and consistent racial, cultural, and intraracial socialization that was provided by their parents as well as support from parents when identity issues arose. As a result, these respondents now have a racial identity that doesn't rely on stereotypes and external validation and that demonstrates an awareness of and commitment to issues in the Black community. They also appear comfortable and confident in terms of their racial identifications and interactions with other Blacks. Furthermore, they exhibit a sense of peace about who they are and how they define Blackness. In these ways, their stories exist in sharp contrast to those in the other two categories of identity.

The Great Middle: Ambivalent Attachments to Black Culture and Community

As evidence of the difficulties of reconciling race and class for middle-class Blacks, the vast majority of Cosby Cohort respondents ($N = 19$) indicated ambivalent attachments to Black people and culture. In their twenties and thirties at the time of this study, this group was still trying to "figure it all out." Perhaps the best metaphor for them is that they are sticking their toes in the water trying to figure out if they want to take the full plunge—that is, immerse themselves in Black culture and in relationships with all Blacks—or sit on the sideline. There is a lot of attitudinal back-and-forth movement amongst this group in that they want to support low-income Blacks but are hesitant to be around them. They acknowledge the role of social structure in the current difficulties that Blacks face but in the same breath will emphasize the role of personal responsibility and often do that to the exclusion of structural explanations. When they perform community service in low-income areas, it is infrequent and usually tied to organizational membership, where they see themselves as "missionaries" who arrive for a short period of time to provide guidance or assistance to poor Blacks and then disappear. Furthermore, this group tended to be sensitive toward how other Blacks judge their "authenticity" but also sensitive to White perceptions that they might be "too Black." Finally, while they claim to maintain a sense of pride in African or African American culture, they also express some shame around it. This group is still trying to figure out their place in the larger Black community, the nature of their relationships with other Blacks, and how personally salient Blackness is to them. In these ways, their childhoods have played an integral role in shaping their racial consciousness.

There were some in the ambivalent group who expressed similar sentiments as those in the strongly attached group. At times, they are almost indistinguishable from those with strong attachments, but in listening close, it becomes apparent that there are some subtle differences in their attitudes. For some, it seemed as if they were transitioning to the strong category but hadn't quite reached that level yet. Others fluctuated back and forth between demonstrating both strong attachments and limited attachments, further indicating the fluidity and changeability of racial identity. However, generally, this group seemed more uncertain about their relationships with other Blacks and various aspects of Black culture than those with stronger attachments. In the following sections, I discuss the cultural attachments of ambivalents, their attitudes toward poor Blacks, their uncertainties over the role of structure versus personal responsibility in the lives of poorer Blacks, the spotlight anxiety they feel among Whites and Blacks alike, and, finally, the way in which all of these harkened back to their childhood experiences.

Love and Loathing for Black Culture
As indicated above, one of the ways in which those with ambivalent attachments were similar to those with strong attachments was in their appreciation

for Black culture and heritage. Even when most indicated ambivalence toward Black people, their cultural attachments were fairly strong. In part, this may be because it is easier to attach to one's self to a culture than to a group of people; the latter requires more emotional investment. This group proved very attached to elements of Black culture and frequented Black exhibits and festivals and patronized Black establishments whenever possible. For example, Layla claims that she goes only to Black doctors, and Ariel always shops in Black stores, noting "my dad is really big on that." They also express pride over Black historical figures like Madame C. J. Walker and other Black inventors who "created something out of nothing." They even express love for Black physicality, like Shayla, who said, "I love Black features. I don't have too many myself, but the high cheek bones, and just lips, and then the complexions of skins." In these ways, ambivalents are proud of Black culture and physicality and are honored to be a part of those traditions.

There were other ways in which the ambivalents demonstrated strong attachments as well. For example, they often indicated a love for educating themselves about issues affecting Black Americans. Ariel discussed taking graduate courses in the Department of African American Studies as a way to "be in the know with my community." She also confessed to going to talks on campus if they featured a Black speaker, even if, "I don't have a clue and they are in forestry or something." What makes her statement interesting is the fact that she grew up as a military child and received extremely little racial, cultural, and intraracial socialization. As discussed in chapter 4, she even endured a nasty bout with racial identity issues as a teenager. Her case indicates that even those who are not raised with a strong sense of racial identity can acquire a deep desire to know more about their people, perhaps even more so because they have been denied the opportunity in childhood.

Indeed, the desire to learn more about Black heritage and Black issues was a characteristic evident in many of the ambivalents. Several respondents who were graduate students or professors devoted most of their empirical research on a range of topics related to Black people and culture, including Black interactional styles, colorism in the Black community, or Black linguistics. They also voluntarily taught courses on the African American experience at the university in town—a task that was especially difficult at an institution that is over 90 percent White and located in the Deep South and where racial tension on campus is quite palpable. Nevertheless, these respondents have dedicated their academic careers to educating others on Black culture and a host of other issues representing the many facets of the Black experience. In part, this may again be the result of a desire to (re)connect with their heritage after having spent a childhood fairly disconnected.

To be sure, dedicating one's academic career to racial/cultural exploration is no small issue. As most academics know, the road to a master's or a PhD is inherently fraught with difficulty. For graduate students and faculty of color, the road is significantly bumpier because of their token status in universities, the affirmative action stigma to which they are subjected, and the pressures to mentor and assist undergraduate and graduate students of color (Guiffrida 2005; Guttierez y Muhs et al. 2012; Niemann 1999; Niemann and Dovidio 2005; Rockquemore and Laszloffy 2008). Black academics who study or teach issues around race (or Blackness in particular) are also subjected to additional scrutiny where they are automatically discredited because they are perceived as being biased and self-interested rather than as experts in the field (Moore 1996). As such, the decision for Black academics to pursue research and teaching careers around issues of race and Blackness is no small matter, and while it may reflect the ambivalents' desire to (re)connect with Black people and culture, this particular connection does come at some cost.

Despite that cost, becoming educated and educating others about Black people and culture was important to many of the ambivalents, including those in this category who weren't academics. Chuck, now a physician, likes to expose his White colleagues to Black culture whenever possible and encourages others to do the same:

> The whole point is to just remember where you came from, to do what you gotta do. Take some of your White counterparts [to cultural activities]. So, when we're at a Soul Food restaurant [I ask them], "Why are you so uncomfortable?" What happens is you can ask them why, but they don't know why. We'll eat Mexican, we'll eat Italian, we'll eat Chinese, we'll eat Japanese. [But I say], "I'm going to a soul food restaurant." Or Caribbean or Jamaican. [I ask them], "Hey, why don't we ever do that?" That's how you keep [the culture] going by taking other people to be exposed to it.

Challenging Whites to step out of their comfort zone and eat at places associated with Black culture and people suggests high levels of affinity. By doing so, Chuck even risks his professional relationship and alienating himself from his White colleagues. Nevertheless, this practice is his attempt to keep people aware of the culture, and thus the risk appears worth it to him. Chuck's example demonstrates the way in which educating others about Black people or culture, either formally or informally, helped these Cosby Cohort members stay connected to the Black community.

However, in both subtle and obvious ways, the cautiousness of the ambivalents toward Black culture eventually emerged. For example, in general, the ambivalents were much more likely to feel disconnected from Africa and

African culture and expressed a halfhearted desire to connect with that part of their heritage. For instance, although some said that they preferred to be called "African American" because of the way in which the term emphasizes the link to Africa, there were more who were tentative about this connection and dismissed it altogether. Will said rather insistently, "We're really just *Black*. We really can't trace where our culture comes from." Similarly, Chuck stated, "We are in the minority because we have no true roots in Africa. And my thing is, we're trying to make up one, and Africa is all we know. It's not like we're Hispanic where we can go back." Camille declared rather emphatically, "It's like, yeah, my ancestors may be from Africa but that was a *long* . . . like I can't even think back that far." Their statements reveal not only a sense of loss toward African roots but also a tentativeness or even trivializing of them. This was a noticeable difference from those in the strongly attached group. Their statements further bring to light the need for a cultural socialization that includes the richness and value of African culture and heritage, as this may be a way for Blacks of all social classes to acquire a sense of common rooting. However, for these members of the Cosby Cohort who received little of this type of socialization, there was a cautiousness and hesitance toward African/Black culture that also manifested in some fairly critical attitudes toward other aspects of Black culture and also toward their low-income counterparts.

The Poor Are Always with Us

Many of the ambivalents expressed rather derisive attitudes toward working-class and low-income Blacks, which in large part was attributable to a childhood of privilege. At least one respondent, Olivia, explicitly identified obliviousness to privilege as a distinct disadvantage to growing up Black middle class and admitted that this has become the lens through which she sees other Blacks. Michael who was profiled in the last section on strongly attached respondents also noted that growing up Black middle class often means that "you assume every other Black person has your same experience," but unlike Olivia, he grew up with parents who provided frequent positive racial, cultural, and intraracial socialization and heavily encouraged service to poorer members of the community. In part, this resulted in his having stronger attachments to Black people and culture in adulthood. Olivia's parents, on the other hand, offered no racial and cultural socialization and largely negative intraracial socialization (including a desire to ban Blacks from their neighborhood and a disparaging view of HBCUs, discussed in chapter 3). Childhood experiences like Olivia's lend themselves to a greater sense of ambivalence toward Blacks and Blackness in adulthood.[5]

This tentative quality toward other Blacks came across frequently in the interviews of the ambivalent group. Essentially, this group desires to connect with other Blacks but mostly on their terms. This was revealed in Felicia's interview. As a child of Caribbean heritage, her parents offered extremely negative assessments of African Americans as inferior but stated that these messages were lost on her because "I never identified with being West Indian. I was born and raised here." Nevertheless, some statements from her interview revealed a more discriminating and conditional attitude toward other Blacks:

> I like being around Black people. I like that. There's a sense of empowerment, especially if I'm around positive Black people, and they don't necessarily have to be educated Black people but just about developing their own consciousness. I enjoy being around people who are thinking about the things that I am thinking about—who have something to offer in that regard.

This statement from Felicia expresses a sense of conditionality, where she bases her interactions and relationships with other Blacks on whether they think the same way she does or have something to offer her personally. The statement feels as if it is based on a sense of *how will these other Blacks either add to or subtract from me?* rather than a sense of seeing all Blacks' intrinsic worth. In many ways, it reflects a rather White middle-class, capitalist sensibility where an individual's worth is based on a relative sense of usefulness and a devaluing of those who are perceived to have little or no worth. In comparison to those with strong attachments, her attitude appears far more provisional.

Moreover, while Felicia states that she likes to be around all Blacks regardless of their educational background (often a proxy for social class), she offers the caveat that they need to be "about developing their own consciousness." She was actually in the process of doing so as a thirty-year-old doctoral student studying the Black experience. However, in a society established on a White racial frame (Feagin 2010) and one frequently attempting to bill itself as "postracial," developing one's Black racial consciousness is rarely encouraged, save for Black spaces like the Black Church, where Blackness as a racial identity may be highlighted and celebrated in the form of music, dance, Black History Month programs, or sermons about the difficulties of racial oppression. There are also community centers and majority Black schools or schools in urban centers that may emphasize and celebrate Black heritage as well. Yet in a society centered on Whiteness where other experiences and histories are moved to the margins (or are invisible altogether), there isn't always a great deal of opportunity for Blacks to "develop their own consciousness." Perhaps the first time that many Blacks are offered the opportunity to do so is when they get to college and take a course on the Black/African experience or join a cultural affinity group (e.g., the Black Student Union) on campus. In these ways, Felicia may be setting up an unreasonable standard for her interactions and relationships with other Blacks. This again points to the ways in which the ambivalents largely desire to interact with non-middle-class Blacks on their terms, which further underscores the tensions between race and class that continue to exist for the Cosby Cohort.

Similar to Felicia, other respondents also expressed a conditional attitude toward their relationships with other Blacks. For instance, in Chuck's interview, he stated that he insists that his mostly low-income patients call him by his first name because "[they] don't have to be putting me on a pedestal." He then went on to state the following:

> I am here to help [them] with whatever I can do. That's just my personality. . . . You know, I definitely don't want you pulling me down, but I sure as hell will pull you up if you are willing to climb and help me with that. The thing you have to look at is how many people can you help? I do have a limit. I can't save the world. That's not my job. If I can [help] ten, sorry the bus is full. So, I'm comfortable with that for the ten who would not have otherwise gotten it, you know.

Although he seems to sincerely care about his Black patients, there is a way in which his statement reads, *I am willing to help poorer Blacks so long as they operate within my idea of what they should be doing and so long as it doesn't inconvenience me.* To be clear, in many ways, Chuck's statement is both reasonable and realistic; there aren't unlimited amounts of time to help all people who need it, particularly when one has a busy career and home to which they must attend.[6] However, comparatively speaking, the ambivalents expressed more of these types of statements than respondents in the strongly attached category, who offered no caveats regarding their efforts to give back to other Blacks. The tentativeness toward non-middle-class Blacks in the adult attitudes of the ambivalent group is reflective of a childhood focused on social class, meritocracy, and the dogged pursuit of class goals as a way to compensate for racial discrimination. It is also reflective of an intraracial socialization warning them of the troublesome nature of poorer Blacks. In this case, Chuck's statement echoes his father's warnings of "different mentalities in the race" and not letting other Blacks "get over" or "pull you down" (see chapter 3).

The cautiousness in Chuck's statement was fairly typical of those in this category. They envisioned themselves more as "missionaries" to low-income Blacks who are there to "save" them from themselves, and thus they perform community service in that spirit. This was particularly true of those who were active members of a historically Black sorority or fraternity, where they engaged in short-term group community service activities in low-income areas as part of their organizational membership.[7] This is a distinct contrast from those in the strong category, who were more likely to participate in long-range, grassroots types of community service that they took on themselves. Performing community service in a group context offers a protective mechanism in which the people they are helping are less likely to question their identity, authenticity, and sincerity. This then allows Greek participants the satisfaction of doing service while remaining in the company and security of their middle-class fraternity brothers and sorority sisters.

On the other hand, Greek participation in community service could be read more positively. Members pay a great deal of money (in both the initial membership and the annual dues) and devote much time to these organizations, which often include a community service component. This indicates some measure of desire to connect with other Blacks. Indeed, in the sample area from which these respondents were drawn and in which they did most of their service, the vast majority of Blacks in the town are working class or low income. Respondents participated in many different types of volunteer work in the area, even with busy careers, graduate studies, and families to balance. In these ways, service work required dedication and a significant time commitment on their part. Examples of their activities included adopt-a-family programs and weekly mentoring or tutoring programs for low-income Black children. Yet most participated in service that required more of a minimal time commitment, such as AIDS fund-raisers, canned food drives, Christmas parties for children living in public housing, or collecting school supplies for children in poor families. These were more likely to be annual or biannual events. Nevertheless, paying a great deal of money to be a part of an organization that emphasizes community service suggests some level of attachment to non-middle-class Blacks. Also, Black Greek membership indicates an attachment to Black culture, as these organizations have long and prestigious histories and traditions of their own and also typically celebrate Black culture through fashion shows, art exhibits, step shows, theater trips, and the like.

Nonetheless, the attitudes toward poorer Blacks and toward community service described in this section reflect the generalized ambivalence toward other Blacks that was present among respondents in this category. In large part, this is reflective of their childhood intraracial socialization that transmitted negative messages about other Blacks that cast their problems as a function of personal responsibility rather than a failing social structure.

Personal Responsibility or Structure?

Perhaps there is no greater example of middle-class Blacks' internal struggle between structure and personal responsibility than Barack Obama himself. Obama is often roundly criticized by Black scholars and community leaders for not taking a stronger stance on the structural issues Blacks face. As Joseph (2010) explains,

> Despite overwhelming African American support, there remained a vocal minority of progressive and radical activists, pundits, intellectuals, and writers who have pointedly criticized Obama for failing to speak tough racial truths to his white supporters. Why, for instance, does Obama insist on preaching the politics of personal responsibility and the meaning of fatherhood to black churches without corresponding tough-love symposiums to white law enforcement officials whose eagerness to criminalize black defendants has left the criminal justice system bursting at the seams with African American prisoners? (193)

In another example, Joseph argues that in President Obama's book *The Audacity of Hope*, he lauds welfare reform even while recognizing its injurious impact on the working poor (199). In these ways, "Obama has been reluctant to directly address the racial roots behind black America's perpetual economic crisis, one marked by failing schools, poverty, and crumbling inner cities" (192–93).

The ambivalent members of the Cosby Cohort are no different than Obama in their understandings and explanations for the problems Blacks face. While respondents in the strongly attached category offered more structural explanations for the challenges Blacks face, those with ambivalent attachments frequently waffled back and forth as to how much responsibility Blacks bear for their own predicament and relied heavier on explanations of personal responsibility. For example, a critique offered by several respondents was that Blacks fail to practice delayed gratification and focus too much on material items. After hearing this message consistently in childhood and having the values of sacrifice and delayed gratitude stressed by their parents, many appeared to have adopted these values wholeheartedly in adulthood. For instance, in chapter 2, Zara told the story of a lesson she got in delayed gratification after she complained that she did not have the same material items as her friend. Her mother drove her to her friend's dilapidated house in a poorer neighborhood and told her that she could either have those material items and live there or have fewer material items and live in a nice house and have money for college. Given the lessons learned in childhood, it is not surprising that, as an adult, Zara identified delayed gratification as a value she believes is missing in the Black community:

> Sometimes I see a failure to plan for the long term. I think there are quite a few people who go for the short term, and they don't have this whole thing of delayed gratification. And sometimes, I think that when I'm out in the community, people really focus on the short term. You know, I work with parents who will spend hundreds of dollars buying Sean John designer outfits and Jordan shoes, but when I ask them, "Do you have a computer in the house?" they are like, "No. It costs too much."

Marissa expressed a similar sentiment when she said,

> I feel ashamed of the Black people who are in low SES [socioeconomic status] kinds of situations. I don't really feel that they take advantage of some of the opportunities that are available. So, I guess the lack of faith or the lack of persistence in trying to get ahead, that kinda makes me feel ashamed. . . . I just don't think we're willing a lot of the times to do whatever it takes, you know, even if we have to walk ten blocks to work. . . . So, that makes me ashamed, because those are the kinds of things that White people notice.

Other respondents remarked on the lack of "drive" among lower-class Blacks or "whatever that intangible it is to go out and do it" (Will).

These statements are ripe with class bias but well reflect the socialization into the Black middle-class culture of mobility and its cornerstone values of sacrifice and delayed gratification. These were the tools that both respondents and their parents used to ascend the class ladder. As such, they express frustration and shame toward lower-income Blacks for supposedly not practicing these values instead of identifying the role that structure might play in hindering their progress. For instance, the parents to whom Zara refers likely witness their friends and relatives working hard for a living, to no financial avail. For them, delayed gratification may appear to have little purpose, and temporal objects and status symbols take on added value. Additionally, the ability to buy a computer that costs several hundred dollars may be completely outside of these parents' financial capabilities. These are factors Zara fails to take into account in her critique.

Marissa's statement expresses actual shame and embarrassment toward poorer Blacks. She even uses distancing language by referring to the group as "*the* Black people," as if she is not also Black. Marissa's Caribbean background

and the negative intraracial socialization provided by her relatives partly explain this distance; however, Zara isn't of Caribbean descent, received fairly
positive racial and cultural socialization, and received fairly positive intraracial
socialization but expressed the same attitude. Both women's statements can be
traced back to their socialization into a culture of mobility as well as the class
privilege they take for granted when casting aspersions on other Blacks.

Even institutions and aspects of culture on which the Black middle class
is built didn't escape the scrutiny of the ambivalent respondents and their
reliance on notions of personal responsibility. For example, in her interview,
Gabrielle offered an analysis of the hardships faced by Morris Brown College, an HBCU. In many ways, she was typical of those in this group in that
she evidenced some strong attachments toward Black people and culture,
including volunteering at predominantly Black elementary schools, regularly
donating to the United Negro College Fund, and defining Blackness for
herself ("I don't always feel the need to go with the crowd"). While there are
many things that Gabrielle is proud of about Black culture and people, she
was critical of some aspects as well, like the serious financial trouble Morris
Brown College was experiencing at the time of our interview:

> Morris Brown College is pretty much not going to exist anymore. When we have
> the All-Star Game in Atlanta, there are so many parties, so many gatherings
> with your rap artists, your R&B artists, your actors . . . so when you're paying
> $200 to get into a party at a warehouse that Jay-Z is throwing during All-Star
> Weekend, the only people that can pay that kind of money to get into the party
> are first, your drug dealers, your rappers, and anybody else who probably has
> saved for an entire two months to be able to pay. If you can donate that money
> to go into that party, that money could have been saved and given to Morris
> Brown, and it could still be up and running today. So, that's the struggle.

Conflicting notions abound in Gabrielle's statement. On the one hand, she
expresses serious concern that a historic Black institution might close because of its financial issues. Gabrielle didn't attend an HBCU, but sees the
intrinsic worth of these institutions and donates her money to the United
Negro College Fund. However, she lays the blame for the college's demise
on Blacks themselves and also indicts hip-hop culture for not doing more to
advance the Black agenda. Noticeably missing from her analysis is any acknowledgment of the social structure and/or political economy that puts HB-
CUs at risk, namely, that they are underfunded, lack the larger endowments
of predominantly White colleges and universities, and are tuition dependent
on a population of largely low- and middle-income Black students who have
difficulty financing the expensive tuitions. Instead, Gabrielle reduces the

problem to an issue of personal responsibility and the notion that Blacks as a community spend their time, energy, and money on frivolous endeavors that are part of hip-hop culture.

This reliance on notions of personal responsibility was very common among those in the ambivalent group, where many also offered criticisms about the supposed lack of cooperation in the Black community. Generally, the criticism was that Black people do not help each other like other racial and ethnic communities. Some mentioned how White people, in general, will patronize each other's businesses and maintain dense networks of economic and social cooperation but that Blacks don't. A few specifically referenced the Jewish community as operating this way and attempted to draw contrasts between Jewish people and Black people, like Camille, who said, "And that's another thing that irritates me about Black people. A lot of us don't like to turn around and help that next person up. . . . Like the Jewish community—if one got it, all of 'em got it."

This critique (offered by other respondents in this category as well) is considerably shortsighted. The history of Jewish Americans who arrived as voluntary immigrants and were able to immediately convert their business acumen into capital, establish enclaves and dense networks of cooperation, and benefit from policies designed to benefit Whites (Brodkin 1998; Healey 2003) contrasts sharply with Blacks' experience as a colonized minority group. This status precluded Blacks from converting their skills into capital or accumulating wealth and bequeathing it to future generations (Oliver and Shapiro 1995). Thus, the situation of Jewish Americans is not comparable to African Americans. The critique also ignores the myriad ways in which Black Americans *have* acted cooperatively in the past and present (see Endnote 2 in chapter 4). Consequently, this criticism of the Black community expressed by those in the ambivalent category suggests not only a lack of knowledge about the history of racial and ethnic groups in America[8] but also a tendency to hold Blacks to an unrealistic and unreasonable standard. It further reflects the meritocratic themes of their childhood socialization and the negative intraracial socialization they received.

In both subtle and obvious ways, the above accounts also represent a sense of hyperawareness among ambivalents of how Blacks appear to Whites and thus the spotlight anxiety that many middle-class Blacks feel.

I Don't Like Living under Your Spotlight

Cross (1991) refers to "spotlight anxiety" as being overly sensitive toward Black stereotypes. Essentially, while they may not necessarily buy into Black stereotypes, middle-class Blacks are hypersensitive to the fact that some Whites do and, as a result, become nervous about people or situations that appear stereotypically Black or cast Blacks in some negative way. Genevieve, a twenty-seven-year-old teacher at the time of the study, expressed this sentiment when she said,

> I find myself trying to make sure when I am in the presence of White people that I am alert to what's going on and that I'm not doing "Black" type of things or [things that] stereotype us. . . . I want to make sure they understand I'm not some little dumb Black girl. . . . I become a little more dominant which is really not in my character, but I become a lot more dominating in their presence.

Being concerned about the judgments of Whites is common for Black middle-class people in White settings (Cose 1993; Feagin and Sikes 1994). However, when I asked her about what types of stereotypical things she avoids when Whites are around, she said that she might avoid "lingo" and gave the phrase "Yeah, girl, what's up?" as an example of something she would avoid saying. This is a fairly benign phrase that's even said among some Whites and contains no form of Black English or hip-hop slang. Yet this is a phrase she would try to avoid for fear that it might be taken as stereotypically Black.

Hyperawareness of the public performance of Blackness in front of Whites was frequently a topic of conversation amongst the respondents in the ambivalent category. Damon offered the following observations:

> When I see a lot of young Black guys go out and buy all those diamonds, like all the rappers and stuff, like that shit makes me embarrassed. And I know a lot of it is not their fault because people may not have shown them how to invest and spend money or even behave in public, so to speak. It's almost like it's so cool to be real ghetto now. That like Black people have no pride. . . . Like, look how many guys think it's cool to walk around wearing a doo-rag. I remember growing up as a little kid, a Black person would *never* wear a doo-rag out in public like that. You just would never do that. I think we've seen a real deterioration of our people. We don't have any shame. We really don't. We put on this minstrel show for ourselves, for White people. It's just really bad.

Damon's statement is indicative of many ambivalents' spotlight anxiety and concerns over public representations of Blackness. Notably, he acknowledges the structural roots of Blacks' financial attitudes and orientations but is nevertheless embarrassed of them and disparages the "ghetto" mentality. Even the wearing of a "doo-rag" (a head scarf used for creating waves in one's hair or holding the hair in place) is worthy of derision and a sense of having "no pride" in Blackness. His statement portends a Eurocentric bias that fails to recognize or find value in the particulars of African hair care or Afrocentric hairstyles. Finally, his labeling of these behaviors as a "minstrel show" is further indication of the disdain many in this group showed toward low-income counterparts and their shame over behaviors or characteristics associated with them—a disdain that their parents indicated through much of their childhood.

In addition to being concerned about how they (and essentially all Blacks) appear to Whites, this group was also concerned with how they as middle-class Blacks appeared to other Blacks. In short, they expressed a sense of spotlight anxiety when among other Blacks that seemed particularly derivative of the negative experiences and identity events they experienced as children. For example, Debra, a twenty-seven-year-old graduate student at the time of the study, said she does not have the same anxiety she used to have as a teenager around other Black people, but then stated the following:

> Depending on the group of Black people—and it has everything to do with stereotypes—but depending on how I see them communicate or just how they look to me, there's something that goes through my mind that says, "Hmm. I wonder how they're going to take me." Not that I care, whereas when I was younger I cared, but it crosses my mind, "Hmm, I wonder if they're going to think I'm not Black." And I don't care whether or not they do, but it actually pops into my mind. I wonder if they're going to think I'm not Black enough. I wonder if they're going to think I'm acting White. So, it affects my relationships with other Black people on that level. . . . I guess I'm kinda sensitive. I'm very hyperaware of those things.

Debra proves honest about her feelings and readily admits to stereotyping other Blacks and using that as a basis for deciding whether they will accept her. Also, although she insists that she does not care what other Blacks think of her, she admits several times that she wonders about it when she walks in a room and confesses to being "hyperaware" of their judgments. This was similar to what Alexis said in her interview when I asked her whether she was concerned about these judgments: "I am always conscious of . . . it's really sad because I've really been trying to think about like what is authentic Black and how should you act if you're Black. . . . I think those images play in my mind, and so I think it probably does affect me to some degree of how others perceive me." Comments like these demonstrate the ways in which some of the ambivalents are still looking for external validation of their Blackness.[9]

This stands in marked contrast to the strongly attached group who had defined Blackness for themselves and eschewed stereotypical representations and performance expectations. The respondents in the ambivalent category more frequently had their identity and "authenticity" attacked during childhood and lacked a feeling of connectedness to other Blacks throughout the life course.

Perhaps feeling insecure about their own racial identity and still in the throes of trying to define it for themselves, a few ambivalents went on to question the identity of others and had, to some extent, bought into narrow constructions of Blackness. In her interview, Marissa (who earlier said she was embarrassed of low-income Blacks), criticized the Black middle class in general and her own relatives specifically for not being "Black enough":

> I find a lot of Black people who are middle class to be kind of shady with identifying with who they are. I find like some of them almost don't even want to be Black. They want to be as White as possible. Like I have relatives like that, and I don't get along with them whatsoever. I refuse to go visit those people because I feel like they are just too much on that side.

Later in her interview, she went on to say that she believes her family members want to be White because one of her male cousins did not want to attend an HBCU, while a female cousin pledged her love for Harry Potter (the young, White, boy-wizard in the J. K. Rowling book series). Her concern over her cousins' racial identity is particularly ironic considering her own confession of sometimes feeling embarrassed of being Black.

Even I, as the researcher, was not immune from the identity judgments of one of the respondents in the ambivalent category. Twenty-three years old and pursuing a master's degree at the time of the study, Will and I had never met prior to his interview. He knew nothing about me except that I needed interviewees for this study. Nevertheless, for him, my Blackness was reducible to one criterion only: whether I had visited the Martin Luther King Museum in Atlanta. When I said I hadn't, he jumped in immediately and said, "Okay, you're not Black. You're not even Black! You're not Black if you've been in [the Atlanta area] for more than six months and haven't gone to the King Center! . . . What's wrong with you?" For Will, it did not matter that I had spent the last four years educating a predominantly White student population on race and topics related to the Black experience, that my research revolves around Black issues, or that I even took a seminar on Martin Luther King in college, which probably gave me a more extensive knowledge of his life and work than Will. What mattered to him was that I had not gone to the museum. He was indicative of the ways in which ambivalents struggled with defining and understanding racial identity.

Childhood Connections

Overall, the childhood racial and cultural socialization of this group was a mixed bag. In childhood, the vast majority received confusing and/or negative racial, cultural, and intraracial socialization or none at all. However, a substantial portion of respondents in this category received very strong racial and cultural socialization. Respondents like Gabrielle, Zara, Jamika, and Alexis had parents and family members who regaled them with accounts of Black history, dispelled Black stereotypes, taught them about prejudice and racism, or signed them up for community activities where they could interact with Blacks of other class backgrounds. Their families celebrated Black cultural holidays, bought them books by African American writers and Black Cabbage Patch dolls, and took them to Black museums, festivals, college homecoming parades, and performances of Black dance troupes. They still participate in many of these activities as adults. Essentially, these parents provided a great deal of racial and cultural socialization, and in some cases they received even more than those respondents with stronger attachments. Regardless, while there were quite a few accounts of racial and (positive) cultural socialization, the majority received a great deal of negative intraracial socialization where their parents frequently cast other Blacks as "ghetto," untrustworthy, unintelligent, and a poor reflection on all Blacks.

The identity events that this group faced in childhood further complicated their feelings toward Blacks and Blackness. Indeed, these respondents were more likely to relay their identity events to me with some emotion, namely, anger and sadness. The pain came across in their stories. For example, when Camille's Black peers kept ridiculing the way she talked (and intimated that she must have White parents), she told me rather sadly that she ended up clinging to her White friends because "the White students never asked me to change." Gabrielle said that being accused of acting White made her feel rather lonely and "was a source of me feeling as if I was set aside from the rest." The identity events and feelings of being rejected by other Blacks in childhood yielded residual effects that caused this group of respondents to be hesitant toward Black people and conflicted about aspects of Black culture in adulthood.

Nevertheless, while the respondents profiled in this section are more tentative about their relationships to Black people and culture, they desired a connection. Even though there may be a push–pull relationship to Blacks and Blackness, the pull factor always exists, and they still feel drawn toward the community and culture. For the final set of respondents, those with limited attachments, this pull factor was largely absent.

Full Retreat: Limited Attachments to Black Culture and Community

Participants with limited attachments (N = 7) were far less likely to have a personally salient view of race, expressed great shame over being Black, and had virtually detached from Black people and culture altogether. They expressed anti-Black attitudes that were much more vehement than the ambivalent group; where the ambivalents were somewhat critical of low-income Blacks, this group showed utter disdain. They likewise showed disdain for Black culture and Black institutions. Moreover, they tended to be the most sensitive to the judgments of both Whites and Blacks. They also demonstrated little understanding of the implications of race in their adult lives. In childhood, these respondents were most likely to have received little or no parental racial, cultural, and intraracial socialization and tended to experience traumatic identity events that were difficult to overcome. The cumulative impact of these factors has led to a segment of the Cosby Cohort who have turned their backs on Black people and Black culture altogether.

Notably, five of the seven respondents in this category were children of military parents. There were eleven in the study altogether, and of those eleven, only one (Jeremy[10]) demonstrated strong attachments to Black people and culture in adulthood. The remaining five fell into the ambivalent category. One possible explanation for the prevalence of military children in the limited attachments category is that, at an early age, they internalized the military values of color blindness and meritocracy (see Moore and Webb 2000; Moskos and Butler 1996; Wertsch 1991) transmitted to them by their parents, something that caused them to downplay or even ignore the significance of race (Wertsch 1991). In examining the limited attachments to Black people and culture by these respondents, it is clear that a lack of racial, intraracial, and cultural socialization had a significant bearing on their adult attachments.

In the following sections, I detail select respondents' stories individually in order to illustrate the multiplicity of factors that brought them to a place of detachment from other blacks. Four of them grew up as military children, while one (Scott) did not.

Vivian's Story: "Martin Luther King Was a Womanizer!"
Vivian is a good example of what happens to Black middle-class children who aren't provided with strong racial, intraracial, or cultural socialization. Like several others in this category, she also grew up as a military child. Her stories have appeared several times throughout this book. In chapter 3, I discussed how she learned lessons about Blackness as a minority status through her father's experience in the workplace. However, by and large, she received few racial messages and admitted that she was never raised with "a strong sense of the Black community" and was simply taught to treat all people as individuals. When I asked her if her parents took her to any Black cultural activities or events, she said, "That's just not the kind of people they are." Although this may have been the case, Vivian did mention that she tried to learn some things about Black culture on her own by going to an exhibit if it came to town or would take some friends with her to see a Black play, but these instances were few and far between.

In childhood, Vivian was teased often about talking White. As a twenty-three-year-old graduate student at the time of the study, she angrily discussed a number of identity events like this in her interview. For example, in her senior year of high school, she went to a Black hairdresser for a relaxer (a chemical hair-straightening process). During her perm, the hairdresser asked her if she had ever been called "bourgie," suggesting that she was putting on airs. While recounting this story to me, Vivian became incensed, and her voice became louder, to the point where I was nervous that she was disturbing people in offices adjacent to mine. She angrily declared, "The only reason I didn't walk out was because the relaxer was on my hair. . . . If I could, I probably would have!" Her adult reaction to this childhood identity event existed in sharp contrast to the strongly attached group and even the ambivalent group. When discussing identity events, the strongly attached discussed them in a dismissive way, while the ambivalents tended to discuss them with a little more emotion. However, the group with limited attachments were extremely emotional, as if the event happened yesterday. For this group, there appeared to be more scars surrounding racial identity than those in any other group. Here, Vivian was very excited about an event that happened at least four years ago.

Another characteristic of those with limited attachments was that they offered uncritical assessments of social phenomena in the Black community. While the ambivalents offered explanations that indicated a more critical thought process, the statements made by many of those in the limited category sounded more like ill-considered snap judgments. For example, in Vivian's interview, she discussed the Blacks she admired, including both Diddy (then known as "Puff Daddy") and Supreme Court Justice Clarence Thomas:

> Granted, I do listen to Puff Daddy's music, but you got to give the man his props. He went from being like a runner, an intern who will work for free [and] he runs his own kit and caboodle now. Granted, he got the new 2003 White trophy through J-Lo,[11] but he went and got his, and I can't fault the man for that. . . . With Clarence Thomas—now I don't agree with the man's politics, but dog-gone-it, he is a Supreme Court justice. He is accomplishing things [so] he obviously did something correctly.

A number of indicators emerge in this statement. First, while she gives Diddy credit for having worked his way to the top, she simultaneously criticizes him for dating singer/actress Jennifer Lopez, going so far as to cast her as a "White trophy." Where it has often been stated in the Black community that successful Black men "sell out" by choosing White women as trophy wives, she likens the Puerto Rican Lopez to being the new White trophy wife, which is a (not so) subtle way of questioning Diddy's identity and loyalty.

Perhaps the most surprising part of her statement is her appreciation for Clarence Thomas. Ostensibly, her statement reads as a balanced assessment of the justice. However, this particular figure is frequently perceived by other Blacks as an individual who avoids embracing Black people, interests, or institutions (see Graham 1999; see also Feagin 2010, 190).[12] Hence, her statement suggests that perhaps she hasn't considered the larger implications of her admiration and what Thomas's accomplishments have truly meant for other Blacks. Of primary concern to her is Thomas's educational and occupational achievement, which reflects not only a childhood of socialization into a culture of mobility but also a level of assimilation where class is privileged over and above racial identity and community advancement.

Much like others in the limited group, Vivian denigrated Black leaders, institutions, and culture. For example, while she had admiration for Clarence Thomas, she reserved her scorn for Blacks like Rodney King (the motorist who was severely beaten by the Los Angeles Police Department in 1991) and civil rights leader Dr. Martin Luther King Jr.:

> Like, it trips me out how Black people are so accepting of some things. Like, we're okay with Rodney King. He should not have been beaten, and I'm not condoning that, but he was high [on drugs], okay! Martin Luther King—he did wonderful things, but he was a womanizer and we're accepting of that. . . . And so, I really get

ashamed of how we're so accepting of certain behaviors and how we are not want-
ing to take responsibility to a certain extent for where we are and who we are.

While Rodney King had a history of drug abuse,[13] Vivian's statement almost
suggests that this takes greater precedence over the fact that he was nearly
beaten to death by several White police officers who were caught on camera
yet acquitted of the crime. Instead of criticizing a social structure that allowed Rodney King to be beaten and ultimately acquitted the officers of the
crime, she chooses to focus on Mr. King's personal problems.[14]

Vivian used a similar one-dimensional reasoning in regard to Martin
Luther King Jr. While there have been suspicions that Dr. King was unfaith-
ful to his wife, she directs her attention to his alleged infidelity rather than
the fact that he was an instrumental architect of the civil rights movement,
which led to the destruction of Jim Crow. These comments demonstrate the
extent to which Vivian has adopted an ideology that relies completely on
notions of personal responsibility and individual failings and mostly absolves
the social structure of racism and discrimination. Ultimately, she was in good
company with other respondents in this category who offered similarly shal-
low analyses of Black people and culture and therefore distanced themselves
from both.

Michelle's Story: "I Will Not Go to a Place Where There Are Just a Lot of Black People"

Michele's childhood and adolescent history reads similarly to Vivian's. Her
father was in the military, and, as such, she too received no formal or informal racial socialization, in part because of growing up outside the United
States. In addition, her parents never took her to any Black cultural events
or activities, which she attributed to the fact that "my parents worked *hard* to
make sure me and my brother had everything we needed and wanted." Out
of the thirty-three respondents in this study, Michele experienced the most
jarring and horrific identity event when two Black girls ripped an earring out
of her ear, tearing her earlobe in half (see chapter 4). She confessed to having a "mental breakdown" and being extremely affected by these experiences.
When I asked her if these childhood events had any effect on her presently,
she said,

> It sure does. I won't say that I won't deal with Black people a lot. I mean, if I
> know them, I will. But if I don't—like, I will not go to a place where there are
> just a lot of Black people. Like college parties, I just didn't fool with them that
> much. It was all stemming from [my childhood]. . . . I still had that thought in

my mind that if I get around a lot of Black people, they're going to say something about me, they're going to make fun of me, they're going to try and hurt
me, and I don't want to deal with it.

As a result of her childhood experiences, Michele has categorized all Blacks
as being like the girls who teased her in school, which has, in turn, caused
her to avoid the entire group.

This avoidance of Blacks as a group was particularly evident in an anecdote
Michele offered about a recent trip to an upscale mall in Atlanta. This mall is
rather notorious for its wealthy Black clientele, often clad in expensive brand-
name clothes and strolling through designer stores (it is a favorite of celebrities
as well). When Michele entered this mall, she felt immediately uncomfortable: "I was just like, *oh wow, there's a lot of Black people in here!* I didn't feel
like they were going to hurt me or anything, I was just not . . . I wasn't in my
element. I wasn't real comfortable." The sheer number of Blacks caused her to
immediately leave the mall. Strikingly, these are Blacks who weren't working
class or low income and actually have class backgrounds and experiences more
comparable to her own, but she still felt out of her "element." Accordingly, like
other respondents in this category, she has rejected most Blacks, even middle-
class Blacks, because of fear and potential discomfort.

Also characteristic of those with limited attachments, Michele showed
disdain for Black institutions and cultural symbols. One of the institutions
that drew her derision were HBCUs. Michele declared that she didn't ap-
prove of her brother going to an HBCU. When I pushed her as to why, she
said that it was "unrealistic" and that, while they may instill Black pride in
their students (which she claims to appreciate), "it's done in the context of
just themselves, [so] I don't like it." Here, she overlooks all of the benefits
of the HBCU experience (e.g., the camaraderie, networking opportunities,
smaller student populations, and so on) and even seems to minimize the idea
of them providing a sense of Black pride to their students.

Michele's limited attachments to Black culture were further evident in
her statement about cultural garb and artifacts:

> I feel like I'm a cultured person, but you're not going to see me walk around in
> a Kente cloth. That's just not my thing. And people may find fault with me,
> but that's not my thing. You're not going to make me walk around in that.
> So, when they have the specialty stores, that's not going to do me any good
> because I don't wear that stuff or I'm not going to have that stuff in my house.

Certainly, the decision to wear African garb like Kente cloth might simply
be a matter of personal taste and indicate nothing about one's attachments

to Black culture. It could even be argued that this is an indicator of strong
identity because she rejects the notion that wearing a Kente cloth makes
one "authentically" Black. Yet the latter half of her statement, where she
repeatedly refers to Black/African cultural artifacts as "that stuff" that she
wouldn't even want in her house, is noteworthy. In the context of her statement, the phrase "that stuff" suggests that these cultural symbols are, in some
way, inherently objectionable; at the very least, it is distancing language. In
addition, there is a qualitative difference between wearing a Kente cloth in
public and having, for instance, African artifacts in one's home. Clothing is
worn in public spaces and is an object from which people discern personal
cues about the person with whom they are interacting. However, the home
is a private space where an individual can choose who to let in or keep out.
Therefore, the home is the safest place to express one's culture without fear
of public objection or ridicule. Still, Michele wouldn't consider having "that
stuff" in her home either.

Michele also demonstrated a preoccupation with White approval and dis-
proving Black stereotypes. She relayed this in a story she told me about her
friend Jonathan, who was riding in an elevator with a friend of his (who was
Black middle class) and some Whites. Jonathan's friend made a statement
along the lines of, "Yeah, you know Black people. We don't pay our bills."
Of this statement, Michele loudly and angrily said to me,

> I really don't like when Black people perpetuate stereotypes about us. . . . And
> he was trying to be funny about it. I mean [Whites] already think we don't pay
> our bills, so why would you say it? Why would you go perpetuate that? You
> know, we make it bad for ourselves. We make it bad for ourselves.

Here, she indicates that she is concerned about perpetuating Black stereotypes and appears horrified that someone else would not be as concerned
about the opinions of White people. In this way, she exhibits the same
spotlight anxiety as the ambivalents but imbued with much more emotion
and concern. She overlooks the fact that the friend's statement may have
been his way of satirizing Black stereotypes by poking fun at them. As such,
his remark might have been an act of resistance against commonly held
Black stereotypes. She also overlooks the fact that if there is any truth to the
stereotype of Blacks not paying bills, in many ways, this can be explained
by the poverty that many Blacks face, which is a function of several other
structural constraints, such as a lack of education and lack of access to jobs
and social networks. Instead, Michele's focus was that Jonathan's friend was
perpetuating Black stereotypes in front of potentially racist White people. In

these ways, Michele seemed to be living a life in which she was distancing herself from all things Black. She had much in common with Belinda, who is profiled below.

Belinda's Story: "It Kinda Makes My Skin Crawl Just a Bit"

Belinda, who was another military child in this category, grew up without any racial and cultural socialization. She also received no intraracial socialization (e.g., "My mom and dad never taught us the rules in terms of communicating within [the Black] community"). Her childhood relationships with other Blacks were fraught with difficulties, where she was largely excluded by other Blacks, particularly once she transitioned to high school, where there were larger numbers of Black children. Belinda said, "I wanted to hang out with everybody [but] that was kinda difficult." It was particularly difficult for her to find her footing in Black social circles when she spoke a very proper Standard English, received good grades, and appeared to be the only Black child in the school with a rather eclectic musical collection that included a love for a popular (White) rock band. She admitted that it was emotionally difficult for her to be cast out of Black social circles (she was also cast out of White circles, as discussed in chapters 2 and 4). The sum of these experiences was emotionally difficult for her, and as a result, she seems to have very limited attachments to Black people and culture in adulthood. Unlike other respondents with strong or even ambivalent attachments, she has not yet become comfortable with her Blackness and reacts strongly when people question her identity. Like Michele, Belinda admits that her strong reaction has much to do with her childhood: "I think to some extent [my childhood] was bothersome because I didn't feel like I totally fit into Black culture, and I still feel the repercussions of that now."

In order to avoid feeling out of place among other Blacks, Belinda, a thirty-five-year-old professor at the time of the study, chooses not to go to places where Blacks are likely to frequent, nor does she desire to be involved in Black political activities. She readily admits to not being a part of the Black community on the campus where she works, where most of the Blacks with whom she interacts are middle class. Indeed, her distance extends to *all* Blacks, particularly those from a low-income background, whom she views with some contempt. For example, Blacks often complain about portrayals of themselves in the mass media (see Williams 2000), yet when Belinda complained about these portrayals, she appeared embarrassed about these Blacks' class background:

Okay, let's say we're watching the news, and they go and pick somebody who's not the most intelligent person to represent. I mean, they're not calling on them to represent the entire African American community, but they choose someone to give their commentary on some news event. And they speak and I'm just like a little bit embarrassed. But at the same time, I understand that maybe they're coming from a different location in life. I mean, so, it kinda makes my skin crawl just a bit.

First, Belinda equates the way a person speaks with their intelligence level and diminishes their opinion because of the manner in which they express it. As chapters 2 and 3 indicate, for Cosby Cohort Blacks raised under the culture of mobility, Blacks without formal education and/or who speak in the vernacular are frequently characterized as unintelligent. Her final comment about their speech making her "skin crawl" indicates that she is ashamed of Black people who come from "a different location in life." While she appears somewhat sympathetic toward the lack of resources and opportunity they have been afforded, she lacks a full appreciation of these structural limitations. Because Belinda implies that speaking in a Black dialect is one of the ways in which Blacks lose face in front of White people, her comment about understanding the circumstances of low-income Blacks emerges more as a sense of embarrassment than sincere sympathy for those who are less privileged. Her withdrawal from Blacks of all class backgrounds, combined with her disdain for low-income Blacks and her sensitivity to Black stereotypes, all suggest limited attachments to Black people and Black culture. This could be attributed partially to her military upbringing, but even respondents who didn't grow up in military families exhibited similar patterns. One of those respondents was Scott.

Scott's Story: "I'm Really Not That Connected"

In chapter 4, I discussed Scott's experience in the cafeteria where he would stand at the door trying to decide whether to sit with his Black friends at one table or his White friends at another. He struggled throughout his childhood and adolescence with trying to form a viable racial identity and received no racial, cultural, or intraracial socialization to help him in the process. For these reasons, Scott decided to get his bachelor's degree at an HBCU. While most respondents who attended HBCUs regarded this experience as helpful in strengthening their racial identity, this was not the case for Scott. During the interview process, I found Scott to be very detailed and explicit when answering my questions about his childhood. However, when asked about his current attitudes toward Black people and culture, his answers became much shorter and less coherent. This perhaps demonstrates the extent to which he hasn't given a great deal of critical thought to issues of racial identity in his adult life or is simply uncomfortable or reluctant to discuss these issues.

A twenty-three-year-old master's student at the time of the study, Scott appeared to have shut the door on Black people and Black culture. He doesn't seek out Blacks and says that nearly all of his friends are White—an issue that causes fights between him and his family. Scott also believes that Blacks make excuses for why they haven't achieved more and that many are just "complacent" with their current situation and have no desire to try harder to improve their circumstances. His limited attachments to Black people were further evident in this statement at the end of his interview: "I'm really not a social activist, so I really don't have any specific responsibilities that I feel motivated to. . . . So now, other than talking to the Black friends that I have, I'm really not that connected." There is a level of indifference toward other Blacks that comes across in his statement that wasn't present in those with strong or even ambivalent attachments. Also, as other respondents' stories indicate, activism is not the only way to stay connected to the community, as many participate in different cultural activities or events as a way to stay connected. However, Scott maintains no point of connection or attachment to the Black community by way of social activism or cultural experiences. In this way, it is clear that the identity challenges that Black middle-class children face in childhood often carry on into adulthood.

A final respondent in this category, Tim, proved interesting on multiple levels and well illustrates the ways in which those with limited attachments seem unable to reconcile their childhood experiences.

Tim's Story: "I Would Rather Have My Accolades Based on Merit"

Like Vivian, Belinda, and Michelle, Tim also grew up as a military child but ultimately joined the military himself. Growing up, he led a very middle-class existence and admitted to being a "nerd" who got good grades and was a fan of classical music, ultimately becoming classically trained while in high school. He was perhaps the only male respondent who wasn't involved in sports. His "nerdiness," affinity for classical music, and membership in the school band, along with his lack of sports prowess, evoked some scrutiny from low-income Blacks at his high school, which meant, "I wasn't 100 percent in that clique."

In childhood, Tim received no racial socialization: "I don't remember [my mom] telling me anything like, 'You may be disadvantaged because you're

Black' or 'White people don't like Black people and might try to hold you down.' I don't remember any type of messages like that." He received no cultural socialization either. When I asked him about the cultural socialization in his family, he jokingly said, "I don't recall anything like that. . . . There was no Black power type of movement going on in my family. . . . I don't recall any necessarily strong ethnic ties." As further example of his lack of cultural socialization, he said that even now, people "clown him" because he has never seen the film *The Color Purple*. He also said that he did not know who Malcolm X was until he was in his teens. During that time, he saw a Malcolm X medallion (a popular fashion accessory in the 1990s) and thought Malcolm X was a rapper. Given these factors, it is also no great surprise that when I asked Tim if he received any kind of intraracial socialization (i.e., messages about other Blacks), he said, "Not that I can recall."

At the time of our conversation, Tim was a twenty-eight-year-old graduate student who had gained access to college through enrollment in an officer training program that encourages young soldiers to earn degrees and become officers. However, because he believed it was simply a preferential program, he quit during his freshman year:

> I realized that it was an affirmative action type of program, and I realized that I didn't want to be considered in that type of program. I would rather have my accolades based on merit. I had a very low SAT score—I got like a 900 on the SAT.[15] And there was a kid who applied for the program who was White, and he got like a 1,300, and I was selected along with that person. And I remember being very disappointed and I remember thinking [that] being Black, I get stuff handed to me, and I didn't want it to be that way.

Perhaps because Tim had not received any racial socialization, several alternative explanations never occurred to him. For instance, he doesn't consider that he might have other qualities besides his SAT score that the military considers important in officers or that his experiences as a person of color have provided him with a valuable worldview that the White soldier didn't have. Moreover, his argument that Blacks get opportunities handed to them rings false in the face of a mountain of sociological research as well as simple daily observation. Furthermore, he doesn't appear to recognize that affirmative action has been responsible for the ascension of many Blacks into the middle and even upper class and that it was probably integral to his own father's military success and therefore may require greater consideration. Finally, his explanation for quitting doesn't account for the possibility that through his training in this program, he could become an officer who could help other young Black soldiers rise through the ranks as well. Instead, he reduces the program to a racial handout and goes so far as to drop out in order to distance himself from his racial status.

On the whole, it appeared that Tim was unwilling to acknowledge the difficulties Blacks face as a result of their minority group status and was dismissive of identity-related concerns. He was one of the few respondents to say that he most strongly identifies with the Black upper-class (i.e., the Black elite) who make up the smallest part of the Black population and a group to which he currently doesn't belong. Moreover, to identify oneself so strongly with such a small, exclusive, and exclusionary part of the Black population (see Graham 1999) and to "aspire to be one of them" (as he claimed in his interview) further indicates a distancing from the majority of Black Americans. He tended to view most Blacks as troublesome and by way of example claimed that Blacks invented the term "African American" simply to "find something else to fuss about." His racial and cultural attitudes are even more surprising considering that he attended an HBCU and was once an active member of a Black fraternity. Nevertheless, like the other respondents profiled in this section, a lack of racial, cultural, and intraracial socialization may bring long-range identity issues that are difficult for some middle-class Blacks to reconcile.

Conclusion

Some call them the "Afristocracy" (Dyson 2005), and others call them "the mainstreamers" (Robinson 2010), but what the Cosby Cohort represents is a group of well-educated Blacks who grew up in the changing racial landscape of the 1980s and 1990s and continue to occupy a peculiar space in the American social structure that has impacted their racial identity in significant ways. As the parents in Tatum's (1999) study feared some twenty years ago, for Black middle-class children raised in predominantly White spaces, something indeed has been "lost in the process." To be sure, their parents were faced with a daunting task: ensuring their children's upward mobility while imbuing them with a sense of what it means to be Black and a member of the Black community. However, the former task appears to have been much easier to accomplish than the latter. Because social class was placed at the center of their childhoods, for most, class occupies a greater space in their adult identities than race. In part, because they have always had class privilege, they take it for granted and rarely acknowledge it. And, while they understand the role race plays in their own experience, by and large they tend not to see the role it plays in the experiences of Blacks who *aren't* middle class. To these respondents, it appears as if other Blacks simply made the choice not to work hard and, thus, are undeserving of assistance. They look at the sacrifices and hardships (e.g., the discomfort and isolation in White surroundings) they endured to become upwardly mobile and cannot understand how other Blacks haven't made the "choice" to make certain sacrifices as well. These sentiments are only reinforced by similar messages included in the intraracial socialization of their childhood.

To be sure, in a society dominated by the White racial frame, all Blacks are subject to adopting the ideals of meritocracy and bootstraps theory, not just middle-class Blacks. For instance, Bonilla-Silva (2010) argues that dominant racist ideologies that have been woven into the fabric of American society cause Blacks to accept racist premises about Black people (e.g., "Black people are lazy") while simultaneously believing that racism is a central factor in the current status of Black Americans (158). This is due to the fact that as a minority group, Blacks are socialized into and forced to operate within the four central discursive frames that make up America's color-blind ideology: (1) abstract liberalism (e.g., an emphasis on "equal opportunity," individualism, and lack of government intervention in social policy), (2) naturalization (e.g., explanations that excuse racial phenomena as natural occurrences), (3) cultural racism (e.g., reliance on cultural explanations for minorities' position in society), and (4) minimization of racism (e.g., a discourse suggesting that racial discrimination is no longer a central factor affecting minorities' life chances). With this ideology, "contemporary racial inequality [is explained] as the outcome of nonracial dynamics" (Bonilla-Silva 2010, 2). Essentially, all Blacks are susceptible to ignoring, minimizing, or being oblivious to the extensive effect of racism on Blacks' life chances. This bears out in recent polling from political scientist Frederick Harris, whose survey of 1,032 Blacks in 2008 revealed that a majority (44 percent) believed that Blacks' difficulties are due to their own lack of initiative, while 37 percent attributed these difficulties to racism, and the remaining 13 percent attributed it to both racism and a lack of initiative (Harris 2008, 3). Blacks, regardless of class, tend to minimize the varying and far-reaching effects of racism.

But for Cosby Cohort Blacks, in particular, the combination of intraracial socialization from their families that emphasized Bonilla-Silva's four frames and the class privilege they have always taken for granted has predisposed them to dismissing the concerns of the larger Black community. Growing up in a world that is drastically different from their Black counterparts, being separated from them, receiving negative messages about them, and having negative interactions with them has meant that their attachments to Black people and culture in adulthood have been compromised. Thus, according to the findings of this study, what has been lost for many of these respondents is (1) a firm understanding of the extensive reach of institutional racism that leaves other Blacks bound to poor neighborhoods, failing school systems, and a generalized lack of options and (2) a belief that their relationships across class lines can be fulfilling and productive or that such relationships are even necessary.

These findings contradict an abundance of research and data chronicling the Black middle class's supposed strong attachments to other Blacks. A fairly extensive body of research, most of which was conducted in the 1990s and thus likely focusing on first-generation adults, suggests that this is a strong pattern amongst the middle class (Billingsley 1992; Dawson 1994; Higginbotham and Weber 1992; Hochschild 1995; Pattillo-McCoy 1999; Pattillo 2007). Yet a recent study by Hams (2008) indicates that nearly a third of Blacks (32 percent) don't believe that their fates are tied to other Blacks. Harris's report suggests that for a sizable segment of Blacks, there is little sense of group unity and an understanding based on shared experiences. The Cosby Cohort may be heavily present among this group because they have "compose[d] their racial identities at a time of largely implicit rather than explicit racial tension" (Watkins 2005, 263) and grew up with significant spatial, experiential, and emotional distance from other Blacks. Moreover, this is a group who grew up in households where class interests were central to everyday life and as a result may be hesitant to give back to poorer Blacks, especially if this will impact their own wealth and asset accumulation.[16] This may also particularly be the case if they have reduced other Blacks to doo-rag wearing do-nothings with poor linguistic skills and questionable values that they believe reflect poorly on all Blacks. The Cosby Cohort's childhood experiences and tentative attachments to other Blacks over the life course seem to translate into a young, privileged segment of the community who distance themselves from the rest of Black America.

Nevertheless, from the interviews presented here, the majority maintain a partial understanding of the structural barriers to advancement that working-class and low-income Blacks face. For those with strong attachments, this is absolutely true. It is also true of those in the ambivalent category, except that they find themselves in a tug-of-war with their class-centered socialization and inconsistent (or negative) racial, cultural, and intraracial socialization. For these reasons, they tend to discuss structure but inevitably fall back on notions of personal responsibility.[17] The fact that twenty-six of the thirty-three ended up with ambivalent or limited attachments is an indicator of just how difficult it is for middle-class Blacks to reconcile issues of race and class.

A significant space of uncertainty persists for most of the respondents, even for those who were provided with fairly consistent levels of (positive) racial, cultural, and intraracial socialization. While this study represents a snapshot of how racial identity development and various life events can alter racial identity over the life course (see Parham 1989 on "Nigrescence recycling"), the stories presented illuminate the complexities of racial identity development for Blacks who occupy a marginal status in both the White and the Black world.

Their marginal status highlights the need for consistent and positive racial, cultural, and intraracial socialization in childhood for middle-class Blacks. Listen closely to the voices of these Cosby Cohort respondents and one can hear the messages and attitudes of their parents permeating their own personal beliefs. In the voices of the strongly attached, one can hear the parental messages emphasizing the richness of Black culture and stressing to them that "it's your job to give back" and that "every member of our community is important." In the voices of the ambivalents, one can hear the generalized appreciation for Black heritage instilled in them by their parents but also their parents' slight embarrassment over poor Blacks and current components of Black culture as well as their fleeting desires to distance themselves from both. And, in the voices of those with limited attachments, one can imagine the silence on issues integral to race and culture and the ways in which these respondents have pieced together a racial worldview on their own or perhaps with some help from media images and dominant discourses that demonize Black people and culture. In sum, those provided with frequent and positive racial, cultural, and intraracial socialization in childhood felt more at ease with being Black and the varying implications of this status in both White and Black America. Those who received the opposite spent a lot of time distancing themselves from Blackness and being embarrassed of their status, culture, or both. This latter group essentially lost the ability to appreciate Black culture and heritage as well as the ability to examine it critically, instead relying on stereotypes, snap judgments, and dominant ideologies. Such a phenomenon demonstrates why consistent and positive racial, cultural, and intraracial socialization is critical to the racial identity development of Black middle-class children if they have any hope of reconciling the status inconsistency of being Black and middle class.

Also of significance to adult identity are the identity events that Black middle-class children experience. Episodes of isolation and rejection by other Blacks significantly impacted their childhoods to the point where many carried such memories into adulthood and were still deeply affected by them. The childhood emotional trauma resonates so powerfully and deeply that it keeps the ambivalents in a push–pull pattern in their relationships with other Blacks, while it keeps those in the limited category completely distanced from them. It is extremely important that parents, teachers, and clinicians pay attention to these emotional scars as they appear to affect long-range social psychological functioning. Indeed, a 2011 study from psychologists at Michigan State University emphasized that those Blacks who identify more strongly with their racial identity have greater levels of life satisfaction (Yap et al. 2011). The study also found that Blacks who define themselves primarily in terms of race and view their racial group more positively are more satisfied with their lives. In these ways, the personal salience of racial identity cannot be underestimated.

In the end, what remains is a generation of middle-class Blacks whose lives, shaped in response to systemic racism, have ultimately resulted in varying degrees of alienation from self and community. Their primary engagement with other Blacks has always been that of outsiders. As a result, they are most comfortable nurturing interactions with other Blacks on their own terms and usually from a position of power. Their mostly ambivalent adult identities reflect a lifetime of existing in the space between Whites and Blacks, the middle class and the poor, and finding no peaceful or secure existence in either.

CHAPTER SIX

~

Passing the Baton

In many ways, the story of the Cosby Cohort reads like a complex fairytale with something other than a "happily-ever-after" ending:

Once upon a time, the children of the civil rights movement were able to use the social, political, and economic gains of the movement to move into the middle class and have children of their own. They dreamed of the very best opportunities for their children—the same kinds of opportunities that White children had. In this pursuit, they moved heaven and earth to make sure that their children had safe, White neighborhoods in which to grow up. They also saw to it that they had the best schools to attend with the most challenging courses and any number of extracurricular activities available. At home, they reinforced these strategies with a tireless socialization that reminded their children that they live in a world in which upward mobility is always more difficult for Blacks, and because of this, they were going to have to make certain sacrifices in order to get ahead. Out of love for their children and in recognition of a social structure dominated by an unyielding systemic racism, first-generation Black middle-class parents did everything possible to give their children a chance to succeed.

While these children benefited from opportunities that their Black counterparts might only dream about, they would pay a significant price for the privilege. Much of their childhood was spent compensating for their racial minority status where they found themselves consumed by accelerated courses, challenging workloads, and a steady diet of extracurricular activities. In their picturesque neighborhoods and top-notch schools, they had few concerns about safety and security but were unprepared for the discrimination and ostracism they would receive from Whites. And when they finally had the opportunity to be around other Black children, they didn't anticipate the ostracism that they would receive there as well. For them, that rejection was particularly painful, as the warm welcome they anticipated receiving turned into slammed doors barring them from contact with those whom they most wanted to belong. So they went about their daily lives, achieving the levels of success that their parents wanted for them while feeling left out and on the margins of both the White and the Black world.

In adulthood, these kids received the keys to the kingdom. They became the lawyers, doctors, and professors that their parents dreamed they would be and now reap the benefits of their belabored childhoods. Still, their childhood experiences haunt them. They continue to sit on the margins of White and Black America, knowing that they will probably never receive full acceptance from Whites and wondering if they'll ever fit in or sit comfortably among their own. At times, they seek out other Blacks, feel somewhat connected to them, and even seek their acceptance. At other times, they don't see the connection at all and avoid them altogether. Their adult lives are now frequently marked by an arm's-length distance from other Blacks, a reluctance to form connections with them, and a skeptical attitude toward them based on the experiences of their childhood.

From the childhood accounts and adult attitudes of these thirty-three Cosby Cohort members, it is clear that a lifetime spent trying to overcome systemic racism carries an enormous weight, including abbreviated childhoods, fractured racial identities, and a lack of connectedness to Black culture and community. Essentially, like all Blacks, they live a life shaped by discrimination, but the coping mechanisms that they have been forced to adopt in response serve to distance them from other Blacks. Moreover, the negative messages about Black counterparts given to them by their parents as a result of the parents' own class insecurities translate into racial insecurities for the children who become uncertain about their racial status and tentative about their membership in the larger Black community and their relationships with other Blacks. In these ways, it is clear that the status inconsistency of growing up Black and middle class is extraordinarily difficult to reconcile and, for some, results in alienation from self and community.

In looking at the price the Cosby Cohort paid and comparing it to the price that poor Blacks pay every day as victims of systemic racism, our temptation is to want to downplay or even dismiss the challenges of middle-class Blacks. In many ways, we are conditioned not to feel sympathy for privileged groups, even when its youngest members are experiencing difficulties. We want to believe that since they are largely exempt from the crime and poverty of the inner city, they can't possibly have problems or at least any that merit serious attention. Yet, certainly, the stories of the respondents in this book tell us that their lives do, in fact, merit serious attention, particularly when they are burdened by inequality in important and unanticipated ways. Their stories reinforce the research that indicates that even privileged Blacks experience a life that is encumbered by the complex intersections of race and class—status contradictions that they will have to reconcile, negotiate, and renegotiate throughout the life course.

Ultimately, middle-class Blacks may not face the same challenges as poorer Blacks, but much like poor Blacks, they must contend with the dictates of systemic racism and pay the price for having to wage the war. In a world where race prevents low-income Blacks from gaining access to quality housing and schooling, it operates in a different way for the middle class. Structural racism and personal prejudices mean that Whites have the power to deny even the most qualified Blacks access to quality education and jobs. In knowing this and in also drawing on their own experiences, Black middle-class parents are prompted to exhaust all options when it comes to preparing their children to compete in such a world. While the parents' sacrifice is clear, this research makes it clear that the children sacrifice as well. In exchange for the opportunities their parents provide, they are expected to sacrifice precious hours of their childhood studying and participating in extracurricular activities, in near complete isolation from other Blacks and in fairly hostile White spaces. In short, it is much like journalist Leanita McClain so astutely wrote about her experience in the Black middle class before her untimely suicide: "We are simply fighting on different fronts and are no less war weary" (cited in Hochschild 1995, 92).

The war weariness among middle-class Blacks has been well documented among adults, but very little of the available literature discusses the impact on children. Indeed, a great deal of energy is required to fight this war. Joe Feagin (1991) uses an anecdote from a Black professor to illustrate this point. The professor theorized that while Blacks and Whites may be born with the same energy level and while both may spend half their energy dealing with everyday life issues, Blacks spend perhaps another 25 percent fighting all of the problems that come with being Black. As a result, middle-class Blacks are expected to do just as much with their 25 percent of leftover energy as Whites do with their 50 percent. According to this professor, "You just don't have as much energy left to do as much as you know you really could if you were free, [if] your mind were free" (Feagin 1991, 115; see also Feagin and McKinney 2003). When we extend this analogy to the childhood experiences of the Cosby Cohort who at young ages were pushed to achieve in order to compensate for impending discrimination while simultaneously struggling to develop a strong and viable racial identity, it becomes clear that they expended most of their energy on the challenges and inequalities born out of their curious location in the Black and White social worlds. This perhaps makes children the most vulnerable segment of the Black middle class.

Ironically, it is how the Cosby Cohort was forced to wage the war against racism that caused distance between them and other Blacks. In addition to the spatial separation they experienced as children, they were further separated philosophically and experientially as a result of the opportunities they were afforded. Moving to White neighborhoods, attending predominantly White schools, speaking Standard English, taking trips to Spain, and wearing conservative styles of hair and dress became the things that distanced them from their brothers and sisters fighting institutional racism in the inner cities. Additionally, because class was the primary mode of socialization in their families where most of the lessons taught were in the spirit of social reproduction, feelings of closeness to Blacks and attachments to Black culture became lost. As a result, the Cosby Cohort were left trying to figure out what Blackness is and what it means to them and must also constantly negotiate their interactions with non-middle-class Blacks.

Their stories also offer insight into the often uneasy marriage of sociology and psychology and how the intersections between play a critical role in racial identity development. Because of the peculiar social location of the Black middle class at the bottom of the racial hierarchy and the middle of the class hierarchy, they must constantly deal with the social and psychological stressors associated with both statuses. The psychological stressors, in particular, are striking when listening to the childhood memories of these respondents and the accompanying emotion. If high levels of distress are indeed occurring among Black middle-class children, then they may require more support than what they are currently receiving. Parents must consider the cumulative impact of the pressures of achievement and the stressors of racial identity on their children. Clinical intervention might even be necessary. None of the respondents in this study reported receiving therapeutic help even though a good number reported deep-seated feelings of anxiety and sadness. This reflects much of the ambivalence over mental health help seeking among all Blacks and the middle class in particular (Boyd-Franklin 2003; Mays et al. 1996; Poussaint 2001; Tatum 1997). Boyd-Franklin (2003) points to the keeping up of appearances and a reluctance to admit difficulties as one reason why Black middle-class parents are reluctant to seek help for their children and families. Further, Tatum's (1997) research reports that

Black middle-class parents are very reluctant to get help for their children because, as one parent said, "It would be very hard for a White counselor, I'd say to reach into a Black individual's mind, understand what this person is talking about, know exactly where he or she is coming from" (107).

Still, help seeking seems all the more important given the achievement pressure these children are under and the identity-related stressors that both parents and children struggled to negotiate. For parents, the idea that their child should be worried about being "Black enough" seemed illogical especially when the characteristics that they were being criticized for (e.g., succeeding academically, speaking Standard English, involvement in activities, and so on) were largely positive. For these reasons, identity events seemed trivial to some parents whom, as a result, often mishandled them. In part, it appears that this was also a function of the generational difference between Black middle-class parents and their children. In these parents' formative years of the 1950s and 1960s, the Black community was not as stratified by class (see Wilson 1980), so the extent of one's Blackness often went unquestioned. At present, however, this is not the case, and a great structural and cultural gap exists—a gap that was problematic for the Cosby Cohort as children and one that continues to be challenging for all Blacks.

For members of the Cosby Cohort, one of their greatest challenges was understanding Blackness as a minority status and adopting it as a cultural identity. Their stories prove that understanding the varied implications of race is imperative for Black middle-class children. Positive and consistent racial, cultural, and intraracial socialization appear to go a long way toward helping children understand what it means to be Black and their affinity toward Black people and Black culture. Where racial socialization is concerned specifically (and as the stories of many of the military children illustrate), minimal or nonexistent socialization can prove extremely confusing and jarring to a child who inevitably plows into a racial brick wall early on in their childhood, especially when living and interacting in mostly White environments. Thus, they need to be able to understand what a racialized society and minority status means for their lives and all of the possible negative implications. Yet this knowledge about the negative implications of race must be counterbalanced with more positive messages that don't frame Blackness as inherently problematic. This is where cultural socialization can play a key role by exposing children to Black cultural events, education about Black/African history, or any other activities that emphasize the richness of the culture and having pride in it. From the stories of the Cosby Cohort, it appears that Black middle-class children have a better chance of reconciling the positive and negative aspects of Blackness when provided with positive and consistent cultural socialization. Many of those who received such socialization proved to have stronger attachments to Black people and culture in adulthood.

Still, to be sure, the situation is very complex. There are obvious structural and cultural differences between middle-class and non-middle-class Blacks that cause both groups to pull away from each other. The distance amounts to a type of showdown between the oppositional culture and the culture of mobility regardless of the fact that both are responses to a racist social structure. Oppositional culture evolves out of the loss of hope that Black lower-class young people experience when they have been shut out of opportunities for quality education and jobs. Similarly, the culture of mobility is also born out of structure where middle-class children overachieve and adopt assimilationist attitudes and behaviors in order to defeat a racist structure that discriminates against all Blacks regardless of class background. Misunderstandings ensue between the classes because this connection is difficult to detect and fully realize.

What results is a type of border patrolling from both groups. In *Tripping on the Color Line*, Heather Dalmage (2000) describes "borderism" as "a unique form of discrimination faced by those who cross the color line, do not stick with their own, or attempt to claim membership (or are placed by others) in more than one racial group" (40).[1] Middle-class Blacks' seeming affinity for Whites and White culture (as evidenced by their existence in White spaces and adherence to White "mainstream" values) places them outside the realm of Black society in the eyes of many Blacks. This leads to what Dalmage (2000) refers to as "border patrolling":

> The belief that people ought to stick with their own is the driving force behind efforts to force individuals to follow prescribed racial rules. Border patrollers often think (without much critical analysis) that they can easily differentiate between insiders and outsiders. Once the patroller has determined a person's appropriate category, he or she will attempt to coerce that person into following the category's racial scripts. . . . Border patrollers tend to take race and racial categories for granted. Whether grounding themselves in essentialist thinking or hoping to strengthen socially constructed racial categories, they believe they have the right and the need to patrol. (43)

Dalmage goes on to state that for Black border patrollers, specifically, loyalty to the race is their chief concern: "If an individual is not being loyal, then he or she is explained away as weak, acting in ways that are complicit with the oppression of other black Americans" (57). For non-middle-class Blacks, it appears as if middle-class Blacks don't understand how to do Blackness correctly and, perhaps more important, have "sold out" and now are part of the oppressor group. Children, in particular, make these connections in uncritical fashion and hold other children to their mythical standards of Blackness, perhaps out of class jealousies or some fleeting sense of superiority. However, the knife cuts both ways, as the middle class perceives poorer Blacks as doing Blackness in ways that are harmful not only to them as individuals but to the community as a whole.

In order to bridge this gap, both the external social structure and the internal definition of Blackness must change. Presently, what is passing as Black culture and "authentic Blackness" among the masses involves performing and/or behaving poorly in school, wearing brand-name designer clothes, adhering to hip-hop culture, speaking slang and/or Ebonics, being violent, having an "I don't care" attitude, and being openly rude to others (Peterson-Lewis and Bratton 2004). An internal redefining of Black culture that emphasizes the intellectual tradition, Black achievements, and the rich Black/African cultural heritage must occur in order to reinvent what currently constitutes Blackness. This may balance out a steady diet of commercialized hip-hop culture and its present emphasis on sex, violence, and anti-intellectualism. These ideas certainly aren't new. Peterson-Lewis and Bratton (2004) promote a four-pronged strategy for redefining what it means to "act Black" that includes the following:

(1) teaching children about the precedents of Black achievement using historical and contemporary materials

(2) exposing children to accounts of achievement that emphasize the behind-the-scenes labor and perseverance that underlie significant achievements

(3) acquainting children with Blacks who exemplify both positive racial identity and high achievement, and

(4) strategically using Black youths' sensitivity to racial loyalty to emphasize achievement as a cultural and historical obligation. (97–98)

These four strategies represent an important step toward changing the conversation and redefining Black culture and "authentic" Blackness.

However, one factor the authors don't emphasize is that the structure must change as well in order for the culture to change. In other words, it is difficult for a young person to adopt an ethos of achievement and Black excellence if they don't have the proper tools with which to do so, including an accommodating opportunity structure. Without additional funding for teachers, computers, books, and educational programming in the predominantly Black schools that most Black children attend, we would be asking a great deal of children to adopt an ethos of achievement when that would be next to impossible to accomplish without these structural changes. To be clear, research shows that some disenfranchised Black students are very concerned about their academics and continue to study hard despite a lacking opportunity structure (Carter 2005; Theoharis 2013). Regardless, it is not enough to ask individuals to change their attitudes; the structure has to provide opportunities that make it possible for them to do so. In addition, because the acting-White accusation is about much more than academic achievement, children in particular need a definition of Blackness that extends beyond how one walks, talks, behaves, or dresses.

Ideally, redefining Black culture in such a way that embraces the following may prove a better conceptualization of Blackness: (1) the aspects of hip-hop culture that stress social justice and political activism (while retaining hip-hop culture's emphasis on self-expression); (2) the diasporic history of peoples of African descent, including the intellectual tradition; and (3) an appreciation for all members regardless of ethnicity, class, sexuality, skin tone, and other socially constructed categories. This conceptualization may transcend the present emphasis on stylized Blackness and any other points of separation that serve to divide Blacks on the basis of socially constructed categories. If community advancement is the goal, it will become necessary for all to feel a shared sense of struggle as well as a sense that the groups' fates are tied regardless of social class. In both the present and the future, this will be a significant challenge.

The Present and Future

At this point in time, the Cosby Cohort are in their thirties and forties with homes, careers, and even with children of their own. They are part of a growing population of middle-class Blacks who have become the topic of an emerging body of sociological research. Perhaps the bulk of this research discusses middle-class Blacks in regentrifying areas—research that well reflects the tensions between race and class that the Cosby Cohort has spent a lifetime negotiating. In the past, researchers like William Julius Wilson (1980, 1987) have cast the middle class as uninvolved in the lives of other Blacks and that their departure from Black neighborhoods had a detrimental effect on Black communities. This suggests that their return would benefit and rebuild these communities.

The present narratives on Black gentrification indicate that the situation is much more nuanced than this. Derek Hyra (2008), for example, looks at Black gentrification in Harlem and Bronzeville (Chicago) and concludes that the middle class's political activities in these communities are motivated mainly by middle-class interests that frequently result in the disenfranchisement and displacement of the poorer Blacks. As Hyra (2008) says, "On average, the black middle class moving into these communities does not put the concerns of the poor over the goal of protecting their property values" (148). Thus, "rather than acting as a support mechanism to the poor; they use their heightened political power to remove the undesirables" (148). While Hyra casts middle-class Blacks' motivations as distinctly class based, Boyd (2008) and Pattillo (2007) emphasize the racialized nature of Black gentrification and neighborhood revitalization. In studying two neighborhoods in Chicago, both authors concede that class interests are an important factor in the middle class's political activities. However, Boyd (2008) grounds their actions and attitudes in an (often reimagined) history of a thriving Black metropolis under Jim Crow, while Pattillo (2007) maintains that "a deep sense of racial responsibility" (301) and "a strategy of racial uplift" (130) guide the middle class's return migration to and activism in these neighborhoods.

The above accounts well illustrate the conflicted feelings that middle-class Blacks have between preserving their class interests and pursuing a progressive, multiclass racial agenda. However, most of these accounts appear to discuss first-generation middle-class Blacks who "have glimpsed, and sometimes even attained, the comforts of money and prestige . . . [and] do not plan to give those up" (Pattillo 2007, 122). Yet given the ages of the Cosby Cohort, it is quite possible that some of them are included in the group of middle-class Blacks now entering urban areas or that they will be in the future, perhaps searching for feelings of connectedness to other Blacks or chasing the histories of Black metropolises, much like Boyd's respondents.

If the second-generation Cosby Cohort moves into these areas, will their activities and attitudes be similar or different from the first generation? The distinction is made clear when Pattillo (2007) says, "The gentrifying black middle and upper class act as brokers, well-connected to the centers of elite power *but grounded by their upbringings and socialization in more humble black surroundings*" (297, emphasis added). If the second-generation Cosby Cohort migrated to these communities, they wouldn't be "returners" who were raised with a strong pro-Black orientation and have been firmly grounded in Black community and culture. Their identities have been shaped largely around social class and assimilation and in the absence of strong racial and cultural attachments. They aren't Evans's (1993) proverbial "homecomers" looking to reestablish social ties with the larger Black community after a brief estrangement; they represent a group who haven't firmly established these ties in the first place. Nevertheless, this might not deter them from entering these communities, particularly for those looking for a sense of Blackness that they felt was missing from their childhoods. Given their strong class identity and orientation, if they entered these communities, they might arrive with little desire to invest in the needs of poorer residents or to balance them with the needs of middle-class residents. It is perhaps more likely the case that this group would opt out of multiclass Black communities and choose White or multiracial middle-class communities instead.

What is certain is that racial identity will play a key role if and when they decide to move to regentrifying communities. If they do move to these areas, they might be more likely to have the "middle-class-minded" orientation iden-tified in Kesha Moore's (2008) study of regentrification in the Philadelphia area. Middle-class-minded Blacks have a class identity that is "solidly middle class" and use the White and Black middle class as their primary reference groups (505). They are likely to adhere to an integrationist ideology, are more accepting of the class differences between them and other Blacks, and "gener-ally surround themselves with environments in which most of their peers are also middle class" (505). Notably, according to Moore, they are also more likely to be second generation. By contrast, "multiclass-minded" Blacks are almost always first-generation Black middle class, have experienced social mobility within their lifetime, and thus "search for a means to maintain and reconcile the class identity formed during childhood and the one they have acquired in adulthood" (Moore 2008, 505). The multiclass minded carry a specific outsider-within perspective in *both* low- and middle-income Black communities and are strongly attached to Black people and culture. Moore poses the key ques-tion, "What life factors make one middle class person multi-class and another middle-class minded?" (513). The data presented in this book give us some answers as to how and why the middle-class-minded, second generation come to form this orientation. Surely, lives lived in White contexts and focused sin-gularly on running toward achievement as a way to escape systemic racism lend themselves to an orientation that is more middle-class than multiclass minded.

The political ramifications of a middle-class-minded population aren't to be underestimated. As avid voters, there are questions about the extent to which middle-class Blacks will support policies that affect poorer Blacks, such as Head Start Programs, welfare policies, and sensible drug laws. Will they recognize the structural challenges faced by the community as a whole, or will they fall back on the theories of meritocracy and personal responsi-bility with which they were raised and that ultimately cast poorer Blacks as victims of their own "bad" behavior? As Tatum (1997) states, "Certainly the political progress of the group is hindered if those with leadership potential, at least in terms of education and some economic clout, no longer make a connection between their own advancement and that of their group" (125; see also Holt 1995; Spencer 1993; Walzer 1992). While an abundance of research suggests that Blacks will consistently vote for a pro-Black agenda regardless of class (Dawson 1994; Hajnal 2007; Hochschild 1995; see also Sears 2008; Sears et al. 2003), the question may not actually be whether they vote for a pro-Black agenda but instead how *strongly* they will support it. For instance, simply voting for Black issues may be less effective than active, grassroots-level organizing and support.

Will this generation be willing to use their resources for the good of the entire community in light of the socialization they received and the feelings of distance from other Blacks that they have experienced? Will their lukewarm racial identities translate into lukewarm support for the issues that affect poor Blacks? Do they *really* see themselves as having a "linked fate" (Dawson 1994; see also Hochschild 1995) with these Blacks? Research presented here raises questions about the cohesiveness of the Black community and the collectivist and activist spirit among the younger generation, many of whom grew up with a great deal of privilege. To be sure, this is not to lay the responsibility solely at the feet of the middle class, thereby absolving the social structure of its responsibility in creating social justice. As Pattillo (2007) rightly argues, "Middle class blacks *cannot* on their own ameliorate the woes of unemployment, over-aggressive policing, underfunded schools, disparities in access to health care and in health outcomes, or inadequate housing" (103). Nevertheless, their economic, social, and political capital can go a long way toward advancing the community as a whole. Without middle-class Blacks' support and commitment to social justice for all segments of the community, systemic racism and Black exceptionalism will continue to position Blacks behind all other minority groups. As the Black middle class continues to grow and becomes more normative over time, we must continue to explore the varied nature of racial identities, the social facts and patterns that shape them, and the sociopolitical implications that affect all Blacks regardless of social class.

We must also look at how the complexities of race and class will affect future generations of middle-class Blacks. Given that the Cosby Cohort are now in their thirties and forties, they have children of their own and must figure out the best ways to ensure their upward mobility. Their own childhood socialization was heavily influenced by the sociopolitical and economic structure of the 1980s and 1990s—a time of fairly rapid social change with an improving opportunity structure but one still hostile toward Black advancement. As a result, their parents had to take extraordinary measures to help them thrive in this context and ultimately be in a position to take advantage of any opportunities for upward mobility in the future. The 1980s and 1990s were also a time that proved fairly injurious to working-class and low-income Blacks who fell further behind, thus indicating the vulnerability all Blacks faced at that point in time. The question is, has the structure changed enough in the last twenty to thirty years to allow the Black middle class to thrive, or is the Cosby Cohort now saddled with the same challenges their parents faced when attempting to raise upwardly mobile children?

Unfortunately, as indicated in a variety of statistics and measures, there doesn't appear to have been a great deal of progress for Blacks as a whole. Indeed, Blacks as a group appear to lag behind most other groups of color on important measures. Consider the following examples:

- In 2009, the annual median income for White households was $51,681, while for Black households it was $32,584—a decline of 4.4 percent (in constant dollars) from 2008. Moreover, the annual median income for both Asians and Latinos was higher than that for Blacks, where the median income for Asians was $65,469 and $38, 039 for Latinos (Bureau of the Census 2010).
- In 2009, nearly 30 percent of Whites held bachelor's degrees versus 19 percent of Black Americans, 52 percent of Asian Americans, and 13 percent of Latinos (Bureau of the Census 2011).
- Blacks of every economic and educational background are more highly segregated from Whites than Hispanics or Asians (Iceland and Wilkes 2006; Massey and Denton 1993). Where residential segregation is concerned, an analysis of recent census data by demographers William Frey and Dowell Myers indicates a Black–White dissimilarity index of 58.7 for all metropolitan areas, meaning that almost 60 percent of Blacks would have to move in order to achieve a distribution across neighborhoods that reflected their actual proportion of the population. For Asians, the dissimilarity index is 42.9; for Hispanics, it is 42.2 (cited in Patterson 2009).
- At the end of 2009, the unemployment rate for Whites was 8 percent, while it was 15.5 percent for Blacks, 12.5 percent for Latinos, and 7.8 percent for Asians (Pew Research Center 2010).
- In 2008, 34 percent of White men worked in management or professional jobs, compared with 50 percent of Asian men, 23 percent of Black men, and 15 percent of Hispanic men. Forty-one percent of White women worked in management or professional jobs, compared with 46 percent of Asian women, 31 percent of Black women, and 24 percent of Hispanic women (Bureau of Labor Statistics 2009).
- For every dollar of wealth held by the median White family in 2002, similar Black families had seven cents, while Latinos had nine cents.

By 2007, Black families had 10 cents for every dollar of wealth held by White families, and Hispanics had 12 cents (Wright 2009).

- In 2007, the average middle-income White household had accumulated $74,000 of wealth, where the average high-income Black household had only $18,000 (Shapiro et al. 2010).
- Sixty-eight percent of Black middle-class households have no net financial assets whatsoever and live from paycheck to paycheck (Wheary et al. 2008).
- According to a 2007 *USA Today* report, 45 percent of children who grew up Black middle class ended up "near poor." For White children who grew up in middle-class families, the statistic is 16 percent (*USA Today* 2007; see also Attewell et al. 2004; Oliver and Shapiro 1995; Pattillo-McCoy 1999).

In the decades since the Cosby Cohort integrated White suburbs, we might have expected to see more progress in these areas. That seems not to be the case, and in some cases the picture for middle-class Blacks might even be bleaker than before. The statistics, particularly those that rank Blacks lowest even among other racial minority groups, indicate the extent of systemic racism and its presence in the lives of all Blacks, including those who have arrived into the middle class.

As a result, what we might see is the Cosby Cohort's story playing out all over again in the third generation. As it was in the 1980s and 1990s, the stakes are still high, and Black downward mobility is still a reality that middle-class parents will have to guard their children against. In these ways, the Cosby Cohort may similarly push their children toward excellence and academic achievement and, to the extent possible, move their children to White areas or immerse them in White schools and spaces in order to ensure their upward mobility. There is perhaps one difference: there are now more Black middle-class neighborhoods (see Lacy 2007), which allows them an additional option. Nevertheless, the same racial realities that drove the first generation's child-rearing practices still exist, and the Cosby Cohort have their own successes to look to in order to see the ultimate fruits of these strategies. In these ways, they may opt to chart a similar course for their children. The question is, however, will they be able to protect their children from the racial identity crises they have experienced, or will the same uncertainties plague their children as well? In telling their stories, this cohort has opened a conversation about Blacks and Blackness that merits further consideration but one that has often been silenced and relegated to the margins.

~

Appendix

A Final Note: On the Importance of Airing "Dirty Laundry"

While conducting the interviews used in this book, I was surprised at how often respondents would speak to me in hushed tones that frequently required me to ask them to speak up so that their voices could be captured on tape and transcribed accurately. Initially, I became rather frustrated by this, particularly while transcribing the first few interviews, where I found myself straining to hear what was being said. Even when we were in the privacy of my office with the door shut, interviewees would speak to me very quietly almost as if whispering. I wondered to myself, *why are they talking to me as if they're telling me a secret?* After pondering the question for a while and having this experience with several interviewees, I realized that the answer was that they were indeed telling me a secret—they were airing their family's "dirty laundry" and, by extension, the community's dirty laundry.

In Black families, it isn't uncommon for parents to tell their children to keep quiet about what happens behind closed doors. This is the case for middle-class families in particular, who don't want to give the appearance of having difficulties in front of Whites and Blacks alike. As a group stuck on the margins of both social worlds, exposing their vulnerabilities opens them up to the scrutiny of the White world, which might view them as weak, and the Black world, which might view them as spoiled, entitled whiners. A sense of self-protection crops up, leading to silencing, considering one's words very carefully, or giving the appearance that all is well despite underlying difficulties. This is especially the case for first-generation Black middle-class parents who, as a result of their difficult experiences integrating White workplaces and their challenges in maintaining ties with poorer Black counterparts, would perhaps have a more acute fear of the judgments that may be levied against them by Whites and Blacks alike. Moreover, Black parenting has always been under scrutiny in the mass media, scholarly literature, and popular discourse. Indeed, whenever I have presented this research in front of Black middle-class parents, an air of defensiveness sometimes permeates the room. To be sure, it isn't their parenting that is on trial; what is on trial is a racist system that is often insurmountable for Blacks regardless of education or social class and that in turn significantly alters middle-class parenting styles and, by extension, the lives and racial identities of their children. Essentially, the tentacles of racism are far reaching and eventually touch the lives of *all* Blacks.

Nevertheless, fearing attack from a number of different sources (including their own children), parents feel a need to protect themselves and their parental labor, thus encouraging a sanitized account of their family life. As a result, scholarly research on the Black middle class that privileges the parents' accounts misses many of the critical and valuable details of the larger picture. This is where the childhood accounts become valuable. Yet even their now-adult children instinctively self-censor in the service of protecting their families and saving face. They similarly desire to hide the dirty laundry and the secrets of their childhood, which basically are reducible to one inescapable truth: their lives haven't been as easy as others might assume. Even so, the Cosby Cohort doesn't feel that they have the right to complain. After all, they are the "survivors" who have been blessed not to experience the poverty that so many of their counterparts have. They worry about being branded "poor little rich girl" or "poor little rich boy." Thus, the hushed tones and reluctant descriptions reflect the silencing of discussions that desperately need to take place—a discussion on the far-reaching effects of racism and another on the class divisions in Black America and the implications for the community at large.

To be sure, these discussions are beginning to take place in both the scholarly literature and the public discourse, but they are also subject to silencing. However, dismissing a counternarrative that indicates the presence of class divisions is counterproductive to community advancement. If no space is created for the conversation, there is no possibility for unification or social change. Moreover, we run the risk of ignoring and trivializing the standpoint of others in the community whose lives frequently go unexamined. The life stories of second-generation middle-class Blacks who spent their formative years in White suburbs represent a different strand of the research on middle-class Blacks that is well in conversation with and no less important than its predecessors. In order to unify the community toward political advancement, all standpoints will have to be considered, honored, and appreciated. For once we understand the roots of sociopolitical leanings, we have the ability to create lasting and meaningful sociopolitical change.

~

Notes

Preface

1. "Buppie" is a term that refers to "Black yuppies." *Merriam-Webster's* online dictionary defines the term as "a college-educated black adult who is employed in a well-paying profession and who lives or works in or near a large city" (http://www .merriam-webster.com/dictionary/buppie).

2. The whole of this generation is often referred to as "the hip-hop generation," born roughly between 1965 and 1984 (Kitwana 2002).

3. The "model minority" image began appearing in the mass media and popular discourse at the peak of the civil rights movement. The concept gained traction through two articles in 1966—"Success Story, Japanese-American Style" by William Petersen of the *New York Times Magazine* and "Success of One Minority Group in U.S." by the *U.S. News & World Report* staff (Zhou 2008, 281).

4. In *Why Are All the Black Kids Sitting Together in the Cafeteria?*, Beverly Daniel Tatum (1997) refers to this as "the birthday party effect," where, in elementary school, birthday parties in multiracial communities reflect the area's diversity, but as children get older, parents' anxiety about puberty raises fears about interracial dating and causes birthday parties to become more racially homogeneous.

5. All names referenced in this book are pseudonyms.

Chapter One

1. Joseph (2010) describes the episode between Sista Souljah and Bill Clinton as another infamous example of Clinton's ambivalence toward Blacks: "Bill Clinton's ease around African Americans, willingness to appoint them to a string of midlevel

cabinet positions, and friendships during his impeachment hearings made him a perennial favorite in the black community. Yet despite this goodwill, there were also preexisting tensions in Clinton's relationship with blacks, including his well-publicized denunciation of rapper-activist Sista Souljah during a 1992 appearance at Jesse Jackson's Rainbow Coalition. Castigating the rap artist's caustic remarks in the aftermath of the L.A. riots, Clinton laid down a racial gauntlet, letting whites know that he would not pander to the politics of black rage, no matter the cost" (184).

2. As Feagin (2010) so rightly points out, "Those who internalize certain elements of the white racial frame well and often operate openly out of it are frequently rewarded by whites, sometimes dramatically so, as appears to be the case for key government figures like Clarence Thomas and Condoleezza Rice" (190).

3. In his analysis, Jacobs cites Jewelle Taylor Gibbs's (1996) *Race and Justice: Rodney King and O.J. Simpson in a House Divided* (209–16).

4. The notion of Black exceptionalism isn't necessarily new. Freedmen and women, civil rights pioneers, and the Black middle class of yesterday and today have always known that there are unique difficulties that accompany having a Black identity. Mentioned earlier, one way that Blacks striving for upward mobility have attempted to overcome these difficulties is through a politics of respectability that would prove their worth to Whites in the context of White racism and hegemony. In these ways, Blacks have always recognized that Black exceptionalism was an unfortunate part of their reality and one that would require extraordinary efforts to overcome. Certainly, middle-class Blacks desiring upward mobility within the anti-Black rhetoric and hostile sociopolitical context of the 1980s and 1990s knew that this was their sobering reality and that extraordinary efforts would be required in order to ensure upward mobility for their families.

5. When I speak of "structural assimilation," I am referring to Gordon's (1964) definition of secondary structural assimilation whereby the minority group enters the major public institutions and organizations of White society (e.g., schools, workplaces, neighborhoods, and so on).

6. For the most part, Blacks have been singled out where people tend to think of them almost to the exclusion of all other minority groups (Feagin 2010; Feagin and Vera 1995; Frankenberg 1993). In her essay "Seeing More Than Black and White," Elizabeth Martinez (2010) offers some insight into why this may be the case. For instance, until very recently, Blacks were the largest population of color in the United States; only in 2000 did the Latino population finally exceed the Black population. Moreover, the institution of slavery has entrenched the Black–White dichotomy in the nation's collective memory for over 300 years and also led to the nation's only civil war (Martinez 2010). In addition, Black Americans have led several important protest movements and thus "have created an unmatched heritage of massive, persistent, dramatic and infinitely courageous resistance, with individual leaders of worldwide note" (Martinez 2010, 90). In these ways, it is unsurprising that White attitudes toward Blacks are "more cognitively accessible, negative, and politically powerful" (Sears 2008, 142).

7. Occasionally (and particularly in the latter years), Theo could be found in colorful clothing akin to the "Cross Colors" line (a line featuring bright and often

mismatched colors in shirts and pants) that was popular at that time or in overalls with the 1990s style of having one side of the bib unhooked and hanging down.

8. Essentially, there was a very specialized Blackness that existed on *The Cosby Show* that was distinctly middle class and also represented the most nonthreatening forms of Blackness, as evidenced by the show's engagement in Black history and culture. Ultimately, the show engaged these aspects of Blackness in very subtle and implicit ways that kept White audiences comfortable. For example, Black history's ugliest chapters (e.g., the history of slavery, lynching, police brutality, and so on) as well as its most progressive chapters (e.g., the Black power movement) were absent from the show. Yet the civil rights movement was referenced several times throughout the show's run; it was alluded to in the inclusion of footage from the March on Washington, in the Huxtable grandparents' recollections of riding the bus on the way to the march, and in Clair's reminiscing about participating in sit-ins with her friends from "Hillman College." Thus, the few engagements with Black history and culture focused largely on the episode in Black history that was led by middle-class Blacks and that emphasized universalism, nonviolence, and forgiveness for racist behavior and activities.

9. My use of this term is not meant to suggest that the lives of the Huxtable children and real-life Black middle-class children were identical in every way. Its use is primarily symbolic and used to differentiate this solidly middle-class cohort of young middle-class Blacks from Pattillo-McCoy's cohort of more fragile members of this population. It is also meant to reflect the fact that this cohort grew up during the 1980s and 1990s, when Black middle-class life was being represented on screen.

10. Select sections of this book have been previously included in the following article: Cherise A. Harris and Nikki Khanna. 2010. "Black is, Black Ain't: Biracials, Middle-Class Blacks, and the Social Construction of Blackness." Sociological Spectrum 30: 639–670. Licensed content date, Octoer 14, 2010. Taylor & Francis Ltd. Reprinted by permission of the publisher (Taylor & Francis Ltd, www.tandf.co.uk/journals).

11. While the respondents were living in southeastern Georgia at the time of the study, they grew up all over the United States. Many landed in this area to pursue their education or a career.

12. This was also a very conscious research choice. Given my own experiences growing up as a member of this racial class, I had an indication that these experiences could provoke powerful emotion. As such, from a human subjects standpoint, I made a conscious decision not to use actual children who could be traumatized by these questions and not have the emotional resources and reserves to cope with feelings that may be lying just below the surface, particularly because they may be currently living the experience. Indeed, during the interviews with adult respondents, they often had very emotional responses to the questions I posed, particularly when discussing their childhoods. Raw emotions of anger and sadness often surfaced, and a few made comments like, "Wow, this is like therapy!" or "It was cathartic to get this stuff out." These emotional responses suggested that I had made the right choice in not interviewing children. From an epistemological standpoint, their reactions indicated that the childhood experiences of middle-class Blacks merit more discussion than what is currently available in the literature.

13. In some cases, it appeared as though respondents were reconstructing events in order to protect their own sense of self. For instance, one respondent said that she did not care about being outcast from her Black peer group all throughout middle school, high school, and college. However, at another point in the interview, she said that the experience caused her to have a mental breakdown. At that point, it appeared as though she was reluctant to admit how deeply the experience had affected her.

14. An additional problem with the use of memory is that women are more likely than men to produce accurate and elaborate accounts of emotional experiences in childhood (Davis 1999). Each interview lasted on average from seventy-five to ninety minutes. However, the interviews with male subjects tended to be shorter by at least fifteen minutes. With few exceptions, the men in the sample tended to give more curt, nondescriptive responses. To counteract this, I increased my use of probe questions in order to get a more textured account of their experiences. I also encouraged men to use stories from their childhood as answers to the questions. For instance, instead of asking, "How important was education to your parents?," I said, "Tell me a story from your childhood that indicates how important education was to your parents." Phrasing the questions this way forced the men (and some of the more reluctant women) to provide a more detailed account of their experience rather than one-word answers.

Chapter Two

1. As suggested by Dickerson's quote in the previous chapter, there are conflicting points of view on how much Obama has successfully mastered the domains of Black private life. Here, Patterson suggests that he has, while others feel he is disconnected from the lives of most Blacks. This is not terribly surprising, as perceptions of one's racial group identification and affinity are socially constructed and therefore subject to interpretation. More on this in subsequent chapters.

2. Commonly used in sociology, the Thomas theorem states that situations defined as real are real in their consequences (Thomas and Thomas 1928). Based on lived experience and a history of oppression, Black middle-class parents believe that the deck is stacked against their children and that all available strategies must be employed in order to help them achieve.

3. Perhaps the Trayvon Martin case, where a seventeen-year-old unarmed boy was shot and killed by an unregistered neighborhood watchman in Sanford, Florida, on February 26, 2012, illustrates the ongoing nature of neighborhood discrimination for Black middle-class children in White neighborhoods. Martin was visiting his father in a seemingly middle-class subdivision community when he was followed by a White Latino neighborhood watchman, George Zimmerman, who shot him and claimed he did so in self-defense. On the 911 tapes, he called Martin "a real suspicious guy" and allegedly used racial slurs in reference to the boy. Martin had gone to the store to buy Skittles candy and an iced tea and had nothing but those items on him when Zimmerman killed him.

4. In *Living with Racism*, Feagin and Sikes (1994) discuss the intense hostility Black middle-class families faced in White neighborhoods in the early 1990s.

They describe in detail the cross burnings, attempted shootings, property damage, and firebombings that these families endured. Beyond violent episodes, their respondents reported receiving "hate stares" and excessive surveillance from White neighbors. They also describe the hostilities shown toward their children, like being yelled at by a White neighbor for having kicked a ball into their yard or being the only child in the neighborhood not invited into a neighbor's house for juice. The interviews presented here support Feagin and Sikes's research but also force us to examine how the children might have internalized and made sense of the treatment they received.

5. It may also be the case that these parents are participating in a politics of respectability where Blacks, particularly those of the Jim Crow era, demonstrated through "manners and morality" that they deserved to be full participants in a White-dominated society (Gross 1997; Higginbotham 1993). Black parents raised under this ideology might view arguing in public or raising one's voice as falling outside the bounds of "respectability." Likewise, their children might have been socialized into the politics of respectability as well and thus were reluctant to offer a negative account of family life.

6. A large segment of the sample ($n = 11$; 33%) were military children. That experience had a fairly profound impact on their childhood experiences and racial identity formation. More on this in the next chapter.

7. See also Boykin and Toms's (1985) notion of mainstream socialization in Black families discussed in the following chapter.

8. This statement also reflects the politics of respectability emphasized in Black middle-class families.

9. Jamika said that she later found out that the brand-name clothes that her peers had were often shared between them and their siblings, which indicated that she wasn't as deprived as she thought.

10. The current study indicates that the same messages are given to daughters as well. However, as the parents in Reynolds's study indicate, the stakes are higher for Black boys because of the stereotyping of Black men as prone to crime and other deviant activities. In her study, the parents recognize that their boys' middle-class status won't protect them from being perceived in these ways.

11. Bourdieu (1985) argues that such networks serve as "social capital," which he defines as "the aggregate of the actual or potential resources which are linked to possession of a durable network of more or less institutionalized relationships of mutual acquaintance or recognition" (248). See Lacy (2007) for extended discussion on how Black middle-class parents provide social capital for their children by exposing them to high-achieving White and Black peer networks.

12. See Lacy (2007) and Reynolds (2010) for other stories of parental interventions in schools on behalf of Black middle-class children.

13. Parents of this generation likely lived in segregated spaces where one's Blackness went relatively unquestioned and racial identity was taken for granted. As such, some may not have fully understood the racial identity challenges their children faced in White-dominated spaces or that they needed to be particularly vigilant of

the messages they sent their children about Blacks and Blackness. More on this in the next chapter.

14. In terms of my own experience, my mother explained that for my sisters and me, encouraging extracurricular activities was a college admissions strategy. She had belonged to an alliance of Black citizens in the neighborhood that kept their finger on the pulse of what mattered most to colleges and universities. As my mother explained, "During the early 1990s, they didn't just want 'brains'; they wanted a well-rounded student who would not only succeed but also bring their talents to the institution to make it better and not just sit back and 'get theirs.'" She further remarked that on the college applications "there was plenty of room to list all the extracurriculars."

15. Vallejo (2009) uses Light and Gold's argument as one of the reasons for why organizations dedicated to Latino upward mobility in corporate America hold golf clinics for their members (see 140–41).

16. The term "spot" is frequently used in reference to Black people. Essentially, as people of color who are far fewer in number than Whites, in American social spaces, Blacks are often perceived as "dark spots" against the backdrop of a White majority.

Chapter Three

1. Regarding racial socialization, family is frequently the most important agent of socialization (Nunnally 2010; see also DuBois 1903b; Lacy and Harris 2008). However, peers (and also media; see Nunnally 2010) become an extremely important agent of socialization in adolescence (Brown 1990). The importance of peer socialization is emphasized in the next chapter.

2. This is consistent with previous research from Parham and Williams (1993) that found that although the majority (80 percent) of their respondents reported receiving racial socialization messages, 50 percent of the sample received neutral or negative messages and 2 percent were taught that being Black wasn't something to be proud of (cited in Lesane-Brown 2006).

3. Research from Thompson (1994) and Lesane-Brown et al. (2005) indicates that while parents are often the primary agents of racial socialization messages, they aren't the only source where messages from extended family members can be especially meaningful to children.

4. Zhou et al. (2008) discuss the cultural memory of immigrants where "being told of economic hardships in the homeland, [like] traumatic escape from war, hunger, and political/religious persecution, and parental toil and sacrifice" cause many children of immigrants to become self-motivated and resilient (58). The data here show that cultural memory serves a similar purpose for middle-class Blacks.

5. This pattern runs somewhat contrary to recent research from James Stewart (2009) that finds that "the pre-military constructions of racial identity and patterns of racial interaction significantly constrain efforts to foster a primary identification with a homogenized military culture" (73). Thus, despite the military's attempts at inculcating a color-blind ideology, soldiers' racial identity and modes of racial

interaction are derived from the outside social world, which then permeates the military "bubble." In addition, Stewart finds that the armed forces have been plagued internally by racial tensions, where in the 1970s, for instance, several race riots broke out on military bases. Furthermore, according to Stewart, Blacks in the armed forces have historically protested against discrimination in on- and off-post housing, promotions, job assignments and the administration of military justice, among other things. Given these findings, it is surprising that most of the respondents who grew up in military families said they received little or no racial, cultural, or intraracial socialization.

6. For an exception, see Nunnally (2010).

7. Alternatively, respondents could have been worried about offending me as a fellow coethnic and thus refrained from defining the term. While I took care to reveal my own middle-class status in subtle ways (e.g., dress, use of Standard English, and so on), they might have been unsure of my own class background and not wanted to have offended me as the researcher.

8. It is important to note that these are sentiments that a parent being interviewed might hide from the researcher, perhaps out of embarrassment from saying them aloud. This is in part why the accounts of their children become so important.

9. Here the term "Caribbean" refers to descendants of or immigrants from the Caribbean and West Indies.

10. In this section of the chapter, I often use the term "African American(s)" to distinguish between Caribbean Blacks and Blacks whose ancestors were enslaved in the United States.

11. In three interviews, it was unclear how much cultural socialization was received.

12. Pattillo-McCoy (1997) shows that racial/cultural socialization isn't as much of a problem for middle-class Blacks who grow up in or in close proximity to Black spaces. In her account of Groveland, Black cultural symbols were readily available. Moreover, the close proximity to low-income Blacks further facilitated their socialization into Black cultural norms and styles. In this way, the racialized nature of space plays a key role in racial and cultural socialization.

13. To be sure, a great deal of literature talks about code-switching in the Black middle class (see Feagin and Sikes 1994; Lacy 2007; Pattillo-McCoy 1999) in which parents likely engaged. However, the extent to which they passed on Black cultural motifs, modes, and styles remains unclear in the existing literature.

14. This is different from the way it exists now, where the hip-hop aesthetic is everywhere and has a large presence in mainstream culture, as evidenced by the use of rap and hip-hop in Burger King commercials and its presence on Top 40 charts. Today's generation of middle-class Blacks likely has more access to stylized forms of Blackness than the second generation.

15. Ogbar (2007) notes the connection between hip-hop and oppositional culture in his book *Hip-Hop Revolution: The Culture and Politics of Rap*: "[Hip-hop] pulled

qualities from the pervasive sensibilities of black 'oppositional culture' that had become increasingly popular in the 1960s and hegemonic in black America in the early 1970s. In essence, oppositional culture is the system of beliefs and practices that operates counter to the dominant culture and ideologies. Oppositional culture was woven into the tapestry of hip-hop from its inception" (39).

16. Carol Stack (1974) argues that Black Americans often have "fictive kin" in their lives or people to whom they aren't biologically related but who by consensus agree to maintain family-like relationships with one another. The "fictive family" term used here is derivative of Stack's concept.

17. Having a strong sense of group identification reflects the underlying tenets of social identity theory, which suggests that social identity is a product of group membership (Hogg 1988; Tajfel and Turner 1979), where group membership is based on members' recognition of a common plight (Herring et al. 1999). If an individual feels as though he or she shares the same struggle with a particular group, they are more likely to see themselves as part of this group and adopt this social identity as part of their self-concept (Herring et al. 1999).

Chapter Four

1. The existence of the oppositional culture is widely debated in scholarly research.

2. Racial scripts change over time because of the socially constructed nature of race. Behaviors perceived as appropriate or "authentically" Black behavior have also changed over time and are not the same now as they were a hundred or even thirty years ago. For example, as indicated in the previous chapter, during slavery, what was considered appropriate Black behavior was sharing food, caring for children whose parents had been sold away, or covering for each other with the overseer (Blassingame 1979; Mellon 1988). Prior to desegregation, when Blacks were more likely to share the same low socioeconomic status (Wilson 1980), typical Black behavior included attending the same churches and schools and getting one's values from these agents of socialization as well as from the family (Kitwana 2002). Additionally, during the points in history where there were multiclass Black neighborhoods because of prohibitive residential segregation, the Black middle class and elite served the members of their community; the Black midwife or doctor being paid in kind for their services (Brown and Stentiford 2008; Humphreys 2001) was commonly accepted as appropriate and typical behavior for Blacks. In these ways, the current manifestations of Blackness are quite different than previous moments in history; they tend to change with social, political, and economic shifts in the community and will likely change again in the near future.

3. Now Forsyth County, Georgia, is slightly more diverse where the population is roughly 80.3 percent White, 2.6 percent Black, 6.2 percent Asian, and 9.4 percent Latino (http://quickfacts.census.gov/qfd/states/13/13117.html).

4. This situation is an indicator of the fragility of Black middle-class status, where two incomes are often required to support a middle-class lifestyle.

5. This is consistent with findings from the Peterson-Lewis and Bratton (2004) study.

6. Pattillo-McCoy (1999) notes the importance of dress as well, where Black middle-class parents in her study were worried that their children dressing as "gangstas" would lead to them being treated as such by authority figures. Style of dress is an important concern for Black middle-class parents.

7. While admittedly "trauma" is a psychological diagnosis that is beyond the scope of this study, there doesn't appear to be a better word to describe the deep emotional pain respondents described in this chapter that appeared to have a fairly dramatic impact on their racialized sense of self and their racial identity development over the life course.

8. According to Stubblefield (2005), for Blacks, basing group unity on a shared downtrodden status is not the most effective way to foster solidarity: "Recognition of common oppression is not a particularly attractive basis for racial solidarity. Thinking of Black identity solely in terms of the experiences of oppression shared by Black people undermines the goal of creating solidarity, in the first place which is for Black people to take pride in themselves and their heritage, to have self-respect, self-esteem, and self-determination. To say, in effect, that what it means to be Black is to have experienced anti-Black oppression is not a good way to foster Black pride for liberatory purposes" (157).

9. Terms like these exist in every group of color to suggest that a member of the group has left their culture and people behind. Native Americans use the term "apple" (red on the outside, White on the inside), Latinos often use "coconut" (brown on the outside, White on the inside), and Asian Americans use the term "banana" (yellow on the outside, White on the inside) (Spencer and Dornbusch 1990, 132).

10. See Tatum (1997) for a full discussion of "the table." See also Carter (1993).

Chapter Five

1. Presently, most have completed their studies and matriculated with these degrees.

2. Emerging in the late 1960s, the study of Nigrescence (a French term meaning the "process of becoming black") began as a way for Black psychologists to address the identity transformation that occurred through an individual's participation in the Black Power movement (1968–1975). Cross's theory of Nigrescence has remained at the center of most analyses of Black identity development. According to him, it is a model that explains "how assimilated Black adults, as well as deracinated, deculturalized, or miseducated Black adults are transformed by a series of circumstances and events into persons who are more Black or Afrocentrically aligned" (Cross 1991, 190).

3. While offering "discipline and morals" to the poor is a bit of an elitist notion that often came across in respondents with more ambivalent attachments, as stated earlier, respondents' placement in these categories is based on the presence of several characteristics. In other words, while respondents sometimes exhibit characteristics

from another category, their designation of having strong, ambivalent, or limited attachments is based on whether they fit the majority of the characteristics in that category. While Langston may demonstrate some of the elitism of the ambivalents, in every other way, he fit the profile of those with strong attachments. Subsequent statements of his later in this chapter also speak to this fact.

4. They are actually in good company with Whites and people of color alike, as research shows that those who subscribe to notions of structuralism also hold notions of individualism (Hunt 2004, 2007; Kluegel and Smith 1986). Also, structural beliefs can be compartmentalized (Wilson 1996) or layered (Hunt 1996) in a way that supports one's beliefs in individualism. The sentiments expressed by these respondents reflect these research findings.

5. Silencing about class also lends itself to an ambivalent racial identity in adulthood. For example, Zara (a respondent in this category) said the following about her childhood observations on social class: "I just learned a lot about race, but I think I also learned a lot about how *class* interacts with African Americans and how we don't like to talk about it. But I think it really is a big issue. Because I can *see* that sometimes there were differences between the opportunities I had and my cousins, per se, would have." Yet this was never discussed in her family. The silence becomes another way that Black middle-class children are forced to draw their own conclusions about race and class in ways that are sometimes detrimental.

6. Ellis Cose (1993) expresses a very sympathetic view toward the service quandary for middle-class Blacks. He suggests that to expect upwardly mobile Blacks to help other Blacks up the ladder while dealing with their own problems of upward mobility is to expect quite a bit: "Countless members of the black middle class are in fact volunteering every spare moment in an attempt to do whatever they can (working in homeless shelters, volunteering in literacy programs, serving as formal mentors) to better the lives of those in the so-called underclass. At the same time, however, many who belong to America's black privileged class are struggling with problems of their own that are largely unseen or dismissed" (71).

7. Some research indicates that middle-class Blacks are more likely to give back to poorer Blacks because they are more likely to participate in organizations that emphasize the importance of doing so (Billingsley 1992; Higginbotham and Weber 1992; Lipset 1997; Pattillo-McCoy 1999, cited in Vallejo and Lee 2009).

8. Feagin (2010) might argue that it reflects a White racially framed history: "The commonplace white narratives of U.S. historical development still accent whites' superiority and courage over the centuries. Implicitly or explicitly, the contemporary white frame accents continuing aspects of this superiority—that is, that whites are typically more moral, intelligent, rational, attractive, or hardworking than other racial groups, and especially than African Americans and other dark-skinned Americans" (96).

9. Willie (2001, 30) also finds that Blacks who grew up in White environments are worried about their performance, particularly in front of low-income Blacks.

10. It is perhaps worth noting that Jeremy's father had children when he was much older and left the military rather early on in his childhood. As a result, Jeremy didn't have as much exposure to military culture as the other respondents in the study, who were more likely to have lived on military bases and had a life structured around that community.

11. At the time of the interview, the two were dating.

12. Likewise, Feagin (2010) characterizes Thomas as an individual who has internalized elements of the White racial frame and openly operates out of it. As a result, he has been well rewarded by Whites (see 190).

13. There are conflicting reports about whether King was under the influence of narcotics or alcohol at the time of his arrest.

14. To be sure, many social scientists might argue that those personal problems were also a function of structure, notably the combination of King's difficult childhood with an alcoholic father who died early in his life, thus leading him down a destructive path and the notoriously aggressive police tactics toward Blacks utilized by then Los Angeles police chief Daryl Gates; both factors appeared to be on a collision course on that fateful night in Los Angeles.

15. This was under the previous SAT system where the maximum score was 1600.

16. This reality bears out in scholarly research, where several scholars note that middle-class minorities who give financial assistance to poorer relatives and coethnics compromise their own wealth accumulation (Cole and Omari 2003; Conley 1999; Oliver and Shapiro 1995; Vallejo and Lee 2009).

17. Alternatively, this could be a sense of "survivor's guilt," where Hochschild (1995) says, "It is all too easy to see how similar one is to friends, cousins, siblings who did not make it; and the urge to justify 'Why me? Why not him?' can propel one far from those rejected origins" (125).

Chapter Six

1. Dalmage refers to border patrolling in the context of biracial Americans, but her theory appears to apply as well to "bicultural" Americans, such as middle-class Blacks who also live somewhere between America's racial lines.

References

Anderson, Elijah. 1990. *Streetwise*. Chicago: University of Chicago Press.
———. 1999. *The Code of the Streets: Decency, Violence, and the Moral Life of the Inner City*. New York: Norton.
Attewell, Paul, David Lavin, Thurston Domina, and Tania Levey. 2004. "The Black Middle Class: Progress, Prospects, and Puzzles." *Journal of African American Studies* 8, no. 1–2: 6–19.
Barajas, Heidi Lasley, and Jennifer L. Pierce. 2001. "The Significance of Race and Gender in School Success among Latinas and Latinos in College." *Gender and Society* 15, no. 6: 859–78.
Baxter, Leslie, and Catherine L. Clark. 1996. "Perceptions of Family Communication Patterns and the Enactment of Family Rituals." *Western Journal of Communication* 60, no. 3: 254–69.
Billingsley, Andrew. 1992. *Climbing Jacob's Ladder: The Enduring Legacy of African American Families*. New York: Simon and Schuster.
Blackwell, James E. 1985. *The Black Community: Diversity and Unity*. 2nd ed. New York: Harper and Row.
Blassingame, John W. 1979. *The Slave Community: Plantation Life in the Antebellum South*. New York: Oxford University Press.
Blau, Zena Smith. 1981. *Black Children/White Children: Competence, Socialization, and Social Structure*. New York: Free Press.
Bobo, Lawrence, James R. Kluegel, and Ryan A. Smith. 1997. "Laissez-Faire Racism: The Crystallization of a Kinder, Gentler, Antiblack Ideology." In *Racial Attitudes in the 1990s: Continuity and Change*, edited by Stephen A. Tuch and Jack K. Martin, 15–42. Westport, CT: Praeger.

Bobo, Lawrence, and Camille L. Zubrinsky. 1996. "Attitudes on Residential Integration: Perceived Status Differences, Mere In-Group Preference, or Racial Prejudice?" *Social Forces* 74: 883–909.

Bonilla-Silva, Eduardo. 2001. *White Supremacy and Racism in the Post-Civil Rights Era.* Boulder, CO: Lynne Rienner.

———. 2010. *Racism without Racists: Colorblind Racism and the Persistence of Inequality in America.* Lanham, MD: Rowman & Littlefield.

Bourdieu, Pierre. 1984. *Distinction: A Social Critique of the Judgment of Taste.* Cambridge, MA: Harvard University Press.

———. 1985. "The Forms of Capital." In *The Handbook of Theory and Research for the Sociology of Education,* edited by J. G. Richardson, 241–58. New York: Greenwood.

Bourdieu, Pierre, and Jean-Claude Passeron. 1979. *The Inheritors: French Students and Their Relation to Culture.* Translated by Richard Nice. Chicago: University of Chicago Press.

———. 1990. *Reproduction in Education, Society, and Culture.* London: Sage.

Bowman, Phillip J., and Cleopatra Howard. 1985. "Race-Related Socialization, Motivation, and Academic Achievement: A Study of Black Youths in Three-Generation Families." *Journal of the American Academy of Child Psychiatry* 24: 134–44.

Boyd, Michelle. 2008. *Jim Crow Nostalgia: Reconstructing Race in Bronzeville.* Minneapolis: University of Minnesota Press.

Boyd-Franklin, Nancy. 2003. *Black Families in Therapy: An African-American Experience.* New York: Guilford Press.

Boykin, A. Wade, and Forrest D. Toms. 1985. "Black Child Socialization: A Conceptual Framework." In *Black Children: Social, Educational and Parental Environments,* edited by Harriette Pipes McAdoo and John Lewis McAdoo, 33–52. Newbury Park, CA: Sage.

Brodkin, Karen. 1998. *How Jews Became White Folks: And What That Says about Race in America.* Piscataway, NJ: Rutgers University Press.

Broman, Clifford L., Harold W. Neighbors, and James S. Jackson. 1988. "Racial Group Identification among Black Adults." *Social Forces* 67, no. 1: 146–58.

Brown, B. Bradford. 1990. "Peer Groups and Peer Cultures." In *At the Threshold: The Developing Adolescent,* edited by S. Shirley Feldman and Glen R. Elliot, 171–96. Cambridge, MA: Harvard University Press.

Brown, Michael K., Martin Carnoy, Elliot Currie, Troy Duster, David B. Oppenheimer, Marjorie M. Schultz, and David Wellman. 2003. *Whitewashing Race: The Myth of a Colorblind Society.* Berkeley: University of California Press.

Brown, Nikki L. M., and Barry M. Stentiford. 2008. *The Jim Crow Encyclopedia: Greenwood Milestones in African American History.* Westport, CT: Greenwood.

Brunsma, David L., and Kerry Ann Rockquemore. 2002. "What Does 'Black' Mean?: Exploring the Epistemological Stranglehold of Racial Classification." *Critical Sociology* 28, no. 1–2: 101–21.

Bureau of the Census. 2010. "Income, Poverty, and Health Insurance Coverage in the United States: 2009." http://www.census.gov/prod/2010pubs/p60-238.pdf (accessed February 4, 2011).

———. 2011. "Educational Attainment by Race and Hispanic Origin: 1970 to 2009." http://www.census.gov/compendia/statab/2011/tables/11s0225.pdf (accessed February 4, 2011).

Bureau of Labor Statistics. 2009. *Labor Force Statistics from the Current Population Survey*. Washington, DC: Bureau of Labor Statistics, 2009. http://www.bls.gov/cps/race_ethnicity_2008_occ_ind.htm. Report (accessed February 4. 2011).

Butler, John Sibley. 2005. *Entrepreneurship and Self-Help among Black Americans: A Reconsideration of Race and Economics*. Albany: State University of New York Press.

Carr, Leslie G. 1997. *Color-Blind Racism*. Thousand Oaks, CA: Sage.

Carter, Prudence L. 2005. *Keepin' It Real: School Success beyond Black and White*. New York: Oxford University Press.

Carter, Robert T., and Janet E. Helms. 1988. "The Relationship between Racial Identity Attitudes and Social Class." *Journal of Negro Education* 57, no. 1: 22–30.

Carter, Stephen. 1993. "The Black Table, the Empty Seat, and the Tie." In *Lure and Loathing: Essays on Race, Identity and the Ambivalence of Assimilation*, edited by Gerald Early, 55–79. New York: Penguin.

Cashin, Sheryll. 2001. "Middle-Class Black Suburbs and the State of Integration: A Post-Integrationist Vision for Metropolitan America." *Cornell Law Review* 86: 729–76.

Celious, Aaron, and Daphna Oyserman. 2001. "Race from the Inside: An Emerging Heterogeneous Race Model." *Journal of Social Issues* 57: 149–65.

Centers for Disease Control. 1998. "Suicide among Black Youths: United States, 1980–1995." *Morbidity and Mortality Weekly Report* 47, no. 10: 193–206. http://www.cdc.gov/epo/mmwr/preview/mmwrhtml/00051591.htm.

Chavous, Tabbye M., Debra Hilkene Bernat, Karen Schmeelk-Cone, Cleopatra H. Caldwell, Laura Kohn-Wood, and Marc A. Zimmerman. 2003. "Racial Identity and Academic Attainment among African American Adolescents." *Child Development* 74, no. 4: 1076–90.

Clasen, D. R., and B. B. Brown. 1985. "The Multidimensionality of Peer Pressure in Adolescence." *Journal of Youth and Adolescence* 14: 451–68.

Coard, Stephanie I., Scyatta A. Wallace, Howard C. Stevenson Jr., and Laurie M. Brotman. 2004. "Towards Culturally Relevant Preventive Interventions: The Consideration of Racial Socialization in Parent Training with African American Families." *Journal of Child and Family Studies* 13: 277–93.

Cole, Elizabeth R., and Safiya R. Omari. 2003. "Race, Class and the Dilemmas of Upward Mobility for African Americans." *Journal of Social Issues* 59, no. 4: 785–802.

Collins, Patricia Hill. 2000. *Black Feminist Thought: Knowledge, Consciousness, and the Politics of Empowerment*. Boston: Unwin Hyman.

———. 2005. *Black Sexual Politics: African Americans, Gender, and the New Racism*. New York: Routledge.

Collins, Sharon. 1997. *Black Corporate Executives: The Making and Breaking of a Black Middle Class*. Philadelphia: Temple University Press.

Coner-Edwards, Alice F., and Henry E. Edwards. 1988. "The Black Middle Class: Definitions and Demographics." In *Black Families in Crisis: The Middle Class*, edited by Alice F. Coner-Edwards and Jeanne Spurlock, 1–10. New York: Brunner/Mazel.

Coner-Edwards, Alice F., and Jeanne Spurlock. 1988. *Black Families in Crisis: The Middle Class*. New York: Brunner/Mazel.

Conley, Dalton. 1999. *Being Black, Living in the Red: Race, Wealth, and Social Policy in America*. Berkeley: University of California Press.

Constantine, Madonna G., and Sha'Kema M. Blackmon. 2002. "Black Adolescents' Racial Socialization Experiences: Their Relations to Home, School, and Peer Self-Esteem." *Journal of Black Studies* 32, no. 3: 322–35.

Cook, Phillip J., and Jens Ludwig. 1998. "The Burden of 'Acting White': Do Black Adolescents Disparage Academic Achievement?" In *The Black-White Test Score Gap*, edited by Christopher Jencks and Meredith Phillips, 375–400. Washington, DC: Brookings Institution.

Cose, Ellis. 1993. *The Rage of a Privileged Class: Why Are Middle-Class Blacks Angry? Why Should America Care?* New York: HarperCollins.

———. 2011. *The End of Anger: A New Generation's Take on Race and Rage*. New York: Ecco.

Crawford, June, Susan Kippax, Jenny Onyx, U. Gault, and Peter Benton. 1992. *Emotion and Gender: Constructing Meaning from Memory*. London: Sage.

Cross, William E., Jr. 1991. *Shades of Black: Diversity in African-American Identity*. Philadelphia: Temple University Press.

Dalmage, Heather M. 2000. *Tripping on the Color Line: Black-White Multiracial Families in a Racially Divided World*. New Brunswick, NJ: Rutgers University Press.

Dasgupta, Nilanjana, Debbie E. McGhee, Anthony G. Greenwald, and Mahzarin R. Banaji. 2000. "Automatic Preference for White Americans: Eliminating the Familiarity Explanation." *Journal of Experimental Social Psychology* 36: 316–28.

Datnow, Amanda, and Robert Cooper. 1996. "Peer Networks of African American Students in Independent Schools: Affirming Academic Success and Racial Identity." *Journal of Negro Education* 65, no. 4: 56–72.

Davis, Penelope J. 1999. "Gender Differences in Autobiographical Memory for Childhood Emotional Experience." *Journal of Personality and Social Psychology* 76, no. 3: 498–510.

Dawson, Michael C. 1994. *Behind the Mule: Race and Class in African-American Politics*. Princeton, NJ: Princeton University Press.

Day-Vines, Norma L., James M. Patton, and Joy L. Baytops. 2003. "Counseling African American Adolescents: The Impact of Race, Culture, and Middle Class Status." *Professional School Counseling* 7, no. 1: 40–51.

DeFazio, William. 2006. *Ordinary Poverty: A Little Food and Cold Storage*. Philadelphia: Temple University Press.

Delpit, Lisa. 1995. *Other People's Children: Cultural Conflict in the Classroom*. New York: New Press.

Demo, David H., and Michael Hughes. 1990. "Socialization and Racial Identity among Black Americans." *Social Psychology Quarterly* 53, no. 4: 364–74.

Dent, David J. 2006. "*The New York Times Magazine* Spotlights Black Suburbaniza-tion, 1992." In *The Suburb Reader*, edited by Becky M. Nicolaides and Andrew Wiese, 412–14. New York: Routledge.

Derricotte, Toi. 1999. *The Black Notebooks*. New York: Norton.

Diamond, John B., and Kimberley Gomez. 2004. "African American Parents' Edu-cational Orientations: The Importance of Social Class and Parents' Perceptions of Schools." *Education and Urban Society* 36: 383–427.

Dickerson, Debra J. 2009. "Class Is the New Black: How I Had to Look beyond Race and Learn to Love Equality." *Mother Jones*, January 16. http://motherjones.com/politics/2009/01/class-new-black.

DiIulio, John J., Jr. 1999. "Black Churches and the Inner-City Poor." In *The African American Predicament*, edited by Christopher H. Foreman Jr., 116–42. Washing-ton, DC: Brookings Institution.

Dillard, Joey Lee. 1972. *Black English: Its History and Usage*. New York: Random House.

Doane, Ashley Woody, Jr. 2003. "Rethinking Whiteness Studies." In *White Out: The Continuing Significance of Racism*, edited by Ashley Woody Doane Jr. and Eduardo Bonilla-Silva, 3–18. New York: Routledge.

Donaldson, Jam. 2010. *Conversate Is Not a Word: Getting Away from Ghetto*. Chicago: Lawrence Hill Books.

Doss, Richard C., and Alan Gross. 1992. "The Effects of Black English on Stereotyp-ing in Intraracial Perceptions." *Journal of Black Psychology* 18: 47–58.

Dougherty, Conor. 2008. "The End of White Flight." *Wall Street Journal On-line*, July 19. http://online.wsj.com/article/SB121642866373567057.html?mod=googlenews_wsj.

Drake, St. Clair, and Horace R. Cayton. 1962. *Black Metropolis: A Study of Negro Life in a Northern City*. New York: Harper Torchbooks.

DuBois, W. E. B. 1903a. *The Negro Problem*. New York: James Pott and Company.

———. 1903b. *The Souls of Black Folk*. New York: Penguin.

———. 1948. "The Talented Tenth: Memorial Address." *Boule Journal* 15: 3–13.

Dyson, Michael Eric. 2004. *The Michael Eric Dyson Reader*. New York: Basic Civitas Books.

———. 2005. *Is Bill Cosby Right? Or Has the Black Middle Class Lost Its Mind?* New York: Basic Civitas Books.

Early, Gerald, ed. 1993. *Lure and Loathing: Essays on Race, Identity and the Ambiva-lence of Assimilation*. New York: Allen Lane/Penguin.

Erikson, Erik H. 1968. *Identity: Youth in Crisis*. New York: Norton.

Etzioni, Amitai. 1973. "A103—The Crisis of Modernity: Deviation or Demise?" *Journal of Human Relations* 21, no. 4: 371–94. Reprinted from *The Human Context* 5, no. 3 (Autumn 1973): 622–37.

Evans, Arthur S., Jr. 1993. "The New American Black Middle Classes: Their Social Structure and Status Ambivalence." *International Journal of Politics, Culture and Society* 7, no. 2: 209–28.

Feagin, Joe. 1991. "The Continuing Significance of Race: Antiblack Discrimination in Public Places." *American Sociological Review* 56, no. 1: 101–17.

———. 2001. *Racist America: Roots, Current Realities, and Future Reparations.* New York: Routledge.

———. 2010. *The White Racial Frame: Centuries of Racial Framing and Counter-Framing.* New York: Routledge.

Feagin, Joe R., and Karyn D. McKinney. 2003. *The Many Costs of Racism.* Lanham, MD: Rowman & Littlefield.

Feagin, Joe R., and Melvin P. Sikes. 1994. *Living with Racism: The Black Middle-Class Experience.* Boston: Beacon Press.

Feagin, Joe R., and Hernan Vera. 1995. *White Racism: The Basics.* New York: Routledge.

Finestra, Carmen. 1986. "Close to Home." *The Cosby Show,* season 2, episode 20, directed by Jay Sandrich, aired March 13.

Fordham, Signithia. 1988. "Racelessness as a Factor in Black Students' School Success: Pragmatic Strategy or Pyrrhic Victory?" *Harvard Educational Review* 58, no. 1: 54–84.

Fordham, Signithia, and John U. Ogbu. 1986. "Black Students' School Success: Coping with the Burden of 'Acting White.'" *Urban Review* 18, no. 3: 176–206.

Frankenberg, Ruth. 1993. *White Women, Race Matters: The Social Construction of Whiteness.* Minneapolis: University of Minnesota Press.

Frazier, E. Franklin. 1957. *Black Bourgeoisie.* New York: Free Press.

Gaines, Kevin K. 1996. *Uplifting the Race: Black Leadership, Politics, and Culture in the Twentieth Century.* Chapel Hill: University of North Carolina Press.

Gans, Herbert J. 2008. "Race as Class." In *The Contexts Reader,* edited by Jeff Goodwin and James M. Jasper, 262–68. New York: Norton.

Garrod, Andrew, Janie Victoria Ward, Tracy L. Robinson, and Robert Kilkenny. 1999. *Souls Looking Back: Life Stories of Growing Up Black.* New York: Routledge.

Gates, Henry Louis, Jr. 1992. "TV's Black World Turns, but Stays Unreal." In *Race, Class, and Gender: An Anthology,* edited by Margaret L. Andersen and Patricia Hill Collins, 310–17. Belmont, CA: Wadsworth.

Gibbs, J. T. 1996. *Race and Justice: Rodney King and O.J. Simpson in a House Divided.* San Francisco: Jossey-Bass.

Giddings, Paula. 1984. *When and Where I Enter: The Impact of Black Women on Race and Sex in America.* New York: HarperCollins.

Gilkes, Cheryl Townsend. 1998. "Plenty Good Room: Adaptation in a Changing Black Church." *Annals of the American Academy of Political and Social Science* 558: 101–21.

Goffman, Erving. 1959. *The Presentation of Self in Everyday Life.* New York: Anchor.

Gordon, Milton M. 1964. *Assimilation in American Life: The Role of Race, Religion, and National Origins.* New York: Oxford University Press.

Graham, Lawrence Otis. 1999. *Our Kind of People: Inside America's Black Upper Class.* New York: HarperCollins.

Grier, Eunice, and George Grier. 1958. *In Search of Housing: A Study of Experiences of Negro Professional and Technical Personnel in New York State*. New York: New York State Commission Against Discrimination.

Gross, Kali N. 1997. "Examining the Politics of Respectability in African American Studies." *Almanac* 43, no. 28. http://www.upenn.edu/almanac/v43/n28/benchmrk.html (accessed October 1, 2010).

Guiffrida, Douglas. 2005. Othermothering as a framework for understanding African American students' definition of student-centered faculty. *Journal of Higher Education* 76: 701–23.

Gutierrez y Muhs, Gabriella, Yolanda Flores Niemann, Carmen G. Gonzalez, and Angela P. Harris, eds. 2012. *Presumed Incompetent: The Intersections of Race and Class for Women of Color in Academia*. Salt Lake City: Utah State University Press.

Gwaltney, John Langston. 1980. *Drylongso: A Self-Portrait of Black America*. New York: Random House.

Hacker, Andrew. 1995. *Two Nations: Black and White, Separate, Hostile, Unequal*. New York: Ballantine.

Haddix, Angela. 2009/2010. "Black Boys Can Write: Challenging Dominant Framings of African American Adolescent Males in Literacy Research." *Journal of Adolescent and Adult Literacy* 53, no. 4: 341–43.

Hajnal, Zoltan L. 2007. "Black Class Exceptionalism: Insights from Direct Democracy on the Race versus Class Debate." *Public Opinion Quarterly* 71, no. 4: 560–87.

Han, Chong-Suk. 2010. "Darker Shades of Queer: Race and Sexuality at the Margins." In *Race, Class, and Gender: An Anthology*, edited by Margaret L. Andersen and Patricia Hill Collins, 255–62. Belmont, CA: Wadsworth Cengage.

Harris, Cherise A., and Nikki Khanna. 2010. "Black Is, Black Ain't: Biracials, Middle-Class Blacks, and the Social Construction of Blackness." *Sociological Spectrum* 30: 639–670.

Harris, David. 1995. "Exploring the Determinants of Adult Black Identity: Context and Process." *Social Forces* 74, no. 1: 227–41.

Harris, Fredrick C. 2008. "Survey on Race, Politics, and Society." In *Center on African American Politics and Society: Black Politics Survey*, 1–7. http://iserp.columbia.edu/files/iserp/caaps_report_9_08.pdf (accessed March 27, 2009).

Harris, Will. 2010. "A Chat with Darius Rucker." *Bullz-eye*, October 7, 2010, http://www.bullz-eye.com/music/interviews/2010/darius_rucker.htm2010.

Hatch, Margaret Beddow. 1983. "Vanessa's Rich." *The Cosby Show*, season 3, episode 8, directed by Tony Singletary, aired November 13.

Hays, Sharon. 2003. *Flat Broke with Children: Women in the Age of Welfare Reform*. New York: Oxford University Press.

Healey, Joseph F. 2003. *Race, Ethnicity, Gender and Class: The Sociology of Group Conflict and Change*. Thousand Oaks, CA: Pine Forge Press.

Heaven, Patrick C. L. 2001. *The Social Psychology of Adolescence*. New York: Palgrave.

Helms, Janet E., ed. 1993. *Black and White Racial Identity: Theory, Research, and Practice*. Westport, CT: Praeger.

Herring, Cedric, and Charles Amissah. 1997. "Advance and Retreat: Racially Based Attitudes and Public Policy." In *Racial Attitudes in the 1990s: Continuity and Change*, edited by Steven A. Tuch and Jack Martin, 121–43. New York: Praeger.

Herring, Mary, Thomas B. Jankowski, and Ronald E. Brown. 1999. "Pro-Black Doesn't Mean Anti-White: The Structure of African-American Group Identity." *Journal of Politics* 61, no. 2: 336–86.

Higginbotham, Elizabeth. 1981. "Is Marriage a Priority? Class Differences in Marital Options of Educated Black Women." In *Single Life: Unmarried Adults in Social Context*, edited by P. Stein, 133–76. Ann Arbor, MI: Institute for Social Research.

Higginbotham, Evelyn Brooks. 1992. "African American Women's History and the Metalanguage of Race." *Signs* 17, no. 2: 251–74.

———. 1993. *Righteous Discontent: The Women's Movement in the Black Baptist Church: 1880–1920*. Cambridge, MA: Harvard University Press.

Higginbotham, Evelyn, and Lynn Weber. 1992. "Moving Up with Kin and Community: Upward Social Mobility for Black and White Women." *Gender and Society* 6: 416–40.

Hill, Shirley A. 1999. *African American Children: Socialization and Development in Families*. Thousand Oaks, CA: Sage.

———. 2005. *Black Intimacies: A Gender Perspective on Families and Relationships*. Walnut Creek, CA: AltaMira Press.

Hine, Darlene Clark, William C. Hine, and Stanley Harrold, eds. 2006. *The African-American Odyssey: Volume 2: Since 1865*. 3rd ed. Upper Saddle River, NJ: Pearson.

Hochschild, Jennifer L. 1995. *Facing Up to the American Dream: Race, Class, and the Soul of the Nation*. Princeton, NJ: Princeton University Press.

Hogg, Michael A. 1988. *Social Identifications: A Social Psychology of Intergroup Relations and Group Processes*. London: Routledge.

Hollander, Jocelyn A., and Judith A. Howard. 1996. *Gendered Situations, Gendered Selves: A Gender Lens on Social Psychology*. Lanham, MD: AltaMira Press.

Holt, Thomas C. 1995. "Marking: Race, Race-Making, and the Writing of History." *American Historical Review* 100, no. 1: 1–20.

Horvat, Erin McNamara, and Kristine S. Lewis. 2003. "Reassessing the 'Burden of Acting White': The Importance of Peer Groups in Managing Academic Success." *Sociology of Education* 76: 265–80.

Hughes, Diane, and Lisa Chen. 1997. "When and What Parents Tell Children about Race: An Examination of Race-Related Socialization among African American Families." *Applied Developmental Science* 1: 200–214.

———. 2003. "The Nature of Parents' Race-Related Communications to Children: A Developmental Perspective." In *Child Psychology: A Handbook of Contemporary Issues*, edited by Lawrence Balter and Catherine S. Tamis-LeMonda, 467–490. New York: Psychology Press.

Humphreys, Margaret. 2001. *Malaria: Poverty, Race, and Public Health in the United States*. Baltimore: Johns Hopkins University Press.

Hunt, Matthew O. 1996. "The Individual, Society, or Both? A Comparison of Black, Latino, and White Beliefs about the Causes of Poverty." *Social Forces* 75, no. 1: 293–322.

———. 2004. "Race/Ethnicity and Beliefs about Wealth and Poverty." *Social Science Quarterly* 85, no. 3: 827–53.

———. 2007. "African American, Hispanic, and White Beliefs about Black/White Inequality, 1977–2004." *American Sociological Review* 72: 390–415.

Hyra, Derek S. 2008. *The New Urban Renewal: The Economic Transformation of Harlem and Bronzeville.* Chicago: University of Chicago Press.

Iceland, John, and Rima Wilkes. 2006. "Does Socioeconomic Status Matter? Race, Class, and Residential Segregation." *Social Problems* 52, no. 2: 248–73.

Innis, Leslie B., and Joe R. Feagin. 1995. "The Cosby Show: The View from the Black Middle Class." *Journal of Black Studies* 25, no. 2: 692–711.

Jackson, John L. 2001. *Harlemworld: Doing Race and Class in Contemporary Black America.* Chicago: University of Chicago Press.

Jackson, Regine. 2010. "Black Immigrants and the Rhetoric of Social Distancing." *Sociology Compass* 4, no. 3: 193–206.

Jacobs, Ronald N. 2001. "The Problem with Tragic Narratives: Lessons from the Los Angeles Uprising." *Qualitative Sociology* 24, no. 2: 221–43.

Jhally, Sut, and Justin M. Lewis. 1992. *Enlightened Racism.* Boulder, CO: Westview.

Jones, Charisse, and Kumea Shorter-Gooden. 2003. *Shifting: The Double Lives of Black Women in America.* New York: HarperCollins.

Joseph, Peniel E. 2010. *Dark Days, Bright Nights: From Black Power to Barack Obama.* New York: Basic Civitas Books.

Kaslow, Nadine J., Ann Webb Price, Sarah Wyckoff, Grall Mamette Bender, Alissa Sherry, Sharon Young, Larry Scholl, Upshaw Venus Millington, Akil Rashid, Emily B. Jackson, and Kafi Bethea. 2004. "Person Factors Associated with Suicidal Behavior among African American Women and Men." *Cultural Diversity and Ethnic Minority Psychology* 10, no. 1: 5–22.

Katz, Michael B. 1996. *In the Shadow of the Poorhouse: A Social History of Welfare in America.* New York: Basic Books.

Khanna, Nikki D. 2011. *Biracial in America: Forming and Performing Racial Identity.* Lanham, MD: Lexington Books.

Kitwana, Bakari. 2002. *The Hip-Hop Generation: Young Blacks and the Crisis in African-American Culture.* New York: Basic Books.

Klein, Alec. 2004. "A Tenuous Hold on the Middle Class." *Washington Post*, December 18, A1.

Klor de Alva, Jorge, Earl Shorris, and Cornel West. 1997. "Our Next Race Question: The Uneasiness between Blacks and Latinos." In *Critical White Studies: Looking behind the Mirror*, edited by Richard Delgado and Jean Stefanic, 482–92. Philadelphia: Temple University Press.

Kluegel, James R., and Eliot R. Smith. 1986. *Beliefs about Inequality.* New York: Aldine DeGruyter.

Kronus, Sidney. 1971. *The Black Middle Class.* Columbus, OH: Merrill.

Kunjufu, Jawanza. 1995. *Countering the Conspiracy to Kill Black Boys.* Sauk Village, IL: African American Images.

Kusmer, Kenneth L. 1976. *A Ghetto Takes Shape: Black Cleveland, 1870–1930.* Chicago: University of Illinois Press.

Lacy, Karyn. 2002. "A Part of the Neighborhood? Negotiating Race in American Suburbs." *International Journal of Sociology and Social Policy* 22, no. 1: 39–74.

———. 2004. "Black Spaces, Black Places: Strategic Assimilation and Identity Construction in Middle-Class Suburbia." *Ethnic and Racial Studies* 27, no. 6: 908–30.

———. 2007. *Blue Chip Black: Race, Class and Status in the New Black Middle Class.* Berkeley: University of California Press.

Lacy, Karyn, and Angel L. Harris. 2008. "Breaking the Class Monolith: Understanding Class Differences in Black Adolescents' Attachment to Racial Identity." In *Social Class: How Does It Work?*, edited by Dalton Conley and Annette Lareau, 152–78. New York: Russell Sage Foundation Press.

Landry, Bart. 1987. *The New Black Middle Class.* Berkeley: University of California Press.

Lareau, Annette. 2003. *Unequal Childhoods: Class, Race, and Family Life.* Berkeley: University of California Press.

Leeson, Michael, and Ed. Weinberger. 1984. "Pilot." *The Cosby Show,* season 1, episode 1, directed by Jay Sandrich, aired September 20.

Lenski, Gerhard. 1954. "Status Crystallization: A Non-Vertical Dimension of Social Status." *American Sociological Review* 19: 405–13.

———. 1967. "Status Inconsistency and the Vote: A Four Nation Test." *American Sociological Review* 32: 298–301.

Lesane-Brown, Chase L. 2006. "A Review of Race Socialization within Black Families." *Developmental Review* 26: 400–426.

Lesane-Brown, Chase L., Tony N. Brown, Cleopatra H. Caldwell, and Robert M. Sellers. 2005. "Comprehensive Race Socialization Inventory (CSRI)." *Journal of Black Studies* 36: 163–90.

Levine, Madeline. 2006. *The Price of Privilege: How Parental Pressure and Material Advantage Are Creating a Generation of Disconnected and Unhappy Kids.* New York: HarperCollins.

Light Ivan H., and Steven J. Gold. 2000. *Ethnic Economies.* San Diego, CA: Academic Press.

Lipset, Seymour M. 1997. *American Exceptionalism: A Double-Edged Sword.* New York: Norton.

Lipsitz, George. 2006. "The Possessive Investment in Whiteness: Racialized Social Democracy and the 'White' Problem in American Studies." In *The Suburb Reader,* edited by Becky M. Nicolaides and Andrew Wiese, 341–44. New York: Routledge.

Manns, Wilhemina. 1997. "Supportive Roles of Significant Others in African American Families." In *Black Families,* edited by Harriette Pipes McAdoo, 198–213. Thousand Oaks, CA: Sage.

Marable, Manning. 2002. *The Great Wells of Democracy.* New York: Basic Civitas Books.

Marshall, Sheree. 1995. "Ethnic Socialization of African American Children: Implications for Parenting, Identity Development, and Academic Achievement." *Journal of Youth and Adolescence* 24 no. 4: 377–96.

Martin, Lori Latrice. 2010. "Strategic Assimilation or Creation of Symbolic Blackness: Middle-Class Blacks in Suburban Contexts." *Journal of African American Studies* 14: 234–46.

Martinez, Elizabeth. 2010. "Seeing More Than Black and White." In *Race, Class, and Gender: An Anthology*, edited by Margaret L. Andersen and Patricia Hill Collins, 87–92. Belmont, CA: Wadsworth.

Massey, Douglas, and Nancy Denton. 1993. *American Apartheid: Segregation and the Making of the Underclass*. Cambridge, MA: Harvard University Press.

Mays, Vickie, M., Cleopatra Howard Caldwell, and James S. Jackson. 1996. "Mental Health Symptoms and Service Utilization Patterns of Help-Seeking among African American Women." In *Mental Health in Black America*, edited by Harold W. Neighbors and James S. Jackson, 161–76. Thousand Oaks, CA: Sage.

McAdoo, Harriette. 1975. "The Extended Family." *Journal of Afro-American Issues* 3: 291–96.

———. 1978. "Factors Related to Stability in Upwardly Mobile Black Families." *Journal of Marriage and the Family* 40: 761–76.

McKnight, Reginald. 1993. "Confessions of a Wannabe Negro." In *Lure and Loathing: Essays on Race, Identity, and the Ambivalence of Assimilation*, edited by Gerald Early, 95–112. New York: Penguin.

Mellon, James, ed. 1988. *Bullwhip Days: The Slaves Remember*. New York: Avon.

Mendez, Linda M. Raffaele, and Howard M. Knoff. 2003. "Who Gets Suspended from School and Why: A Demographic Analysis of Schools and Disciplinary Infractions in a Large School District." *Education and Treatment of Children* 26, no. 1: 30–51.

Merrell-James, Rose. 2006. "Intra-Racial Bullying: An Issue of Multicultural Counseling." In Conference Proceedings of *Persistently Safe Schools 2006: Collaborating with Students, Families and Communities*, Washington, DC, September 19–21. http://gwired.gwu.edu/hamfish/merlin-cgi/p/downloadFile/d/16859/n/off/other/1/name/647Intra-racialbullyingpdf (accessed June 18, 2011).

Miller, David B. 1999. "Racial Socialization and Racial Identity: Can They Promote Resiliency for African American Adolescents?" *Adolescence* 34, no. 135: 493–501.

Moore, Brenda L., and Schuyler C. Webb. 2000. "Perceptions of Equal Opportunity among Women and Minority Army Personnel." *Sociological Inquiry* 70, no. 2: 215–39.

Moore, Kesha S. 2008. "Class Formations: Competing Forms of Black Middle-Class Identity." *Ethnicities* 8, no. 4: 492–517.

Moore, Valerie Ann. 1996. "Inappropriate Challenges to Professorial Authority." *Teaching Sociology* 24: 202–6.

Morrell, Ernest. 2007. *Critical Literacy and Urban Youth: Pedagogies of Access, Dissent, and Liberation*. New York: Routledge.

Moskos, Charles C., and John Sibley Butler. 1996. *All That We Can Be: Black Leadership and Racial Integration the Army Way*. New York: Basic Books.

Murray, Carolyn B., Julie E. Stokes, and M. Jean Peacock. 1999. "Racial Socialization of African American Children: A Review." In *African American Children, Youth and Parenting*, edited by Reginald L. Jones, 209–29. Hampton, VA: Cobb and Henry.

National Association for the Advancement of Colored People. 2005. "Dismantling the School-to-Prison Pipeline." New York: NAACP Legal Defense and Educational Fund. http://naacpldf.org/files/publications/DismantlingtheSchooltoPrisonPipeline.pdf (accessed February 18, 2011).

National Black Parents Association. N.d. http://www.facebook.com/pages/The-National-Black-Parents-Association/64589991851 (accessed February 18, 2011).

Neal-Barnett, Angela, Robert Stadulis, Nicolle Singer, Marsheena Murray, and Jessica Demmings. 2010. "Assessing the Effects of Experiencing the Acting White Accusation." *Urban Review* 42: 102–22.

Neckerman, Kathryn M., Prudence Carter, and Jennifer Lee. 1999. "Segmented Assimilation and Minority Cultures of Mobility." *Ethnic and Racial Studies* 22, no. 6: 945–65.

Nicolaides, Becky M., and Andrew Wiese. 2006. *The Suburb Reader*. New York: Routledge.

Niemann, Yolanda Flores. 1999. "The Making of a Token: A Case Study of Stereotype Threat, Stigma, Racism, and Tokenism in Academe." *Frontiers: A Journal of Women's Studies* 20, no. 1: 111–34.

Niemann, Yolanda Flores, and John F. Dovidio. 2005. "Affirmative Action and Job Satisfaction: Understanding Underlying Processes." *Journal of Social Issues* 61, no. 3: 507–23.

Noguera, Pedro. 2003a. "Anything but Black: Bringing Politics Back to the Study of Race." In *Problematizing Blackness: Self Ethnographies by Black Immigrants to the United States*, edited by Percy C. Hintzen and Jean Muteba Rahier, 193–200. New York: Routledge.

———. 2003b. *The Trouble with Black Boys: And Other Reflections on Race, Equity and the Future of Public Education*. San Francisco: Jossey-Bass.

Nunnally, Shayla. 2010. "Learning Race, Socializing Blackness: A Cross-Generational Analysis of Black Americans' Racial Socialization Experiences." *DuBois Review* 7, no. 1: 185–217.

Ogbar, Jeffrey O. G. 2007. *Hip Hop Revolution: The Culture and Politics of Rap*. Lawrence: University Press of Kansas.

Ogbu, John. 1982. "Socialization: A Cultural Ecological Approach." In *The Social Life of Children in a Changing Society*, edited by Kathryn M. Borman, 253–67. Hillsdale, NJ: Lawrence Erlbaum Associates.

Oliver, Melvin, and Thomas Shapiro. 1995. *Black Wealth/White Wealth*. New York: Routledge.

Omi, Michael, and Howard Winant. 1994. *Racial Formation in the United States: From the 1960s to the 1990s*. New York: Routledge.

Onyx, Jenny, and Jennie Small. 2001. "Memory-Work: The Method." *Qualitative Inquiry* 7, no. 6: 773–86.

Parham, Thomas A. 1989. "Cycles of Psychological Nigrescence." *The Counseling Psychologist* 17, no. 2: 187–226.

Parham, Thomas A., and Paris T. Williams. 1993. "The Relationship of Demographic Background Factors to Racial Identity Attitudes." *Journal of Black Psychology* 19: 7–24.

Parke, Ross D. 2004. "Development in the Family." *Annual Review of Psychology* 55: 365–99.

Patterson, Orlando. 1972. "Toward a Future That Has No Past—Reflections on the Fate of Blacks in the Americas." *Public Interest* 27: 25–62.

———. 2009. "Equality." *Democracy: A Journal of Ideas.* http://www.democracyjournal.org/pdf/11/patterson.pdf (accessed January 24, 2011).

Pattillo, Mary. 2005. "Black Middle-Class Neighborhoods." *Annual Review of Sociology* 31: 305–29.

———. 2007. *Black on the Block: The Politics of Race and Class in the City.* Chicago: University of Chicago Press.

Pattillo-McCoy, Mary. 1999. *Black Picket Fences: Privilege and Peril among the Black Middle Class.* Chicago: University of Chicago Press.

Pessar, Patricia R. 1995. "The Elusive Enclave: Ethnicity, Class, and Nationality among Latino Entrepreneurs in Greater Washington, DC." *Human Organization* 54: 383–92.

Peters, Marie Ferguson. 1985. "Racial Socialization of Young Black Children." In *Black Children: Social, Educational, and Parental Environments*, edited by Harriette Pipes McAdoo and John Lewis McAdoo, 159–73. Beverly Hills, CA: Sage.

Peterson, Christopher. 1980. "Memory and the 'Dispositional Shift.'" *Social Psychology Quarterly* 43, no. 4: 372–80.

Peterson-Lewis, Sonja, and Lisa M. Bratton. 2004. "Perceptions of 'Acting Black' among African American Teens: Implications of Racial Dramaturgy for Academic and Social Achievement." *Urban Review* 36, no. 2: 81–100.

Pew Forum on Religion and Public Life. 2009. "A Religious Portrait of African-Americans." *Analysis*, January 30. http://www.pewforum.org/A-Religious-Portrait-of-African-Americans.aspx (accessed April 3, 2012).

Pew Research Center. 2010. "A Balance Sheet at 30 Months: How the Great Recession Has Changed Life in America." http://pewsocialtrends.org/files-recession.pdf (accessed February 27, 2011).

Phinney, Jean S., and Victor Chavira. 1995. "Parental Ethnic Socialization and Adolescent Coping with Problems Related to Ethnicity." *Journal of Research on Adolescence* 5: 31–53.

Phinney, Jean S., and Mary Jane Rotheram, eds. 1987. *Children's Ethnic Socialization: Pluralism and Development.* Thousand Oaks, CA: Sage.

Pinkney, Alphonso. 2000. *Black Americans.* Upper Saddle River, NJ: Prentice Hall.

Portes, Alejandro, and Ruben G. Rumbaut. 2001. *Legacies: The Story of the Immigrant Second Generation.* Berkeley: University of California Press.

Pouissant, Alvin F. 1988. "The Huxtables: Fact or Fantasy?" *Ebony*, October, 72–74.

———. 2001. *Lay My Burden Down: Suicide and the Mental Health Crisis among African-Americans.* Boston: Beacon Press.

Price, Lisa, and Hilary Beard. 2004. *Success Never Smelled So Sweet: How I Followed My Nose and Found My Passion.* New York: Random House.

Price, Melanye T. 2009. *Dreaming Blackness: Black Nationalism and African American Public Opinion.* New York: New York University Press.

Public Broadcasting Service. 1998. "Children at Risk: Behind the Numbers." Transcript from *The NewsHour with Jim Lehrer*, May 6.

Reynolds, Rema. 2010. "'They Think You're Lazy,' and Other Messages Black Parents Send Their Black Sons: An Exploration of Critical Race Theory in the Examination of Educational Outcomes for Black Males." *Journal of African American Males in Education* 1, no. 2: 144–63.

Robinson, Eugene. 2010. *Disintegration: The Splintering of Black America*. New York: Doubleday.

Robinson, Matt. 1987. "Shakespeare." *The Cosby Show*, season 4, episode 5, directed by Jay Sandrich, aired October 22.

Rockquemore, Kerry Ann, and David L. Brunsma. 2007. *Beyond Black: Biracial Identity in America*. Lanham, MD: Rowman & Littlefield.

Rockquemore, Kerry Ann, and Tracey Laszloffy. 2008. *The Black Academic's Guide to Winning Tenure without Losing Your Soul*. Boulder, CO: Lynne Rienner.

Rooks, Noliwe. 1996. *Hair Raising: Beauty, Culture, and African American Women*. New Brunswick, NJ: Rutgers University Press.

Russell, Kathy, Midge Wilson, and Ronald Hall. 1993. *The Color Complex: The Politics of Skin Color among African Americans*. New York: Doubleday.

Rust, Paula C. 2009. "The Impact of Multiple Marginalization." In *Reconstructing Gender: A Multicultural Anthology*, edited bay Estelle Disch, 289–95. New York: McGraw-Hill.

Scales-Trent, Judy. 1995. *Notes of a White Black Woman: Race, Color, Community*. University Park: Pennsylvania State University Press.

Schuman, Howard, Charlotte Steeh, Lawrence D. Bobo, and Maria Krysan. 1997. *Racial Attitudes in America: Trends and Interpretations*. Cambridge, MA: Harvard University Press.

Sears, David O. 1988. "Symbolic Racism." In *Eliminating Racism: Profiles in Controversy*, edited by Phyllis A. Katz and Dalmas A. Taylor, 53–84. New York: Plenum.

———. 2008. "The American Color Line 50 Years after Brown v. Board: Many 'Peoples of Color' or Black Exceptionalism?" In *Commemorating Brown: The Social Psychology of Racism and Discrimination*, edited by Glenn Adams, Monica Biernat, Nyla R. Branscombe, Christian S. Crandall, and Lawrence S. Wrightsman, 133–52. Washington, DC: American Psychological Association.

Sears, David O., Jack Citrin, Sharmaine V. Cheleden, and Colette van Laar. 1999. "Cultural Diversity and Multicultural Politics: Is Ethnic Balkanization Psychologically Inevitable?" In *Cultural Divides: The Social Psychology of Cultural Contact*, edited by Deborah Prentice and Dale Miller, 35–79. New York: Russell Sage Foundation.

Sears, David O., Mingying Fu, P. J. Henry, and Kerra Bui. 2003. "The Origins and Persistence of Ethnic Identity among the 'New Immigrant' Groups." *Social Psychology Quarterly* 66, no. 4: 419–37.

Sellers, Robert M., and J. Nicole Shelton. 2003. "The Role of Racial Identity in Perceived Racial Discrimination." *Journal of Personal Social Psychology* 84, no. 5: 1079–92.

Sellers, Robert M., Tabbye M. Chavous, and Deanna Y. Cooke. 1998. "Racial Ideology and Racial Centrality as Predictors of African American College Students' Academic Performance." *Journal of Black Psychology* 24, no. 1: 8–27.

Semaj, Leachim Tufani. 1985. "Afrikanity, Cognition and Extended Self-Identity." In *Beginnings*, edited by Margaret Beale Spencer, Geraldine K. Brookins, and Walter R. Allen, 173–83. Hillsdale, NJ: Lawrence Erlbaum Associates.

Shapiro, Thomas M., Tatjana Meschede, and Laura Sullivan. 2010. "The Racial Wealth Gap Increases Fourfold." Waltham, MA: Institute on Assets and Social Policy.

Smith, Emilie P., Katrina Walker, Laurie Fields, Craig C. Brookins, and Robert C. Seay. 1999. "Ethnic Identity and Its Relationship to Self-Esteem, Perceived Efficacy, and Prosocial Attitudes in Early Adolescence." *Journal of Adolescence* 22, no. 6: 867–80.

Snow, David A., and Leon Anderson. 1987. "Identity Work among the Homeless: The Verbal Construction and Avowal of Personal Identities." *American Journal of Sociology* 92, no. 6: 1336–71.

Spencer, Jon Michael. 1993. "Trends of Opposition to Multiculturalism." *Black Scholar* 23, no. 2:16–22.

Spencer, Margaret Beale. 1983. "Children's Cultural Values and Parental Rearing Strategies. *Developmental Review* 3: 351–70.

Spencer, Margaret Beale, and Sanford M. Dornbusch. 1990. "Challenges in Studying Minority Youth." In *At the Threshold: The Developing Adolescent*, edited by S. Shirley Feldman and Glen R. Elliott, 123–46. Cambridge, MA: Harvard University Press.

Stack, Carol B. 1974. *All Our Kin: Strategies for Survival in a Black Community*. New York: Basic Books.

Stevenson, Howard C., Jr. 1994. "Validation of the Scale of Racial Socialization for Black Adolescents: Steps toward Multidimensionality." *Journal of Black Psychology* 20: 445–68.

Stevenson, Howard C., Jr., Rick Cameron, Teri Herrero-Taylor, and Gwendolyn Y. Davis. 2002. "Development of the Teenager Experience of Racial Socialization Scale: Correlates of Race-Related Socialization Frequency from the Perspective of Black Youth." *Journal of Black Psychology* 28: 84–106.

Stewart, Abigail J., Isis H. Settles, and Nicholas J. G. Winter. 1998. "Women and the Social Movements of the 1960s: Activists, Engaged Observers, and Nonparticipants." *Political Psychology* 19: 63–94.

Stewart, James B. 2009. "Be All That You Can Be?: Racial Identity Production in the U.S. Military." *Review of Black Political Economy* 36: 51–78.

St. Jean, Yanick, and Joe R. Feagin. 1998. *Double Burden: Black Women and Everyday Racism*. Armonk, NY: M. E. Sharpe.

Storrs, Debbie. 1999. "Whiteness as Stigma: Essentialist Identity Work by Mixed-Race Women." *Symbolic Interaction* 23: 187–212.

Stryker, Sheldon. 1980. *Symbolic Interactionism: A Social Structural Version*. Menlo Park, CA: Benjamin/Cummings.

Stubblefield, Anna. 2005. *Ethics along the Color Line*. Ithaca, NY: Cornell University Press.

Suarez-Orozco, Carola, and Marcelo M. Suarez-Orozco. 1995. *Transformations: Immigration, Family Life, and Achievement Motivation among Latino Adolescents*. Stanford, CA: Stanford University Press.

Sue, Derald Wing, and David Sue. 2003. *Counseling the Culturally Different: Theory and Practice*. New York: Wiley.

"Sweet Auburn." N.d. http://www.sweetauburn.com (accessed May 26, 2012).

Tajfel, Henri, and John C. Turner. 1979. "An Integrative Theory of Intergroup Conflict." In *The Social Psychology of Intergroup Conflict*, edited by William G. Austin and Stephen Worchel, 33–47. Monterey, CA: Brooks/Cole.

Takaki, Ronald T. 2010. "A Different Mirror." In *Race, Class, and Gender: An Anthology*, edited by Margaret L. Andersen and Patricia Hill Collins, 49–58. Belmont, CA: Wadsworth Cengage.

Tarpley, Natasha, ed. 1995. *Testimony: Young African-Americans on Self-Discovery and Black Identity*. Boston: Beacon Press.

Tatum, Beverly Daniel. 1997. *Why Are All the Black Kids Sitting Together in the Cafeteria? And Other Conversations about Race*. New York: HarperCollins.

———. 1999. *Assimilation Blues: Black Families in White Communities—Who Succeeds and Why*. New York: Basic Books.

Terrell, Francis. 1975. "Dialectal Differences between Middle-Class Black and White Children Who Do and Do Not Associate with Lower-Class Black Children." *Language and Speech* 18: 65–73.

Theoharis, Jeanne. 2013. "I Hate it When People Treat Me Like a Fxxx-up: Phony Theories, Segregated Schools, and the Culture of Aspiration among African American and Latino Teenagers." In *Race, Class, and Gender: An Anthology*, edited by Margaret L. Andersen and Patricia Hill Collins, 408–15. Belmont, CA: Wadsworth.

Thomas, William I., and Dorothy Thomas. 1928. *The Child in America*. New York: Knopf.

Thompson, Gerald. 1991. *Reflections of an Oreo Cookie: Growing Up Black in the 1960s*. Monroe, NY: Library Research Associates.

Thompson, Vetta L. Sanders. 1994. "Socialization to Race and Its Relationship to Racial Identification among African Americans." *Journal of Black Psychology* 20: 175–88.

———. 1999. "Variables Affecting Racial-Identity Salience among African Americans." *Journal of Social Psychology* 139, no. 6: 748–61.

Thompson-Miller, Ruth, and Joe R. Feagin. 2007. "Continuing Injuries of Racism: Counseling in a Racist Context." *The Counseling Psychologist* 35, no. 1: 106–15.

Thornton, Michael C., Linda M. Chatters, Robert Joseph Taylor, and Walter R. Allen. 1990. "Sociodemographic and Environmental Correlates of Racial Socialization by Black Parents." *Child Development* 61: 401–9.

Toliver, Susan D. 1998. *Black Families in Corporate America*. Thousand Oaks, CA: Sage.

Tyson, Karolyn, William Darity, and Domini R. Castellino. 2005. "It's Not 'a Black Thing': Understanding the Burden of Acting White and Other Dilemmas of High Achievement." *American Sociological Review* 24: 582–605.

USA Today. 2007. "Downward Mobility Trend Threatens Black Middle Class." http://www.usatoday.com/printedition/news/20071119/edtwo19. art.htm (accessed November 19, 2007).

Vallejo, Jody Agius. 2009. "Latina Spaces: Middle-Class Ethnic Capital and Professional Associations in the Latino Community." *City and Community* 8, no. 2: 129–54.

Vallejo, Jody Agius, and Jennifer Lee. 2009. "Brown Picket Fences: The Immigrant Narrative and 'Giving Back' among the Mexican-Origin Middle Class." *Ethnicities* 9, no. 5: 5–31.

Vendantam, Shankar. 2005. "Many Americans Believe They Are Not Prejudiced. Now a New Test Provides Powerful Evidence That a Majority of Us Really Are." *Washington Post Magazine*, January 23, W12.

Walker, Juliet E. K. 2009. *The History of Black Business in America: Capitalism, Race, Entrepreneurship: Volume 1 to 1865.* Chapel Hill: University of North Carolina Press.

Walzer, Michael. 1992. *What It Means to Be an American: Essays on the American Experience.* New York: Marsilio.

Waters, Mary C. 2001. *Black Identities: West Indian Immigrant Dreams and American Realities.* Cambridge, MA: Harvard University Press.

Watkins, Celeste M. 2005. "A Tale of Two Classes: The Socio-Economic Divide among Black Americans under 35." In *Race and Ethnicity in Society: The Changing Landscape*, edited by Elizabeth Higginbotham and Margaret L. Anderson, 260–67. Belmont, CA: Thomson Wadsworth.

Wertsch, Mary E. 1991. *Military Brats: Legacies of Childhood Inside the Fortress.* New York: Harmony Books.

West, Candace, and D. Zimmerman. 1987. "Doing Gender." *Gender and Society* 1: 125–51.

Wheary, Jennifer, Thomas M. Shapiro, Tamara Draut, and Tatjana Meschede. 2008. "Economic (In)Security: The Experience of the African-American and Latino Middle Classes." Waltham, MA: Institute on Assets and Social Policy. http://iasp .brandeis.edu/pdfs/byathreadlatino.pdf (accessed February 4, 2011).

Wiese, Andrew. 1993. "Places of Our Own: Suburban Black Towns before 1960." *Journal of Urban History* 19, no. 3: 30–54.

———. 2004. *Places of Their Own: African American Suburbanization in the Twentieth Century.* Chicago: University of Chicago Press.

Williams, Lena. 2000. *It's the Little Things: The Everyday Interactions That Get under the Skin of Blacks and Whites.* Orlando, FL: Harcourt.

Williams, Matt. 1987. "The Shower." *The Cosby Show*, season 3, episode 19, directed by Jay Sandrich, aired February 26.

Willie, Sarah Susannah. 2001. "Performing Blackness: What African Americans Can Teach Sociology about Race." In *2001 Race Odyssey*, edited by Bruce R. Hare, 22–38. New York: Syracuse University Press.

Wilson, Frank. 1995. "Rising Tide or Ebb Tide? Recent Changes in the Black Middle Class in the U.S., 1980–1990." *Research in Race and Ethnic Relations* 8: 21–55.

Wilson, George. 1996. "Toward a Revised Framework for Examining Beliefs about the Causes of Poverty." *Sociological Quarterly* 37, no. 3: 413–28.

Wilson, William Julius. 1980. *The Declining Significance of Race*. Chicago: University of Chicago Press.

———. 1987. *The Truly Disadvantaged: The Inner City, the Underclass, and Public Policy*. Chicago: University of Chicago Press.

Wiltz, Teresa. 2009. "Yee Haw! The Rise of Black Country." *The Root*, April 21. http://www.theroot.com/views/yee-haw-rise-black-country?page=0,1 (accessed June 25, 2012).

Wingfield, Adia Harvey, and Joe R. Feagin. 2010. *Yes We Can? White Racial Framing and the 2008 Presidential Campaign*. New York: Routledge.

Woodard, Michael D. 1997. *Black Entrepreneurs in America: Stories of Struggle and Success*. New Brunswick, NJ: Rutgers University Press.

Wright, Kai. 2009. "The Assault on the Black Middle Class." *The American Prospect*. http://www.prospect.org/cs/articles?article=the_assault_on_the_black_middle_class (accessed February 1, 2011).

Yap, Stevie C. Y., Isis Settles, and Jennifer S. Pratt-Hyatt. 2011. "Mediators of the Relationship between Racial Identity and Life Satisfaction in a Community Sample of African American Men and Women." *Cultural Diversity and Ethnic Minority Psychology* 17, no. 1: 89–97.

Young, Alford A., Jr. 1999. "The (Non) Accumulation of Capital: Explicating the Relationship of Structure and Agency in the Lives of Poor Black Men." *Sociological Theory* 17, no. 2: 201–27.

Zhou, Min. 2008. "Are Asian Americans Becoming 'White'?" In *The Contexts Reader*, edited by Jeff Goodwin and James M. Jasper, 279–85. New York: Norton.

Zhou, Min, Jennifer Lee, Jody Agius Vallejo, Rosaura Tafoya-Estrada, and Yang Sao Xiong. 2008. "Success Attained, Deterred, and Denied: Divergent Pathways to Social Mobility in Los Angeles' New Second Generation." *Annals of the American Academy of Political and Social Science* 620: 37–61.

Zinn, Howard. 2003. *A People's History of the United States*. New York: HarperCollins.

Index

~

About the Author

Cherise A. Harris is an assistant professor of sociology at Connecticut College. Her research focuses on the Black middle-class experience. She has published articles in *Sociological Spectrum*, *Journal of African American Studies*, *Teaching Sociology*, and *Race, Gender, and Class*. Her teaching focuses on race, class, and gender inequality where one of her signature courses is "middle-class minorities." In 2012, she was the inaugural recipient of the Helen Mulvey Faculty Award at Connecticut College in recognition of her teaching success.